ANNE'S WORLD
A New Century of Anne of Green Gables

The recent 100-year anniversary of the first publication of L.M. Montgomery's *Anne of Green Gables* has inspired renewed interest in one of Canada's most beloved fictional icons. The international appeal of the red-haired orphan has not diminished over the past century, and the cultural meaning of her story continues to grow and change. The original essays in *Anne's World* offer fresh and timely approaches to issues of culture, identity, health, and globalization as they apply to Montgomery's famous character and to today's readers.

In conversation with each other and with the work of previous experts, the contributors to *Anne's World* discuss topics as diverse as Anne in fashion, the global industry surrounding Anne, the novel's use as a tool to counteract depression, and the possibility that Anne suffers from Fetal Alcohol Syndrome. *Anne* in translation and its adaptation for film and television are also considered. By establishing new ways to examine one of popular culture's favourite characters, the essays of *Anne's World* demonstrate the timeless and ongoing appeal of L.M. Montgomery's writing.

IRENE GAMMEL is a professor and Canada Research Chair in Modern Literature and Culture in the Department of English at Ryerson University.

BENJAMIN LEFEBVRE has held postdoctoral visiting fellowships at the University of Alberta, the University of Worcester, and the University of Prince Edward Island.

L. M. Montgomery among the Daisies in the "Anne" and "Emily" Country.

L. M. Montgomery was born at Clifton, Prince Edward Island and spent her childhood days in the seashore farming settlement of Cavendish, which is the setting of many of her stories. Although still known to her readers as "L. M. Montgomery" she has for some years presided over a Presbyterian Manse in Ontario, for she is the wife of the Reverend Ewan Macdonald.

L.M. Montgomery in 'Anne' Country. Postcard signed by L.M. Montgomery and sent to Bella Briansky Kalter, 1935. Modern Literature and Culture Research Centre, Ryerson University, Toronto. Gift of Bella Briansky Kalter.

EDITED BY IRENE GAMMEL AND
BENJAMIN LEFEBVRE

Anne's World

A New Century of Anne of Green Gables

UNIVERSITY OF TORONTO PRESS
Toronto Buffalo London

ISBN 978-1-4426-4202-7 (cloth)
ISBN 978-1-4426-1106-1 (paper)

♾

Printed on acid-free paper

Publication cataloguing information is available from Library and
Archives Canada

University of Toronto Press acknowledges the financial assistance to its
publishing program of the Canada Council for the Arts and the Ontario
Arts Council.

 Canada Council Conseil des Arts
for the Arts du Canada   **ONTARIO ARTS COUNCIL**
CONSEIL DES ARTS DE L'ONTARIO

This book has been published with the help of a grant from the Canadian
Federation for the Humanities and Social Sciences, through the Aid to
Scholarly Publications Program, using funds provided by the Social
Sciences and Humanities Research Council of Canada.

University of Toronto Press acknowledges the financial support for its
publishing activities of the Government of Canada through the Book
Publishing Industry Development Program (BPIDP).

Contents

Acknowledgments

Many of the essays included in *Anne's World: A New Century of Anne of Green Gables* take inspiration from the 100th anniversary of *Anne of Green Gables*, which was commemorated across Canada with exhibitions, celebrations, conferences, and the publication of a slew of new books. In Charlottetown, L.M. Montgomery was named 'The Guardian's 2008 Newsmaker of the Year' (3 Jan. 2009). In the late summer of 2009, scholars met at the University of Uppsala in Sweden to celebrate the 100th anniversary of the first Swedish translation of *Anne of Green Gables* and, as we write these acknowledgments, celebrations are being planned by the L.M. Montgomery Society of Ontario to commemorate the author's 100 years in that province, for she had settled in Leaskdale, Ontario, in 1911.

Irene Gammel would like to thank the Social Sciences and Humanities Research Council of Canada for support of the project; the Canada Research Chairs program for invaluable time support; and the Canada Foundation for Innovation and the Ontario Minister of Research and Innovation for infrastructure support for the Modern Literature and Culture Research Centre. Benjamin Lefebvre would like to thank the Social Sciences and Humanities Research Council of Canada for a postdoctoral fellowship (University of Alberta) and the Leverhulme Trust for a visiting fellowship (University of Worcester), which he held throughout the editing of this collection.

We would like to thank University of Toronto Press, in particular our editors Siobhan McMenemy, Patricia Simoes, Ryan Van Huijstee, and Frances Mundy, who have shepherded this book enthusiastically through its various stages. This book would not have been possible without the invaluable, enthusiastic, and professional support of student assistants at Ryerson University: Saeed Teebi, who supported the editorial process; and Keri Kauffman and Beryl Pong, who assisted with the illustration and permission searches. We are also grateful for the support of Juan Ilerbaig, administrative research coordinator at the Modern Literature and Culture Research Centre at Ryerson University, Toronto. In organizing A Ryerson Showcase: The Centenary of *Anne of Green Gables*, the students in Arts and Contemporary Studies 800 laid an important foundation for several of the topics covered in *Anne's World*.

For permission to use images and text we are grateful to the following: Aschehoug (Oslo), Buddies in Bad Times Theatre (Toronto), Chambers Harrap Publishers Ltd. (Edinburgh), Ghadyani Publishing House (Tehran), George Eastman House International Museum of Photography and Film (Rochester, N.Y.), Library and Archives Canada (Ottawa), the Toronto Public Library, McClelland and Stewart (Toronto), the Modern Literature and Culture Research Centre (Ryerson University), Janusz Oblucki (Kanie, Poland), Schildts Förlags AB (Helsinki), V&A Enterprises Ltd. at Victoria and Albert Museum (London), Zhejiang Art and Literature Press (Hangzhou, China). We are grateful to John Sylvester and Tourism PEI (Prince Edward Island) for the photograph used on the front cover and to Regan Winters, who appears in the photograph. We are also grateful to Ainong Ma, Nicole Argyropoulos, Barbara Bell, Laura Brown, Valentina Capuani, Sally Keefe Cohen, Nancy Fay, Nader Ghadyani, Nancy Gruver, Bella Briansky Kalter, Moynan King, Mari Koli, Suzy Malik, Michael Schwartz, A. Audhild Solberg, and Alan Walker.

Quotations from *The Selected Journals of L.M. Montgomery*, vol. 1, 2, 4, and 5 © 1985, 1987, 1998, 2004, by Oxford University Press Canada, are reproduced with the permission of Mary Rubio, Elizabeth Waterston, and the University of Guelph, courtesy of the L.M. Montgomery Collection, Archival and Special Collections, University of Guelph Library. We are grateful to New Moon Girl Media, Sullivan Entertainment (Toronto), and Dolphin Digital Media (parent of Anne's Diary) for permission to use quotations (in Jason Nolan's chapter).

Material written by L.M. Montgomery is excerpted with the permission of Ruth Macdonald and David Macdonald, trustee, who are the heirs of L.M. Montgomery.

L.M. Montgomery is a trademark of Heirs of L.M. Montgomery Inc.

Anne of Green Gables and other indicia of 'Anne' are trademarks and/ or Canadian official marks of the Anne of Green Gables Licensing

Authority Inc., which is owned by the heirs of L.M. Montgomery and the Province of Prince Edward Island.

All reasonable efforts have been made to contact the copyright owners of images. To any owners left unidentified, wishing to establish ownership, you may contact us, and any addenda will be happily made in future reprints.

Dated January 11, 1935, I received a letter from L.M. Montgomery from the Manse, Norval, Ontario, in response to a letter I had written her from Ansonville, Ontario. I had come there as an 8-year-old, on October 29, 1929, from Poland, with my mother and two sisters, reuniting with our father who had emigrated there two years earlier. The walk home from Ansonville post office with that letter is still vividly inscribed in my mind. I was the happiest fourteen-year-old girl in the world hearing from the author to whom I had expressed my gratitude for bringing Anne of Green Gables into my life. I have been writing all my life and while I've not become a successful author like L.M. Montgomery, in the words of a high school teacher of mine who wrote in my autograph book: 'To travel hopefully is better than to arrive, and the true success is to labor.'

[L.M. Montgomery's letter] expresses a special connectedness … linked with the young girl in Ansonville yearning for an expansion of the world. Like Anne, like Lucy Maud Montgomery herself?

– Bella Briansky Kalter to Irene Gammel, August 2008

Introduction: Reconsidering Anne's World

IRENE GAMMEL

> Anyone who has ever encountered her in one of L.M. Montgomery's novels will never forget her, for she is what we're not – and all that we long for and shall never become.
>
> – Jack Zipes about Anne Shirley[1]

Anne is an über-connector. She possesses an exuberance and vitality that spreads from Green Gables to Avonlea and from Avonlea to the world.[2] It is Anne's charisma and intensity, her indomitable spirit in the face of adversity, and her infectious love and need for love that have spread from one generation to the next. Her very vulnerabilities, her dramatic foot-stomping and slate-crashing, have been an important part of her charm. *Anne of Green Gables* has influenced an amazingly broad group of readers across genders and ages, from scriptwriters to housewives, to prime ministers and musicians. Anne fans unabashedly report how they incorporate Montgomery's heroine into their own lives, making Anne an extension of the self, as she is for Jack Zipes, who writes that Anne is 'all that we long for and shall never become.'

In *Lost in Translation: Life in a New Language* (1989), Polish-born writer Eva Hoffman describes her initial encounter with Anne Shirley. When she first read Anne she was a young girl in Krakow far away from the novel's Canadian context:

> One day, I open *Anne of Green Gables* – and for the next few months I'm hooked. I ask the librarian frantically when the next volume might arrive; I'm anxious if there's too much of a pause between them – I can't be left hanging in suspense about whether Anne will become a teacher or

not. My conversation is full of Anne's bon mots and news from her daily life – that her friend, Diana, is tragically dying, and Gilbert invites her for a walk, that she got some dresses with bouffant sleeves for her birthday and was absolutely ecstatic. As long as I am reading, I assume that I am this girl growing up on Prince Edward Island; the novel's words enter my head as if they were emanating from it. Since I experience what they describe so vividly, they must be mine.[3]

In Hoffman's universe, the words themselves become the reality, shaping the cognitive structure of the autobiographical 'I.' 'Like so many children who read a lot,' she explains, 'I began to declare rather early that I wanted to be a writer.' In 1959, during the Cold War, at age thirteen, Hoffman would immigrate to Canada with her parents. She would become a writer.

Fast-forward to 2008, to Mary Lawson, a distant relative of Montgomery who lives in Great Britain but writes about rural Canada. In her book *Crow Lake* (2002), which was long-listed for the prestigious Man Booker Prize, Lawson evokes the world of Anne through the adult narrator-biologist Kate Morrison. As an orphan, like Anne, who lost her parents at age seven, Kate hides her scars behind emotional distance that mirrors her Presbyterian culture at its Eleventh Commandment: 'Thou Shalt Not Emote.'[4] In an illuminating e-mail letter she sent to me, Lawson traced her family connections with Montgomery and described the influence of *Anne of Green Gables* on her writing:

I was well into my thirties when I began writing, but I have to say that at that point I became aware that having an icon in the family can be more hindrance than help; obviously I was never going to be able to be equal to her achievements, and that is a rather discouraging thought when you're first starting out … At a conscious level, I did want to acknowledge Lucy Maud's presence in the background, so to speak, and so I decided to use the surname 'Pye' [in *Crow Lake*]. Somewhere in *Anne of Green Gables* Marilla says something about the Pyes not being able to help themselves; you might say that's true of the Pyes in Crow Lake too, depending on where you stand on the nature/nurture debate.'[5]

'Once a Pye, always a Pye' is the unspoken law of a clannish world of insiders and outsiders that rules Montgomery's Avonlea. Lawson understood something of the darkness of the *pharmakos*, the ritual figure of expulsion; the Pye family in *Crow Lake* is haunted by darkness, including murder and suicide. In our era, the focus has moved to the darker side of Anne.

Like Penelope's web, the story of Anne, itself spun from the quotations Montgomery found in the magazines of the wider world, has been unwoven and reknitted into late-twentieth-century and twenty-first-century texts. For writers like Hoffman and Lawson, who self-consciously dress themselves in reading, Anne stands for that longed-for 'expansion of the world' that Anne fan and writer Bella Briansky Kalter evokes in the epigraph to this book. That expansion of the world is also at the heart of this volume of essays.

Anne of the New Century

Anne's World: A New Century of Anne of Green Gables offers a wide range of new essays sparked by the proliferation of fresh approaches and research in the wake of 2008, the 100th anniversary of the novel's first publication. Culture, identity, agency, ethics, health, reading, branding, home, and globalization are some of topics of research this volume explores as we embark on a new century of L.M. Montgomery studies. The essays collected here provide answers to many probing questions such as: How do we read this early twentieth-century novel in ways that are relevant for readers of the twenty-first century? How do the novel's ethical dimensions fit into our own era? Can *Anne of Green Gables* be read as a therapeutic text, capable of counteracting depression? What is the power and danger of digital encounters with Anne?

Much of the scholarship contained herein will surprise readers. Who would have thought that Anne's exuberant character profile could be read as a code for some startling pathologies, as Helen Hoy's essay documents here, reading the novel, as she does, through the lens of developmental disability? Who would have thought that the novel's celebration of Green Gables resonates with a nomadic sense of home, as Margaret Steffler argues here? Readers may also be intrigued to learn that the Hollywood actress who took Anne Shirley's name became typecast and was stifled by the pervasive Anne Shirley brand. And, for the first time, readers in this country will meet Iranian and Chinese Annes that look quite different from our familiar Canadian Anne.

Several threads run through this reconsideration. First, after a long journey, *Anne of Green Gables* has reached the status of 'classic,' but, ironically, at a time when the notion of 'classic' itself seems to have become redundant. In *Postmodernism, or, the Cultural Logic of Late Capitalism* (1991), Fredric Jameson describes the ways in which, in music, 'after Schönberg and even after Cage, the two antithetical traditions of the "classical" and the "popular" once again begin to merge.' He articulates how postmodern artists no longer just 'quote' texts of mass culture, as Gustave Flaubert had begun to do, 'but they somehow incorporate them' to the point where traditional evaluative terms 'no longer seem functional.'[6] Anne was born by merging the 'popular' with the 'classical,' which is perhaps an apt signal to alert us to the ways in which these categories are constructed and contested, as Anne circulates as a 'classic' into a second century.

In *Toward an Aesthetic of Reception,* Hans Robert Jauss argues that a piece of literature or work of art is always received within what he terms a 'horizon of expectations' (*Erwartungshorizont*), which represents the readers' cultural values and norms, knowledge, and general frameworks for interpretation. Dependent on a broad variety of variables, including socioeconomic and social values, such horizons of expectations are by no means static; they change as society changes, in the process producing new readerships that, in turn, generate eternally changing interpretations, as Jauss observes: 'Here the experience of the first reading becomes the horizon of the second one: what the reader received in the progressive horizon of aesthetic perception can be articulated as a theme in the retrospective horizon of interpretation.'[7] In other words, in order to talk about reception we also have to consider the contexts of the reading publics, including the diverse cultural contexts, as well as the layered responses to the novel over time – in the case of Anne, more than a century.

In fact, formerly *Anne of Green Gables* was presented almost exclusively as a proto-feminist text, as scholars as varied as Gabriella Åhmansson, Elizabeth Epperly, Mollie Gillen, Mary Rubio, Elizabeth Waterston, Rea Wilmshurst, and others challenged the literary establishment by demonstrating how L.M. Montgomery had been marginalized as both a children's writer and a women's writer.[8] These veterans of L.M. Montgomery Studies climbed an 'Alpine Path' in achieving credibility for the author. Thus they were the first to identify Montgomery's sophisticated literary techniques (Epperly, Wilmshurst, Waterston), her use of subversive, double-voiced narration and satire (Rubio), and her layers of subtexts and narrative subtlety (Åhmansson).[9] Mavis Reimer's *Such a Simple Little Tale* (1992) collected many of these early approaches, while *The Annotated Anne of Green Gables* (1997), edited by Wendy E.

Barry, Margaret Anne Doody, and Mary E. Doody Jones, explored the novel's psychological, mythological, and historical dimensions.

Today, the field of Montgomery Studies has matured and become remarkably diverse, so that the novel is no longer discussed exclusively in proto-feminist terms, so much so that ten out of the eleven chapters in this book are concerned with topics that have little to do with Anne's feminist qualities. In fact, while such qualities may have earned *Anne of Green Gables* its historical importance in Western countries such as Canada, the United States, and others, readers in Iran and China, by contrast, may be attracted to very different values – for instance, Anne's family loyalty – that make her a model, of sorts, for a good Iranian or a loyal Chinese daughter. In other words, the specific readership's 'horizon of expectations' determines the interpretation that is applied to the novel in different parts of the world.

As this volume centrally documents, Anne is a global phenomenon, whereby the novel's idea of 'home,' as Jack Zipes also points out in his introduction to the Modern Library edition of *Anne of Green Gables*, is 'a deceptive concept.' Gesturing to the theory of German philosopher Ernst Bloch, for whom 'home' is a place never truly known and so is 'a utopian concept that is progressive,' Zipes highlights Montgomery's nuanced configuration of home as a complex symbol we are always moving towards.[10] Finding the elusive home in a global world is a challenge and may explain the continued worldwide appeal of *Anne of Green Gables*. In the twenty-first century, the world of Anne suggests an alternative spatial rendering, no longer fixed in a particular landscape, but flowing, disjunctive, and migratory. As Anne becomes a building block for contemporary imagined worlds, it is useful too to think about her migration in global terms; as Arjun Appadurai's *Modernity at Large: Cultural Dimensions in Globalization* (1996) points out, the global economy is 'a complex, overlapping, disjunctive order that cannot any longer be understood in terms of existing center-periphery models.'[11] Green Gables was born from different parts of the world, and now brings the world to Green Gables Heritage Site.

Over the past decade, L.M. Montgomery Studies has grown in exciting ways by opening up the field beyond the early, strictly literary models of interpretation, as seen in my own three collections of essays: *L.M. Montgomery and Canadian Culture* (1999; with Elizabeth Epperly) reveals Anne's unique (but by no means uncontested) status as a Canadian cultural icon; *Making Avonlea: L.M. Montgomery and Popular Culture* (2002) explores the spin-off products in musicals, films, and tourism using theories of commodification, film, music, and visual culture (Fiske, Baudrillard); while *The Intimate Life of L.M. Montgomery* (2005) studies Montgomery's performative self-constructions in journals, private writings, and photography. These books have had important scholarly impact and have been widely cited, as well as excerpted and reprinted in the 2007 Norton critical edition of *Anne of Green Gables*, edited by Rubio and Waterston. Moreover, Cecily Devereux's critical edition of *Anne of Green Gables*, published by Broadview in 2004, with its exploration of the fiction's political and ideological dimensions, in particular Montgomery's embedded maternal ideology, has alerted us to the fact that there is no such thing as an 'innocent' children's text. The novel's unspoken and silenced dimensions, its erotic and sexual codes, have also been scrutinized.[12] Crucial work on all aspects of Montgomery Studies has also appeared in a range of Canadian and international journals, including a remarkable number of special dedicated issues, in addition to conference proceedings (such as the 2008 *Storm and Dissonance* edited by Jean Mitchell).[13]

Moreover, scholars have made available a treasure of primary material, including *The Selected Journals of L.M. Montgomery*, edited by Rubio and Waterston in five volumes, the first published in 1985; *My Dear Mr M: Letters to G.B. MacMillan* (1980), edited by Francis Bolger and Elizabeth Epperly; and more recently *After Green Gables: L.M. Montgomery's Letters to Ephraim Weber, 1916–1941* (2006), edited by Hildi Froese Tiessen and Paul Gerard Tiessen. These private writings, in particular, have instigated a shifting of focus in L.M. Montgomery scholarship and a consideration of the darker side found in the sunny Anne novels. Many scholars agree that it was in the journals that Montgomery wrote her truly modernist masterpiece, and many scholars today read her novels beginning with *Anne of Green Gables* through the lens of the journals, the final volume published only in 2004. In this context, the belated and shocking revelation about Montgomery's suicide, which dominated the media headlines in September 2008, also invites a reconsideration of Montgomery's fiction by alerting us to its darker, more adult corners.[14]

Given the wealth of primary and secondary studies, then, the purpose of *Anne's World* is ultimately two-fold: to consolidate a vast amount of information, carefully tracing the previous scholarship and signalling extensions; and to establish new points of departure by locating *Anne of Green Gables* and its production in social, cultural, and historical contexts while also exploring the reception and cultural uses of the novel, thus providing new lines of argument and new domains of study for future research. For the literary landscape has changed, in particular with respect to children's literature, once considered 'a marginalized ghetto' in academia, as Sandra Beckett writes. The successes of Harry Potter have propelled the genre into the mainstream: 'The new status of children's literature and the general phenomenon of crossover literature is one of the most striking and significant cultural markers of our times.'[15] *Anne of Green Gables* is perhaps the quintessential crossover novel, appealing to different generations as readers turn to the book at different points in their lives for different reasons, and even read it in conjunction with the journals, as well as enjoying it with other, related books or media. Further evidence of the wide-reaching appeal of *Anne of Green Gables* to readers of all ages is the range of authors who have noted their debts to Montgomery: in addition to writers for adults such as Margaret Atwood, Margaret Laurence, P.K. Page, Jane Urquhart, and Evelyn Lau (as Margaret Steffler notes in her chapter in this volume), Canadian writers for young people such as Jean Little, Tim Wynne-Jones, Julie Johnston, and Bernice Thurman Hunter have all stated publicly the influence Montgomery had on their careers or have reimagined aspects of Montgomery's fiction in their work.[16]

What most compellingly necessitates a consolidation and reconsideration is the unprecedented crystallization of studies and ideas in 2008 and beyond. *The New York Times* saluted Montgomery as the 'Chick-Lit Pioneer,' while *Newsweek* put Anne Shirley in the American tradition of smart and funny heroines (think Lauren Bacall).[17] A remarkable increase in websites devoted to *Anne of Green Gables* and L.M. Montgomery provided superb research tools, adding to already established sites.[18] Exhibitions across Canada showcased new archival images, research, and approaches.[19] New editions of *Anne of Green Gables* by the Modern Library Classics, the Collector's edition from Penguin Canada, and the New Canadian Library, along with many others; two prequels (Budge Wilson's *Before Green Gables* and Kevin Sullivan's film *Anne of Green Gables: A New Beginning*, also published as a novel); and a plethora of academic studies that appeared in books and journals collectively marked the anniversary. Among the slate of new books are Epperly's *Through Lover's Lane* (2007), a study of Montgomery's visual imagination, and *Imagining Anne* (2008), an attractive annotated edition of Montgomery's Island scrapbooks; my own *Looking for Anne* (2008), an account of how *Anne of Green Gables* came about based on a study of magazines and unpublished journals; and Rubio's long-awaited biography *Lucy Maud Montgomery: The Gift of Wings* (2008). Among exclusively literary studies, Waterston's *Magic Island* (2008) provides snapshot views of the entire Montgomery library, while Holly Blackford's *100 Years of Anne with an 'e'* (2009) offers intertextual readings along with an excellent introduction situating Anne within childhood studies.[20] My co-editor Benjamin Lefebvre's edition of Montgomery's rediscovered final book, *The Blythes Are Quoted* (2009), likewise prompts new questions about the existing Anne series, given that this Anne book was submitted to her publishers on the day of her death. Collectively, these studies have paved the way for several paradigm shifts: alerting us to Montgomery's fragmentary approach to writing that resonates with postmodern cut-and-paste approaches to writing; identifying major new resources that require examination; and inviting an appreciation of Anne's modernity, a modernity that remains to be shared with the world.

Consequently, *Anne's World: A New Century of Anne of Green Gables* is the result of an unprecedented number of international symposia, conferences, and panels that allowed the editors to recruit the best and most diverse contributors, beginning with A Ryerson Showcase: The Centenary of *Anne of Green Gables*, held at Ryerson University on 7 April and organized by my Arts and Contemporary Studies students as a capstone course with support of the president's office (see colour plate 1).[21] Original essays were prepared exclusively for inclusion in this collection. Our fifteen contributors engage a broad range of interdisciplinary perspectives, including geography, fashion, ethics, clinical psychology, film studies, new media studies, early childhood education, and translation studies. By mobilizing feminist, cultural, historical, spatial, educational, and psychological theories, these studies collectively showcase a new Anne – or rather a multiplicity of new Annes – that transforms our understanding of the familiar freckle-faced redhead and allow us to see new sides of Anne, as channelled through different media, cultures, and perspectives. A brightly coloured thread in this collection is Anne herself as a polymorphous figure, revealing how she has been absorbed into readers' identities.

The Essays in This Book

The book begins with Carole Gerson's 'Seven Milestones: How *Anne of Green Gables* Became a Canadian Icon,' which not only reviews a full century of Anne, but argues that Anne's longevity is partly the result of a series of 'institutional, commercial, and grassroots interventions.'

This is an important correction to views of the unmediated powers of this text that have been maintained in Montgomery criticism for a long time. Providing also a trajectory into the future, Gerson studies how Anne achieved her status by way of an institutional process in which the interests of academia, public media, and the reading public diverged and converged.

In '"Matthew Insists on Puffed Sleeves": Ambivalence towards Fashion in *Anne of Green Gables*,' fashion scholars Alison Matthews David and Kimberly Wahl argue that the text allows Anne Shirley to have it both ways: others want her to be fashionable and ambitious, whereas she wants to fit in. In the course of the novel, the heroine is transformed from an ugly duckling dressed in ill-fitting linsey-woolsey to a beautiful swan in stylish puffed-sleeved dresses. While L.M. Montgomery scholarship has begun to take an interest in dress, this chapter's focus on fashion theory and history presents a social and historical analysis of Anne's performative approach to dress, where markers of distinction, theatricality, and self-fashioning play a role in her transformation from awkward outsider to accomplished aesthete.

In her essay '"I'll Never Be Angelically Good": Feminist Narrative Ethics in *Anne of Green Gables*,' Mary Jeanette Moran also focuses on transformation. She reveals that the novel conforms to a feminist ethical paradigm because it tends to value those ethical choices that preserve or maintain relationships, to support the principle that those who nurture others must also care for themselves, and to challenge the assumptions that women naturally care for others or that they alone bear the responsibility to do so. The novel depicts these feminist ethical ideals not simply through the characters' actions, but also through the narratives Anne tells herself, others, and the reader, showing how stories link narrator, audience, and tale into a web of ethical responsibility.

By focusing on Anne's 'disorganized' narration, Helen Hoy's study '"Too Heedless and Impulsive": Re-reading *Anne of Green Gables* through a Clinical Approach' argues for the possibility of reading Anne Shirley as a psychological case study. The character's unpredictability, loquacity, passion, impulsiveness, and risk-taking, along with her talents for drama, fantasy, and story-telling, are all consistent with the behavioural features of what is now known as Fetal Alcohol Spectrum Disorder (FASD). Such a reading revises our understanding of the character and of the novel's trajectory, as well as of simplistic taxonomies of able and mentally challenged. Deliberately political, this provocative essay is a tour de force that shakes up received beliefs about Anne.

My own essay 'Reading to Heal: *Anne of Green Gables* as Biblio-therapy' is concerned with the reader's cognitive transformation. This is the first consistent argument for reading Montgomery's fiction within the important context of bibliotherapy, or the use of books in the treatment of personal and mental disorders, a growing field of study. By shining a light on how Anne effectively models powerful strategies of bibliotherapy, this essay pursues a line of inquiry about how the novel functions as a tool in cognitive intervention and self-help.

How carefully a 'classic' is constructed within the prescriptive rules of cultural institutions is revealed in Leslie McGrath's 'Reading with Blitheness: *Anne of Green Gables* in Toronto Public Library's Children's Collections.' Using as her case study the children's collections of the Toronto Public Library (TPL) from the formal organization of its children's services in 1912 to the present day, McGrath examines how Montgomery's literary reputation endured wide swings of critical opinion. Though their initial endorsements were tactfully phrased, TPL children's librarians did not waver in providing access to the book, giving it the test of time. Current library reviews call *Anne of Green Gables* a 'classic,' affirming both the initial selection of the book, and the librarians' awareness of what children enjoy.

De-institutionalized learning is the focus of Jason Nolan's essay 'Learning with Anne: Early Childhood Education Looks at New Media for Young Girls.' The essay looks closely at *Anne of Green Gables: The Animated Series*, Anne's Diary, and New Moon Girls as prominent examples of how *Anne of Green Gables* and the work of Montgomery in general have been taken up as locations for formal and informal learning, through the identification of Anne as variously a marketing icon, as an ideal young girl, and through the way Montgomery constructed learning environments within her novels. The focus is specifically on very young readers, who have not yet been considered thoroughly by scholars.

We return to the familiar yet unfamiliar world of Green Gables in Alexander MacLeod's 'On the Road from Bright River: Shifting Social Space in *Anne of Green Gables*.' The essay studies the ways in which the characters inside the novel, like the readers outside of the text and the real-world visitors to the Green Gables National Park site in Cavendish, Prince Edward Island, are all engaged in a complex process of reading and rewriting social space. Using the theoretical writings of cultural geographers such as Edward Soja and Tim Cresswell, the chapter examines the socio-spatial transformations that swirl in and around

Montgomery's text and argues that the same tensions and the same competitions between different readings of real-and-imagined geography active in Cavendish today are also staged inside Montgomery's story itself, and might even be interpreted as the central conflicts of the novel.

Margaret Steffler's study 'Anne in a "Globalized" World: Nation, Nostalgia, and Postcolonial Perspectives of Home' is framed by personal reflections on the cross-cultural appeal of *Anne of Green Gables*. This essay critically explores the impact of the novel and character both outside and within Canada, arguing that the attraction of Montgomery's work continues into the twenty-first century because it resonates with conditions in contemporary lives and culture, specifically the emotions and activity involved in migratory patterns of losing and creating home. Nostalgia and the pastoral contribute to ongoing desires and needs to come home.

'An Enchanting Girl: International Portraits of Anne's Cultural Transfer' features interlinked portraits of Anne in four different countries, Iran, China, Japan, and Germany. Researched and written by Andrew O'Malley (Iran), Huifeng Hu (China), Ranbir K. Banwait (Japan), and myself (Germany), these portraits shine a light on the crossover points from one culture to another, identifying cultures that have 'appropriated' Anne for very different purposes. Whereas Western countries may appreciate in Anne similar values as Canadians do, we argue that Iranian, Chinese, and Japanese readers, in contrast, are not witnessing or imagining a 'sameness with a few small differences' with Anne; instead, 'they are experiencing a difference, coming from a "dominant" and sought-after culture, that they can claim and transform into their own cultural property.'

In 'What's in a Name? Towards a Theory of the Anne Brand,' Benjamin Lefebvre draws on film and cultural theories to consider paratextual Annes in terms of authorial ownership, control, and narrative pleasure. Rather than focus on the process of adapting Montgomery's fiction for the big screen, the essay looks at the brand power of the name 'Anne Shirley,' particularly as it circulates in a range of early Hollywood film texts whose strongest link to Montgomery's work is in the image of Anne. The brand power of this name created both rewards and challenges for the actors who portrayed Anne on screen, particularly Dawn Paris, who adopted 'Anne Shirley' as her screen name in an attempt to reinvent herself as a Hollywood star.

Richard Cavell's afterword, 'Mediating *Anne*,' closes off the book by providing a jumping-off point, looking forward to future research exploring the global Anne.

Finally, sharing editorship of this collection between myself and Benjamin Lefebvre not only presents a much needed gender balance, but allows the book to capitalize on the diverse perspectives of two long-time scholars in the field. Ultimately, it is our hope that this book provides the scholarly templates for a consolidation and for new departures, while also facilitating useful discussions for the graduate and undergraduate classroom. Of course, this book has also been researched and written for the many fans of Anne, whose passion for their heroine will help communicate the message. As a connector, Anne is a carrier of emotions and values. In the end she is the perfect communicator, whose message can be translated into different media, languages, and cultures – an ideal icon for our own era. If Anne's village is global, as Richard Cavell asserts, her universe is ours.

NOTES

1 Zipes, 'The Anne-Girl,' ix.
2 According to Malcolm Gladwell (*The Tipping Point*, 15–88), fashions and revolutions are communicated by a few exceptional people called connectors.
3 E. Hoffman, *Lost in Translation*, 28.
4 Lawson, *Crow Lake*, 9.
5 Mary Lawson, e-mail message to author, 2 July 2008.
6 Jameson, *Postmodernism*, 63–4.
7 Jauss, *Toward an Aesthetic of Reception*, 141–3.
8 See Åhmansson, *A Life and Its Mirrors*; Epperly, *The Fragrance of Sweet-Grass*; Gillen, *The Wheel of Things*; Rubio, '*Anne of Green Gables*'; Waterston, 'Lucy Maud Montgomery 1874–1942'; Wiggins, *L.M. Montgomery*; Wilmshurst, 'L.M. Montgomery's Use.' See also Rubio's collection of essays *Harvesting Thistles*; Bolger, *The Years before Anne*; Nodelman, 'Progressive Utopia'; and many others listed in our bibliography.
9 Epperly, *The Fragrance of Sweet-Grass*; Wilmshurst, 'L.M. Montgomery's Use'; Waterston, *Kindling Spirit*; Rubio, 'Subverting the Trite'; Åhmansson, *A Life and Its Mirrors*.
10 Zipes, 'The Anne-Girl,' xviii.
11 Appadurai, *Modernity at Large*, 32.

12 See Gubar, '"Where Is the Boy?"'; Robinson, 'Bosom Friends.'

13 Special issues devoted to all work by Montgomery have appeared in *Canadian Children's Literature / Littérature canadienne pour la jeunesse*, *CREArTA* (Australia), and *The Lion and the Unicorn* (U.S.); contributions can also be found in a range of academic journals such as *British Journal of Canadian Studies*, *Canadian Literature*, *Children's Literature Association Quarterly*, *English Studies in Canada*, *Essays on Canadian Writing*, *Mosaic*, and *Studies in Canadian Literature / Études en littérature canadienne*. See also the many excellent book chapters devoted to the topic of *Anne of Green Gables* and L.M. Montgomery, as seen in Hammill, *Literary Culture and Female Authorship*; Hammill, *Women, Celebrity, and Literary Culture*; Jones and Stott, *Canadian Children's Books*; and L. York, *Literary Celebrity in Canada*.

14 Butler, 'The Heartbreaking Truth'; see chapter 5 for more details. Darker and more adult topics were also emphasized by Mary Rubio at the L.M. Montgomery, *Anne of Green Gables*, and the Idea of Classic conference in Charlottetown, 25–9 June 2008, and in Doody, 'L.M. Montgomery.'

15 Beckett, *Crossover Fiction*, 252.

16 For essays dealing with Montgomery's influence on their careers, see Little, 'But What about Jane?'; Hunter, 'Inspirations.' For examples of recent fiction for young people that revisits or rewrites Montgomery's work, see Julie Johnston's *Adam and Eve and Pinch-Me* (1994) and Tim Wynne-Jones's story 'The Anne Rehearsals,' part of *Lord of the Fries and Other Stories* (1999).

17 Kate Bolick, 'Chick-Lit Pioneer,' *New York Times*, 15 Aug. 2008, http://www.nytimes.com/2008/08/17/books/review/Bolick-t.html; Setoodeh, 'It's Still Not Easy.' See also Margaret Atwood, 'Nobody Ever Did Want Me,' *The Guardian* (London), 29 Mar. 2008, http://www.guardian.co.uk/books/2008/mar/29/fiction.margaretatwood.

18 See, e.g., the *Shining Scroll* newsletter published by the L.M. Montgomery Literary Society, http://home.earthlink.net/~bcavert/id4.html; the Anne Centenary webpage at Ryerson University's Modern Literature and Culture Research Centre, http://www.annecentennary.com/; the Lucy Maud Montgomery Research Centre at the University of Guelph Library, http://www.lmmrc.ca/; and the L.M. Montgomery Research Group, http://lmmresearch.org/.

19 Exhibitions include Creelman and Gammel, *Reflecting on Anne*; Gammel, *Anne of Green Gables*; and Epperly, *Imagining Anne: Celebrating the Creation*. See also Goddard, 'The Genesis of Anne'; Ljunggren, 'New Exhibit Reveals.'

20 Blackford's *100 Years of Anne* had not yet been published as we worked on this collection of essays, but Blackford graciously made the manuscript available so it could be engaged in this study.
21 Later events include '*Anne of Green Gables*: New Directions at 100,' an ACCUTE panel that I co-organized and co-chaired with Benjamin Lefebvre, 31 May; *Anne of Green Gables* at 100: Exhibit Symposium, University of British Columbia, 31 May, a symposium I organized to accompany my *Anne of Green Gables* exhibition installation; L.M. Montgomery, *Anne of Green Gables*, and the Idea of Classic, Charlottetown, 25–9 June (organized by the L.M. Montgomery Institute); '*Anne of Green Gables*, Globalization and Cross-Over Fiction,' Dublin, Ireland, 18 Oct. (organized by the International Board on Books for Young People Dublin); From Canada to the World: The Cultural Influence of Lucy Maud Montgomery, Guelph, 23–6 October (organized by the University of Guelph President's office); '*Anne of Green Gables:* Past, Present, Future' (special session), Modern Language Association Conference, San Francisco, 29 Dec. (organized by the Children's Literature Association); and L.M. Montgomery – Writer of the World, Uppsala University, Sweden, 20–3 Aug. 2009.

1 Seven Milestones: How *Anne of Green Gables* Became a Canadian Icon

CAROLE GERSON

Anne Shirley would be outstanding anywhere, but her presence is particularly distinctive in Canada because our literature features few memorable children. None appeared in the nineteenth century, which saw the birth of Lewis Carroll's Alice, Mark Twain's Huck Finn and Tom Sawyer, Louisa May Alcott's March sisters, and the young heroines of Frances Hodgson Burnett. Brian O'Connal of W.O. Mitchell's *Who Has Seen the Wind* arrived in the 1940s and Mordecai Richler's Duddy Kravitz a decade later. No Canadian author of the twentieth century created a girl with the staying power of L.M. Montgomery's Anne.

When she initially disembarked from the train at Bright River, however, Anne Shirley did not lack company. In the first decade of the twentieth century, *Anne of Green Gables* had many competitors in two major categories that inflect the book's position in the construction of Canada's cultural history: Canadian best-seller lists and fiction for girls. Because best-seller lists were not invented until 1899, earlier accounts of blockbuster success rely on hearsay rather than data. The first Canadian-authored novel believed to have sold over a million copies was also by a Maritime author, Margaret Marshall Saunders's *Beautiful Joe* (1894). This story of an abused dog remains in print today, but neither the book nor its author generated the runaway success of Anne and the ongoing charisma of her creator. For a picture of the larger context of Canadian best-sellerdom we are indebted to Mary Vipond's study of English Canada's best-seller lists from 1899 to 1928; these compilations name many novelists whose popularity once matched Montgomery's but who are seldom read now, such as Gilbert Parker, who charmed readers with his historical romances; Charlottetown-born Basil King, who wrote popular moral fiction; and Ralph Connor, whose stories of western Christian adventure generated spectacular sales figures.[1]

Anne arrived amid the upsurge in Anglo-American stories for girls that offered readers of a century ago an array of appealing adolescent heroines. One such American classic was Kate Douglas Wiggin's *Rebecca of Sunnybrook Farm* (1903); on the Canadian side, Anne's most obvious competitor was Nellie McClung's Pearlie Watson of *Sowing Seeds in Danny* (1908). The eldest in a large impoverished Irish family living in Manitoba, Pearlie engaged readers with her lively chatter and her devotion to her younger siblings. *Sowing Seeds in Danny* actually bested *Anne of Green Gables* on the 1909 list of the top ten sellers in Canada. However, this direct comparison is somewhat misleading, as Montgomery was one of the few authors to be named twice in any given year; *Anne of Avonlea* was also on the list for 1909 and appeared again in 1910, when it was joined by *Kilmeny of the Orchard*.[2] The success of these books was a particularly Canadian phenomenon, given that neither Montgomery nor McClung found her way onto American best-seller lists, which included Gilbert Parker in 1901, 1902, and 1908; Ralph Connor in 1907; and Basil King in 1909.[3] McClung published two subsequent Pearlie Watson books in 1910 and 1925, but, like the once-popular novels by Connor, Parker, and King, they have limited appeal today and most are out of print.

While Pearlie Watson's family role generates much of her story, it is Anne's status as an orphan that ignites interest. She was not the only turn-of-the-century young heroine to lack parents: in *Looking for Anne: How Lucy Maud Montgomery Dreamed Up a Literary Classic* (2008), Irene Gammel suggests that some features of Anne Shirley's story and personality were inspired by orphan fiction that Montgomery most likely read in popular American magazines. M.A. Maitland's Charity Ann, who appeared in *Godey's Lady's Book* in 1892, foretells Anne's big hungry eyes and dark history in the poorhouse, while J.L. Harbour's Lucy Ann, whom Montgomery met in *Zion's Herald* in 1903, provides her red hair, her exuberant love of nature, and her ability to charm a reluctant spinster into adopting her. To this list of precursors I would like to add Marshall Saunders's *'Tilda Jane: An Orphan in Search of a Home* (1901). First serialized in *Youth's Companion*, a periodical that Montgomery knew well and that had published some of her poems, *'Tilda Jane* was issued in book form by L.C. Page, the Boston specialist in juvenile titles and series who would soon publish *Anne of Green Gables*. Like Anne, scrawny 'Tilda is convinced that she is unwanted because she is ugly.

Blessed with a spunky personality, innate domestic competence, and a lively tongue that both creates her scrapes and gets her out of them, 'Tilda has to work harder than Anne to earn her new home, yet despite her considerable appeal she lacked Anne's staying power.[4]

Why did Anne follow a different trajectory? In *Literary Celebrity in Canada* (2007), Lorraine York notes that 'there simply is no comparable Canadian literary persona who has filtered into the culture at large in the way that L.M. Montgomery has' due to her 'strategic and remarkably intelligent negotiation with the celebrity processes that surrounded and, in part, tried to define her.'[5] Anne's initial fame owed a great deal to Montgomery's remarkable output of twenty-three books, some five hundred stories, and an equal number of poems, all of which kept her name prominently in print, while her willingness to be available to interviewers, readers, and the general public maintained her presence as a public personality. In line with studies of celebrity figures that show that literary classics and icons are made as much as they are born, Anne's longevity owes as much to timely institutional, commercial, and grassroots interventions as to Montgomery's brilliant blending of the archetypes of the ugly duckling and the unloved orphan into a character who leaps off the page. Continuing the line of discussion that begins with E. Holly Pike's analysis of Montgomery's presence in Canadian popular culture and Lorraine York's examination of her experience of celebrity,[6] this essay argues that when we examine a chronology of seven specific milestones involving publication, adaptation, reconstruction, commodification, and commemoration, we can see how the occurrence of these events at fairly regular intervals over the twentieth century continually renewed and expanded Montgomery's audience, transforming Anne Shirley from a fictional character to a national icon and a cultural industry.

Fame attaches as much to the character of Anne as to her creator, a unique circumstance in Canadian cultural history according to York,[7] and indeed unusual in the international realm of celebrity studies, which focus on the reputation of authors rather than the prominence of their fictional characters. Critics examining the American star system underscore its initiation in the late nineteenth century with the construction of Mark Twain as 'the epitome of all-American values.'[8] This identity developed through his 'cultural performance of authorial personality' and fostered his own self-projection as a national icon: in his notebook, he jotted, 'I am not *an* American. I am *the* American.'[9] Twain's status was later reinforced by the ubiquity of his books as requisite reading in America's classrooms, a route to iconicity that might have opened for Montgomery if Twain's endorsement of Anne, in a personal letter to Montgomery upon the book's publication, had been fully exploited by her publishers.[10] Montgomery's fame eventually acquired national scope through a process marked by distinct milestones demonstrating the inseparability of the status of the author from the renown of her famous character, and culminating in the centennial events of 2008.

1908: Publication by L.C. Page

The first milestone is the publication of *Anne of Green Gables* by the Boston firm of L.C. Page & Company, following a series of rejections by other publishers, as Montgomery tells us in her journal entry of 16 August 1907.[11] Despite her antagonistic relationship with Lewis Page, he and Montgomery proved a good match. Her ambition complemented his aggressive entrepreneurship and their connection might have endured if Montgomery had received a higher royalty rate.[12] Montgomery well knew the competitive nature of her chosen field of popular fiction; her apprenticeship was an arduous climb up the Alpine Path, as she often reminds us, and she basked in the attention she received as a published author. Page, in turn, immediately set her on the serials track with *Anne of Avonlea* (1909) and created what we would now call a Montgomery brand by issuing similar-looking books almost every year from 1908 to 1915. To maintain her regular output, he had Montgomery rewrite and lengthen a previous serial, 'Una of the Garden,' in order to create *Kilmeny of the Orchard* (1910), and asked her to weave some of her best short stories into a thematically linked volume, *Chronicles of Avonlea*, when she had no novel ready for 1912.

Page's canny use of branding is evident in the visual consistency of his Montgomery titles. *Kilmeny of the Orchard* (1910), *The Story Girl* (1911), *Chronicles of Avonlea* (1912), and *The Golden Road* (1913) were all designed to look like Anne books: their covers feature a delicate, full-colour portrait of an attractive and stylish young woman highlighted against a pastel background, with the entire image set off by a thick, dark rectangular frame. Below this picture a squared, capital font declares the title of the book, with the name of L.M. Montgomery asserted on the bottom line. This appearance of continuity was calculated to retain and enlarge Montgomery's readership, but it also led to complex questions about ownership.[13]

1919: Enter Hollywood

L.C. Page's eye for the market soon sent Anne Shirley to Hollywood, when he sold the rights for the 1919 silent film of *Anne of Green Gables*, which was followed by the talkie of 1934. Because the movie industry was hungry for material, film adaptation was common enough for authors of Montgomery's generation and did not automatically guarantee much fame. However, the first Anne film gained considerable attention for casting the well-known star, Mary Miles Minter, in the title role. Faye Hammill notes that 'when the film was released, the names of both Montgomery and Anne were partially eclipsed by that of Minter, even as Minter's fame was used to promote Montgomery's. Her publisher, Lewis Page, used images of the actress to sell books, producing an early example of the film tie-in with his 1920 Mary Miles Minter illustrated edition of *Anne of Green Gables*.'[14] Neither Minter nor the movie was destined to last. When the film's director was murdered in 1922, love letters from Minter found in his home cast aspersions on her character, and both she and the movie dropped out of sight with all copies of the film reportedly destroyed.[15] However, sufficient traces remain in movie magazines and archival publicity images to allow assiduous researchers to salvage much about the first Anne movie. Participants in the centennial conference of 2008 in Charlottetown were treated to Carolyn Strom Collins's reconstruction of the film with reference to a surprisingly substantial trove of reviews, still images, and posters, along with Jack Hutton and Linda Jackson-Hutton's delightful musical performance that partially reconstructs the first, silent appearance of Anne Shirley on film.[16]

The second film of *Anne of Green Gables* arrived as the Depression deepened, when movies had become a favourite distraction of those who could afford the price of a ticket. Despite its deathbed recovery for Matthew (symptomatic of an era when people needed cheering up), Montgomery found this film 'a thousandfold better' than its predecessor.[17] She was eager to see more of her titles turned into movies, and it was in part the success of this film that inspired her to write *Anne of Windy Poplars* (1936), which was made into a film in 1940.[18] The 1934 film of *Anne of Green Gables* has received considerable critical attention. Theodore F. Sheckels argues that this adaptation transformed Anne's story from an account of an orphan creating her place in a community to a conventional courtship romance, thereby turning a distinctly Canadian novel into a generic American movie. Benjamin Lefebvre further notes that some changes made in this film were repeated in later films, with the result that 'these films' systematic misreading of the source text reinscribes Montgomery as a writer of conventional romance and minimizes her work as a social satirist.'[19] Despite her creation of many other heroines, most of the productions in Montgomery's extensive filmography focus on Anne Shirley, from the first silent film of 1919 to Sullivan's fanciful prequel, *Anne of Green Gables: A New Beginning*, in 2008.[20]

1936: Enter Government and Canada's National Parks

Canada does not abound in sites of literary commemoration. The vast majority of places that have been recognized with plaques or preservation are writers' birthplaces, residences, or gravesites; in 1956, Pauline Johnson's family home of Chiefswood, near Brantford, Ontario, was described by the Historic Sites and Monuments Board as 'Canada's first distinctly genuine literary shrine.'[21] Some literary sites are administered locally while others, like Chiefswood, have been officially designated as national historic sites. Sites that merit this formal recognition share similar characteristics. Some revive demolished buildings and vanished communities with reconstructions based on archival and archeological research, such as the fortress of Louisbourg on Cape Breton Island, whose restoration began in 1961. Others involve the preservation of residences or birthplaces of famous individuals such as Alexander Graham Bell, whose estate in Baddeck, Nova Scotia, became a national historic site in 1952, and Louis Riel, whose family home in Saint-Boniface, Manitoba, was acquired by the federal government in 1969.[22] Yet others entail the restoration of nationally significant buildings, such as Province House in Charlottetown, hallowed as the birthplace of Confederation. Sanctification of some sites associated with Montgomery's life fits this pattern, such as the designation of the Leaskdale Manse as a national historic site in 1997, following concerted lobbying by the L.M. Montgomery Society of Ontario. More recently, Lucy Maud Montgomery's Cavendish National Historic Site was created in 2005 to link the foundations and grounds of the now-demolished house in which Montgomery grew up with the nearby farmhouse that is celebrated as the inspiration for Green Gables.

The creation of both a national park and a national heritage site at the supposed home of a fictional character is a unique occurrence, and the anomaly of Green Gables is evident on the home website of Parks Canada. Here, Green Gables House does not appear in the preliminary list of 'the 165 National Historic Sites Administered by Parks Canada' but sits uneasily at the end, in a briefer list of six 'Historic Sites, Heritage places and exhibits' administered by Parks Canada.[23] It took an extraordinary confluence of federal, provincial, and local interests to sanction the faux reality of Green Gables and construct its 'national' value, a process in which Montgomery herself participated. In 1911, she noted in her journal that her cousin David Macneill's house, later known as the Webb farm, served as only a general model for the Cuthbert home. However, when the property was purchased by the federal government in 1936, she publicly acknowledged the farmhouse as the site of her novel and told the press that she was pleased that 'Anne's haunts will be preserved as they are and my old woods will never be sold to someone who might not care for them when the present owner passes on.' Privately, she mourned the desecration of her 'dear woods' by 'hordes of sight seers and by pleasure hunters.'[24]

The process by which an everyday P.E.I. farmhouse was transformed into Canada's answer to Disneyland has been traced in a number of articles that recount how Green Gables took on a life of its own, a topic revisited in this volume by Alexander MacLeod.[25] When the National Parks Service purchased the house, they painted the gables green and added shutters to make it look more 'suitable' before opening it to the public, who flocked in for tea and souvenirs.[26] Period furnishings were added in 1950, the tearoom was moved to another site in the 1960s, and in the 1970s the decision was taken to furnish the house to replicate the Cuthberts' imagined home. In line with John Urry's analysis of the heritage industry's concentration on the visual at the expense of social experience,[27] subsequent notions of authenticity more closely related to the simulated home of fictional characters than to historic life on a P.E.I. farm in the late nineteenth century. In this regard, Green Gables offers a telling contrast to the Grand Pré national historic site in the Annapolis Valley in Nova Scotia, where there is also reference to a fiction, in this case the controversial statue of Longfellow's Evangeline, erected in 1920. While the heroine of Longfellow's poem may have inspired early commemorative activity in the region, Grand Pré's current interactive website pays little attention to the fiction associated with the site and takes the virtual visitor into the extensive archeological work that is under way to establish the history of the Acadians.[28] Following the success of Montgomery's published journals, Parks Canada's focus shifted from Anne to the legacy of Montgomery, with extracts from her journals and letters displayed on interpretive panels. However, there is no archeology at Green Gables, whose website offers a virtual tour of a domestic interior designed to replicate a fiction, and makes the virtual visitor feel as if Anne herself is waiting in the next room.[29] Historian James De Jonge comments that 'after half a century, this interpretive "tradition" may have acquired historical significance in its own right,' a situation whose irony is nicely expressed in Carol Shields's novel *Swann*: 'The charm of falsehood is not that it distorts reality, but that it creates reality afresh.'[30]

1952: Anne Goes to Japan

Over the past century, Anne Shirley has proven to be Canada's most enduring cultural export, enticing flocks of international visitors to Green Gables to experience the environment of the captivating girl they encountered in one of more than thirty languages, a complex phenomenon of cultural transfer and translation discussed in chapter 10 of this volume. Anne's story was first extended to northern Europe in translations into Swedish (1909), Dutch (1910), Polish (1912), Danish (1918), Norwegian (1918), Finnish (1920), French (1925), and Icelandic (1933). After the Second World War, the book's readership became more global as it appeared in Spanish (1949), Hebrew (1951), Japanese (1952), Slovak (1959), Korean (1963), Portuguese (1972), Turkish (1979), Italian (1980), and Czech (1982). A fresh spate of translations followed international sales of the Sullivan films: Anne and Diana learned to speak German (1986), Chinese (1992), Hungarian (1993), Russian (1995), Serbian (1996), Bulgarian (1997), Croatian (1997), Latvian (1997), Arabic (1998), Slovenian (1998), Estonian (1999), Persian (1999), Romanian (2000), Greek (2001), and Lithuanian (2001). *Anne of Green Gables* and its sequels continue to appear in a number of editions around the world (see colour plates 2–11).

While Montgomery's work took on special resonance in Poland,[31] most significant was the 1952 translation of *Anne of Green Gables* into Japanese. In the country where *Akage no An* was regularly read in school for many decades, almost every English-language publication by or about Montgomery has been translated and *Anne of Green Gables* has served as 'a reference book for learning about Western culture,' as Danièle Allard has noted.[32] In 1979, a fifty-episode Anime series further extended Anne's story to a younger audience.[33] In Allard's analysis, 'albeit a fictional character, Anne is also often perceived as charismatic and having an endearing personality. She is admired for her optimism, perseverance in the face of hardship, diligence, imagination, and orientation towards family, as well as for the affection she holds for and receives from those around her.'[34] Critics such as Yoshiko Akamatsu and Calvin Trillin attribute Anne's appeal to her love of nature, her dedication to Marilla, and her opportune arrival shortly after the Second World War, when she offered a vision of recovery to a shattered society, a topic that Ranbir K. Banwait returns to later in this volume.[35] I like to think there is a subversive element as well – that in a highly regulated culture, Japanese women yearn to enact Anne's independence and likewise break a few slates over the heads of annoying boys.

However, the key to Anne's popularity in Japan may be as much literary as social – the intersection of cultural affinity with effective translation. It is well known that successful translations appeal to the norms of the target readership. Most recently, Sean Somers has found that Muraoka Hanako and Kakegawa Yasuko, the renowned original translators of *Akage no An*, both engaged in 'a purposeful intertwining of Japanese poetic classicism' with the story of the redheaded Canadian orphan. Close attention to the style of the Japanese texts reveals that 'when directly compared, many passages from *Akage no An* read similarly, in spirit and also in phrasing, to some of the Japanese poetic classics.' The resulting 'dually registered Anne, one seemingly attuned to both Japanese and Canadian environments,' implicitly appeals to the cultural sensibilities of Japanese readers by framing Prince Edward Island within their own aesthetic values.[36]

1965: *Anne of Green Gables: The Musical*™

As professional and amateur theatre groups proliferated in Europe and North America through the course of the nineteenth century, so too did stage adaptations of popular novels. Live performance constitutes another significant milestone in the construction of Anne's iconicity: a website devoted to Montgomery's theatre legacy cites more than twenty plays and musicals inspired by her writings, from 1937 to 2008.[37] The most successful of these is undoubtedly *Anne of Green Gables: The Musical*, commissioned by the Charlottetown Festival in 1965. Canada's longest-running musical, regularly performed at the Confederation Centre in Charlottetown, began as a ninety-minute CBC television special created in 1956 by writer Don Harron and composer Norman Campbell. The engaging lyrics and text of the subsequent version resulted from the collaboration of Harron and Campbell with Elaine Campbell, Campbell's wife and partner, and Mavor Moore, first director of the Confederation Centre.[38] The musical's ongoing popularity with high school and amateur groups has kept it alive outside of P.E.I.; many who claim not to know the show are nonetheless familiar with some of its songs, such as 'Ice Cream.'

The success of Campbell and Harron's creation seems to have inspired the predominance of musicals over other performance genres in subsequent stage adaptations of Montgomery's work. The small-scale musical of *Emily of New Moon*, created by composer Dean Burry and writer Hank Stinson in 1998 for the Castle Company and Charlottetown's Stage Door Theatre (which also performed the same team's *Rainbow Valley* and *Anne's Tea Party* in 2000), preceded the Confederation Centre's musical version of *Emily of New Moon*, written by Richard Ouzounian (book and lyrics) and Marek Norman (music), which premiered in 1999.[39] *Emily* disappeared from the Centre's programming after its second year and re-emerged in 2006 in a reduced, revised version that played in Barrie, Ontario, and in Richmond, British Columbia. Another recent musical venture into Montgomery's oeuvre – *Anne and Gilbert: The Musical*, an extension of Anne and Gilbert's courtship – was created by Nancy White, Bob Johnson, Jeff Hochhauser, and director and choreographer Duncan McIntosh. After opening in 2005, it successfully toured Ontario in the fall of 2008. As well, a new show based on Montgomery's journals was developed in Prince Edward Island for the centennial of 2008: the first iteration of *The Nine Lives of Lucy Maud Montgomery*, which is considerably less light-hearted than the previous musicals, met with mixed reviews. Seriousness is also the order of the day in Paul Ledoux's *Anne*. Constructed as a memory play, the script is written for youth theatre groups with a cast of five adolescents and three adults.[40] It has enjoyed performances by different troupes across the country from its premiere in 1998 to numerous centennial productions in 2008. Given all this stage activity and the largely female component of Montgomery's audience, it is curious that Anne's charisma has not significantly extended into ballet. In 1989, the Royal Winnipeg Ballet mounted *Anne of Green Gables* with music by Norman Campbell adapted from the musical, but the ballet did not remain in the company's repertoire and was not revived in 2008 for the book's centennial.

1985: Miniseries for Television and *Selected Journals*

By the 1970s, *Anne of Green Gables* was celebrated in international popular culture and tourism, but neither the book nor its author had reached the higher ground of Canada's national canon. By 2000, *Anne* was a fixture on millennial lists of important Canadian books, and as I've outlined previously, this transition was influenced by two divergent enterprises that made their first appearance in 1985.[41] Both Kevin Sullivan's adaptation of *Anne of Green Gables* as a miniseries for television (followed by *Anne of Green Gables: The Sequel* in 1987) and the published editions of Montgomery's journals had.a huge effect on Montgomery's subsequent status by engaging new audiences in two different realms: young viewers and mature readers. Sullivan began with relatively faithful (albeit not undisputed) adaptations of Montgomery's stories before branching into more fanciful narratives such as Anne and Gilbert's fabricated adventures in the trenches of the First World War in *Anne of Green Gables: The Continuing Story* (2000).[42] Tremendously popular, these miniseries have sold around the world and generated many of the recent translations into Eastern European languages as well as spin-off books in English. From his *Road to Avonlea* television series, which ran for seven seasons from 1990 to 1996, with episodes loosely adapted from Montgomery's work, Sullivan launched the Road to Avonlea series of twenty-nine storybooks based on selected episodes from the first three seasons.[43] His productions are now often the first point of encounter for Montgomery's younger audience, who read her books in relation to the versions on the screen.

The popularity of these television productions led to such vast commodification that in 1992, when Canadian copyright on Montgomery's published works expired (fifty years after her death), the province of Prince Edward Island teamed up with her descendants to establish a pair of licensing authorities. The Heirs of L.M. Montgomery Inc. have trademarked the name 'L.M. Montgomery' as well as a number of titles and characters, while the Anne of Green Gables Licensing Authority of Prince Edward Island has trademarked 'Anne of Green Gables,' 'Avonlea,' and other names associated principally with the Anne stories. Before 1992, Sullivan had cannily trademarked 'Road to Avonlea'; epic legal battles ensued regarding his use of Montgomery's name and characters.

Analysis of the effect of Sullivan's films on the current reception of

Montgomery is too complex a topic to attempt here, but I would like to note how their sanitized and generalized visualization of the past, characterized by Patsy Aspasia Kotsopoulos as 'borderless romance,'[44] enhances the mode of nostalgia that imbues the touristic side of the Montgomery industry. In *Through Lover's Lane* (2007), Elizabeth Rollins Epperly comments that *Anne of Green Gables* was published in 'the same year that Ford virtually created a brave new world of assembly-line factory production' and that, in her stories, Montgomery 'seems to capture a way of life that had passed in most places and was passing rapidly in others.'[45] The presentation of Prince Edward Island as pastoral – which Northrop Frye describes as a myth 'identified with childhood'[46] – accounts for a good proportion of Montgomery's enduring appeal, including the avidity with which her fans greeted the ten new collections of her magazine stories that appeared between 1974 and 1995, eight of them edited by Rea Wilmshurst.

Quite a different impulse underlies the eager reception of Montgomery's *Selected Journals*, expertly edited by Mary Rubio and Elizabeth Waterston, the first two volumes of which appeared in 1985 and 1987. Their sales astounded the book's publisher, Oxford University Press.[47] The first volume sold more than 25,000 copies in hardcover before it was issued in paper in 2000, and the second and third proved similarly popular.[48] These volumes appeal to Montgomery's adult readers who want to learn about the inner life of their favourite author. Alongside this large middle-brow readership, the journals' timely intersection with the interest of second-wave feminists in women's self-representation has enhanced their reception by academics involved in the emergence of life-writing as a scholarly field. While general readers devour them in the belief that they relate Montgomery's 'true story,' professors love them for their complex reflection of Montgomery's efforts to shape her biography.[49]

1990s: Launch of L.M. Montgomery Studies

Publication of the first volumes of Montgomery's edited journals provided the groundwork for the establishment of Montgomery studies as a recognized academic field. While articles about Montgomery appeared with increasing regularity in *Canadian Children's Literature / Littérature canadienne pour la jeunesse* and other scholarly journals, beginning in the 1980s,[50] the growing seriousness of the endeavour was firmly signposted by the establishment of the L.M. Montgomery Institute at the University of Prince Edward Island in 1993, aided by a grant from the Social Sciences and Humanities Research Council of Canada. This funding also enabled the first of the Institute's biennial international conferences in 1994, which have led to the publication of several thematically organized collections of essays. Under the initial guidance of Elizabeth Epperly and Irene Gammel, the Institute established multiple mandates. It asserts a high level of scholarship by organizing its conferences to focus on Montgomery through academically significant approaches such as Canadian culture, popular culture, life writing, and conflict, and by ensuring that the resulting peer-reviewed volumes appear with top scholarly presses. At the same time, the Institute recognizes the significance of Montgomery's huge non-academic community, which includes many devoted lay researchers, and welcomes their participation at conferences and other events, while also remaining sensitive to Montgomery's personal position in Prince Edward Island among local residents and her extended family.

Serious commitments to Montgomery scholarship now thrive outside of Prince Edward Island. The University of Guelph, custodian of Montgomery's journals and other materials, is enhancing access to its Montgomery collection through its digital archive. It also houses the Lucy Maud Montgomery Research Centre, whose website is the primary source of information relating to Montgomery's life in Ontario. At Ryerson University, the Modern Literature and Culture Research Centre, established in 2006 by Irene Gammel, maintains an ongoing mandate to further Montgomery scholarship.[51] The scholars associated with these institutions are interviewed regularly by the CBC and other media, whose thirst for news about Montgomery seems unquenchable.

2008: Centennial Commemoration

Anne Shirley's expanding presence in books in many languages, films, television series, stage performances, scholarly endeavours, and commemorative sites culminated in the extensive celebration of the centennial of *Anne of Green Gables* in 2008. The year's remarkable collection of important new books, exhibitions, and special events, as well as a commemorative coin and commemorative postage stamps, resulted from many intertwining interventions involving an array of agents, from souvenir manufacturers to Crown corporations to university scholars. Several years after the centennial flurry has subsided, it will be revealing to study its effect on the subsequent reception of Montgomery and her works. Towards the end of 2008, Anne seemed to be everywhere; a Google search for 'Anne of Green Gables' yielded over 1.6 million hits. This accumulation gives rise to many questions, not the least of which is to ask which Anne was being commemorated. Films, plays, translations, prequels, and reconstructions all involve interpretations, including the visual image chosen for celebration. There have been Anne stamps and coins in the past, but 2008 marked the first coordinated, widely marketed effort, with the image of Ben Stahl's Anne appearing on both the commemorative coin and one of the two commemorative postage stamps.

In the spring of 2008, the Royal Canadian Mint issued an Anne of Green Gables twenty-five-cent piece that is larger than a silver dollar and actually cost $19.95. Its initial edition sold out instantly. In price and appeal, this coin represented quite a different approach from the Mint's previous tribute to Montgomery. In 1994 (which was not a commemorative year for Anne or her author), the Mint created a $200 22-karat gold coin, issued for the price of $399, that was aimed at Japanese collectors. Its image of 'a young girl under a gazebo, daydreaming about the adventures of Anne of Green Gables,' in the words of the Mint's brochure, was designed by Phoebe Gilman, a well-known Canadian children's book illustrator.[52] The previous postage stamp had been issued in 1975 to commemorate the centennial of Montgomery's birth (a year later than the actual date) and was designed for the occasion by Toronto artist Peter Swan. In contrast to these commissioned images, the rendition of Anne created by Ben Stahl, then an American commercial artist who had not yet set foot on Prince Edward Island, originated as one of the thirty-six covers he created for Bantam-Seal's mass-market paperbacks in the 1980s, which are still in print today. Rights to this image were bought by the Heirs of L.M. Montgomery Inc. when they selected his painting as the 'quintessential Anne'[53] for the centennial. There is an aptness to this convergence of the commercial and the institutional, as Canada Post and the Royal Canadian Mint, while both Crown corporations, represent the face of government to the general public. Given the volume of stamps and coins thus generated, Stahl's Anne, with her hands full of flowers, overrides the original Gibson Girl cover of Page's first edition of *Anne of Green Gables* as well as the dreamy photograph of Evelyn Nesbit that Montgomery had chosen as her image of her heroine, both of which look older than the child in the story. How we 'see' Anne is an important component of understanding her creation and reception, as demonstrated by Gammel in *Looking for Anne* and by critics who have studied the covers of various editions of Montgomery's books (see colour plate 3).[54] The official Anne of the twenty-first century escapes the wide-eyed cuteness typical of commercial art; she looks thoughtful, intelligent, and determined to see beyond the horizon.

Despite the prevalence of this official image, conceptions of Anne remain diverse, as demonstrated in the panel of book covers created for the commemorative exhibition, *Reflecting on Anne of Green Gables / Souvenirs d'Anne ... La Maison aux pignons verts*, prepared by Irene Gammel and the staff of Library and Archives Canada. Gammel's other exhibit, *Anne of Green Gables: A Literary Icon at 100*, which traced the popular culture sources that shaped Anne, appeared in simultaneous installations in cities across Canada, from Cavendish to Vancouver.[55] In Charlottetown, the Confederation Centre for the Arts showcased the original manuscript and Montgomery's scrapbooks in *Imagining Anne*, an exhibition coordinated by Elizabeth Epperly to coincide with the publication of her edition of Montgomery's scrapbooks.

Because Montgomery rewrote her journals after she had achieved celebrity, the entry dated 15 April 1914 is probably disingenuous. Her favourite dream, she claimed, was 'to write a book that will live.' 'I can never do it,' she added, 'but dreams don't have to come true.'[56] If she were alive today, L.M. Montgomery would bask in the endurance and expansion of her fame. Since no one who participated in Anne's first centennial will be around to celebrate the next, the extent of Anne's longevity, not to mention the media through which it might occur, remain to be experienced by future generations.

NOTES

1 According to Eli MacLaren ('The Magnification of Ralph Connor,' 508): 'From 1898 to 1906, [Connor's] first five novels sold over two million copies worldwide ... By contrast, Lucy Maude [*sic*] Montgomery ... sold approximately two million books between the publication of *Anne of Green Gables* in 1908 and her death in 1942.'

2 According to Vipond, in 1909 *Sowing Seeds in Danny* was fourth, *Anne of Green Gables* was sixth, and *Anne of Avonlea* was eighth. In 1910, *Kilmeny* was second and *Anne of Avonlea* was ninth. In 1915, *Anne of the Island* was ninth. In 1917, *Anne's House of Dreams* was third, and it was seventh in 1918. Vipond, 'Best Sellers in English Canada, 1899–1918,' 115–18; see also Vipond, 'Best Sellers in English Canada: 1919–1928.'

3 Korda, *Making the List*, 8–12.
4 Like so many early-twentieth-century books for girls, this story was frequently reprinted before the First World War and vanished shortly thereafter. Gerson, Introduction, xi. *'Tilda Jane* was reissued in 2008 by Formac as *Tilda Jane*.
5 L. York, *Literary Celebrity in Canada*, 75, 76.
6 See Pike, 'Mass Marketing, Popular Culture, and the Canadian Celebrity Author.'
7 L. York, *Literary Celebrity in Canada*, 77.
8 J. Moran, *Star Authors*, 20.
9 Glass, *Authors Inc.*, 57; Budd, 'Mark Twain,' 9.
10 This blurb, frequently misquoted by Montgomery and others, appears in a letter dated October 1908 that Montgomery preserved in her journal in the late 1930s: 'In "Anne of Green Gables" you will find the dearest + most moving + delightful child since the immortal Alice.' LMM, 8 May 1939, in *Selected Journals* (hereafter in the notes as *SJ*), 5: 332.
11 LMM, 16 Aug. 1907, in *SJ*, 1: 330–1.
12 For detailed studies of Montgomery's relationship with Page, see Gerson, '"Dragged at Anne's Chariot Wheels"'; Gammel, *Looking for Anne*, 223–40; Rubio, *Lucy Maud Montgomery*, 220–38.
13 Benjamin Lefebvre reveals in his discussion in this volume the numerous occasions when the Anne brand fled from Montgomery's grasp, including the cover of *Further Chronicles of Avonlea* (1920), which Page published without Montgomery's consent with a thematically identical cover.
14 Hammill, '"A New and Exceedingly Brilliant,"' 664.
15 Rubio, *Lucy Maud Montgomery*, 517; see also LMM, 13 Oct. 1929, in *SJ*, 4: 20.
16 Collins, 'Re-creating the Lost'; Hutton and Jackson-Hutton, 'Take Your Girlie.'
17 LMM, 29 Nov. 1934, in *SJ*, 4: 326.
18 Lefebvre, 'Stand by Your Man,' 153; see also his essay in this volume.
19 Sheckels, 'Anne in Hollywood'; Lefebvre, 'Stand by Your Man,' 165.
20 For a detailed list of these adaptations, see Lefebvre, 'L.M. Montgomery.' An expanded version of this filmography is now available at L.M. Montgomery Research Group, 'Filmography,' http://lmmresearch.org/filmography/.
21 S.M.F. Johnston, *Buckskin & Broadcloth*, 225.
22 Parks Canada, 'Management Plan Newsletters,' Riel House National Historic Site of Canada, http://www.pc.gc.ca/lhn-nhs/mb/riel/plan/bulletin01_e.asp.

23 Parks Canada, 'Directory of Designations of National Historic Significance of Canada,' http://www.pc.gc.ca/apps/lhn-nhs/lst_e.asp.

24 LMM, 27 Jan. 1911, in *SJ*, 2: 38–40; 'Anne of Windy Poplars,' 21; LMM, 15 Oct. 1936, in *SJ*, 5: 99–100.

25 See, for instance, De Jonge, 'Through the Eyes of Memory'; Lefebvre, '"A Small World after All"'; Tye, 'Multiple Meanings Called Cavendish.'

26 Tye, 'Multiple Meanings Called Cavendish,' 124.

27 Urry, *The Tourist Gaze*, 110–12.

28 'Archaeology @ Grand-Pré National Historic Site,' http://www.grand-pre .com/GrandPreSiteDevelopment/en/VirtualExcavation.html.

29 Parks Canada, 'Site patrimonial Green Gables / Green Gables Heritage Place,' http://www.pc.gc.ca/lhn-nhs/pe/greengables/.

30 De Jonge, 'Through the Eyes of Memory,' 264; Shields, *Swann*, 205.

31 See Wachowicz, 'L.M. Montgomery.'

32 Allard, '*Taishu Bunka* and Anne Clubs,' 299.

33 L.M. Montgomery Research Group, '*Akage no An* (1979),' http:// lmmresearch.org/filmography/ana-1979/.

34 Allard, '*Taishu Bunka* and Anne Clubs,' 298.

35 Akamatsu, 'Japanese Readings'; Trillin, 'Anne of Red Hair.'

36 Somers, '*Anne of Green Gables*,' 43–4.

37 'Theatre Legacy of L.M. Montgomery,' an L.M. Montgomery Resource Page, http://www.tickledorange.com/LMM/Theatre.html.

38 MacLellan, 'Snapshot,' 216–17.

39 For the script of the *Emily* musical in book form, see Ouzounian and Norman, *Emily*.

40 See Belliveau, 'Paul Ledoux's *Anne*.'

41 See Gerson, '*Anne of Green Gables*.'

42 For responses to these miniseries, see, e.g., Drain, '"Too Much Love-making"'; Hersey, '"It's All Mine"'; Poe, 'Who's Got the Power?'

43 L.M. Montgomery Research Group, '*Road to Avonlea* (1990–1996),' http:// lmmresearch.org/filmography/rta-1990/.

44 Kotsopoulos, 'Avonlea as Main Street USA?'

45 Epperly, *Through Lover's Lane*, 24.

46 Frye, *The Bush Garden*, 239.

47 Rubio, '"A Dusting Off,"' 71.

48 Jennie Rubio, e-mail message to author, 12 Mar. 2008.

49 See Rubio, *Lucy Maud Montgomery*, 272–80.

50 Gerson, '*Anne of Green Gables*.' More recently, *Canadian Children's Literature / Littérature canadienne pour la jeunesse* has published two additional special

issues devoted to L.M. Montgomery criticism. The first, 'Reassessments of L.M. Montgomery,' edited by Benjamin Lefebvre, appeared in 2004; the second, commemorating the centenary of *Anne of Green Gables*, appeared in 2008.

51 Lucy Maud Montgomery Research Centre, http://lmmrc.ca/; Modern Literature and Culture Research Centre, http://www.ryerson.ca/mlc/.

52 Advertisement for 'Anne of Green Gables: A Literary Legacy,' n.p.

53 Sally Cole, 'In Anne's Footsteps,' *The Guardian* (Charlottetown), 18 Apr. 2008, http://www.theguardian.pe.ca/index.cfm?sid=127959&sc=100.

54 Hutton and Jackson-Hutton, 'Images of Anne.' For a gallery of international covers of books by L.M. Montgomery, see 'Picturing a Canadian Life: L.M. Montgomery's Personal Scrapbooks and Book Covers / Images d'une vie canadienne: Cahiers de coupures personnels et pages couvertures de livres de L.M. Montgomery,' http://lmm.confederationcentre.com/.

55 See Gerson, 'Anne's Anniversary.'

56 LMM, 15 Apr. 1914, in *SJ*, 2: 146.

2 'Matthew Insists on Puffed Sleeves': Ambivalence towards Fashion in *Anne of Green Gables*

ALISON MATTHEWS DAVID AND KIMBERLY WAHL

'It would give me such a thrill, Marilla, just to wear a dress with puffed sleeves.'

– Anne Shirley to Marilla Cuthbert[1]

The September 1903 cover of *The Delineator* depicts two 'bosom friends' who look strikingly like Anne and Diana (see colour plate 12). It is dusk and the pair has spent the day together harvesting the final fruits of summer – 'Blackberries,' as the title of the colour illustration by Emilie Benson Knipe specifies.[2] The mood is romantic and wistful, appropriate for an early fall issue of the magazine reminding its readers of the fading freedoms of the season. 'Diana,' whose dark brown locks are swept up into a stylish braid, is the more conventionally elegant of the two. Her muslin dress, which includes a high Edwardian collar, a pearl necklace, bishop sleeves, and a scarf dubbed a 'Vandyke bertha,' is at the height of fashion. Her gaze is frank and direct.

Her counterpart, 'Anne,' is a more enigmatic presence. She gazes dreamily into the distance, her long, flowing locks and sensuous ruby lips reminiscent of a Pre-Raphaelite beauty painted by John Everett Millais or Dante Gabriel Rossetti. Her hair seems to have a life of its own and also recalls the stylized organic undulations of Art Nouveau illustrations by Alfons Mucha. The redheaded maiden wears no jewelry and her loose, simple, lilac-coloured wrap dress is bordered with delicate floral embroidery. The peasant smocking at her shoulders serves the practical function of gathering the sleeve fabric as well as suggesting associations with the folk art and pastoral inspirations of Aesthetic forms of dress popular from the 1870s to the 1880s. The girls on the *Delineator* cover suggest two concurrent ideals of beauty at the turn of the twentieth century. The 'Diana' figure is up to date and chic, her dress and hairstyle signalling the contemporary world of fashion; in contrast, the 'Anne' figure connotes a timeless and artistic mode of visual address, referencing the pastoralism of the Pre-Raphaelites and the dress reform movement of the late nineteenth century.

The two iconic figures represented on the *Delineator* cover serve as a point of departure for examining the ambivalent role of fashion in *Anne of Green Gables*, a topic that has only begun to be explored. For a central tension represented by Anne and Diana in the novel, just as it is visualized by the *Delineator* cover, involves opposing beauty ideals available to young women at the turn of the century: one of modern fashionability drawing on the most up-to-date fashion magazines of the era, and the other of artistic expressiveness drawing on the legacy of the dress reform movements of the late nineteenth century. Modern fashion is referenced in the text, focused in particular on Anne's desire for puffed sleeves, but so is the rural quaintness that resonates with more timeless values and with the artistic expressiveness of the Arts and Crafts Movement, as we shall see. Moreover, we propose that a key aspect of the novel is the presence of fashion itself as a structuring element and narrative tool that is largely disavowed but which remains central to Anne's transformation and subsequent acceptance into the community of Avonlea. Ultimately, we argue, the presence of fashion is a subversive force that must be contained within the required traditional codes and social values in order to 'write' Avonlea as a pastoral and timeless community.

Aestheticism, Anti-Modernism, and Dress Reform

Within the past decade, the study of fashion history and theory has burgeoned as an academic discipline. Scholars such as Elizabeth Wilson, Christopher Breward, Joanne Entwistle, and Valerie Steele have complicated and enriched the terrain of fashion history and theory, imbricating social theory and material culture perspectives and the study of dress with sophistication and intellectual rigor. Yet while many authors have recently published on national fashion cultures and cultural geography in Great Britain, Australia, and the United States, there is still very little work with a specific focus on Canadian fashion.[3] Fashion's relationship to literature has also been a subject of interest for scholars, but the theme of dress in fiction aimed at children and young adults has not been thoroughly explored,[4] although Virginia Careless and Irene Gammel have begun the process of exploring the role of fashion in *Anne of Green Gables*.[5]

In *Looking for Anne*, for example, Gammel has revealed the silently embedded influence of fashion magazines such as *Godey's Lady's Book*, *The Delineator*, and *Modern Women* in Montgomery's fiction. An avid consumer of magazines, Montgomery distilled in her fiction the magazine influences of the Victorian and Edwardian eras while omitting any reference to these magazines in the novel. But how do we account for fashion in the world of Avonlea, where direct references to the consumer worlds of the fashion industry – from dressmaking supplies to the acquisition of desired textiles, from retail outlets or catalogues – are curiously absent in the novel? Why is it that Anne herself is not seen sewing her fashionable puffed sleeves dress or shopping for one? The answers have to do with the ambivalent status of fashion in *Anne of Green Gables*.

At the turn of the twentieth century, modern life itself was viewed with a sense of ambivalence, with fears and anxieties centreing on the development of mass-produced goods, increasing mechanization, urban crowding, and, most crucially, a growing level of commercial materialism. In response to this supposed decay of culture, many artists and intellectuals felt the necessary antidote was a self-conscious adherence to lost human values and a renewed attention to the way in which daily life was undertaken and lived. The anti-modern impulse, theorized by T.J. Jackson Lears, considers anti-modernism a retreat from an industrialized present that was perceived as over-civilizing and ultimately capable of spiritual and moral corruption. More importantly, Lears connected the rise of anti-modernism with artistic and intellectual leaders in the late nineteenth century who had the power to reshape social values and cultural trends.[6]

The dress reform movements, along with artistic and Aesthetic forms of dress, were an important expression of anti-modernism. The Arts and Crafts Movement, an idealizing brand of socialist thinking, held that the simple pleasures of those who lived close to the land or in small, tightly knit communities were preferable to the complexities and conflicts of industrialization. Design reformers of the late Victorian period wrote extensively on the quaint and becoming nature of dress inspired by folk costume, and by rural and pastoral settings. In 1882, *The Magazine of Art* asserted: 'By many who make their gowns according to their own idea of beauty, and not according to the regulation fashion of a French or English milliner, an artistic Old English costume will perhaps be preferred to one imitated from the antique.'[7] This comment was accompanied by a suggestion for smocking not only in children's clothing but for women's gowns as well.

Smocking, a varied and occasionally difficult technique where the fabric is gathered in repeated patterns to form a kind of quilted effect, invoked a rural countryside ideal. Its importance for the spread and popularity of artistic forms of dress was largely due to Kate Greenaway's illustrations for children's books, as well as some of the more fanciful drawings by Walter Crane. 'Old English' was a vague term that could refer to anything in the distant English past from medieval modes to eighteenth-century models, particularly those taken from rural or picturesque settings. This image of playful innocence and the representation of rural traditions tended to be very popular in British and Canadian lifestyle and literary journals widely read by young women, such as *The Girl's Own Paper*. The sense of timeless tradition and elegant innocence invoked by this rural ideal of 'Old England' seemed to blend harmoniously with received notions of Pre-Raphaelite domestic harmony to form a strong historical strain within Aesthetic dress.

Puffed sleeves had been worn in the 1850s and 1860s by many women in the Pre-Raphaelite Movement, at a time when they were not popular in mainstream fashion. Their adoption was originally linked with notions of utility, mobility, and freedom of movement, so that women could easily engage in artistic and useful pastimes such as embroidery, book-binding, and other traditional craft-based practices.[8] As the Pre-Raphaelite ideal was popularized and widely disseminated, it became clear that such notions of beauty could provide a viable alternative for women who did not fit into the standard beauty ideals of the day, both in the time of the Pre-Raphaelite brotherhood and later, when artistic and Aesthetic forms of dress were popularized in such journals as *Queen* and *Lady's Pictorial*. Eliza Haweis, in her famous 1878 text *The Art of Beauty*, acknowledged the importance of an alternative set of beauty ideals provided by the Pre-Raphaelites, who are 'the plain girls' best friends.'[9] Such notions of artistic style were incorporated into turn-of-the-century magazine and poster imagery such as the 1903 lilac gown worn by 'Anne' on the *Delineator* cover. Of crucial importance was the dissemination of some of these design principles and aspects of artistic dress into the mainstream fashion literature of the 1880s and 1890s (see colour plate 13). Smocking and puffed sleeves were two distinct and important features that characterized folk dress and other forms of 'pastoral' clothing in the dress reform literature of the period.

The pastoral setting of *Anne of Green Gables* can easily be situated within this trend in the visual and literary arts of this era.

Fashion theorist and historian Joanne Entwistle has argued that Romanticism in artistic and literary circles was primarily a response to capitalism and the rise of consumer culture. A Romantic world view allows individuals to retreat behind the 'debris of modern life.'[10] Fashion is inherently contradictory: at the same time that it allows a woman (or a man) to express her (or his) personality, it is also a force that is driven by mass culture, both economically and in terms of shared or communal preferences. Anne's characterization in the novel embodies the inherent contradiction between individual distinctiveness and mass-produced fashionability. Her relationship with public life and the era's 'modern' world is always mediated through the safety of community values and practices as well as her own individual preferences and distinctive personality.

Anne, despite her impoverished and neglectful upbringing, appears to be inherently attuned to the beautiful and poetic aspects of the visual realm and is equally sensitive to those things that are jarring or ugly. Eloquent and expressive, she expounds on the world around her, and at times seems consumed by her own imagination, all of which is suggestive of an artistic temperament, as Gammel notes: 'With her love of wildflowers and celebration of beauty for beauty's sake, Anne is an aesthete.'[11] Yet, as Gammel has also acknowledged, the conflict between Anne's desire for a unique sense of individuality and her urge to belong to a larger community is nowhere more apparent than in her interest in fashion, and more particularly, in puffed sleeves.[12] Connected with modern fashionability and with social empowerment, puffed sleeves offer Anne the opportunity to merge her physical self with her sartorial fantasies.

The inherent contradiction between the pastoral, timeless associations of artistic forms of dress and contemporary modishness signals fashion in general and puffed sleeves more particularly as important sites of discursive tension in the novel. Fashion theorists have often pointed out the conflicted yet central role of fashion in the construction of identity. Entwistle has argued that fashion allows for the individual expression of identity while simultaneously providing access to wider community codes and conventions that are shared. Similarly, clothing can both reveal and conceal aspects of a person's character, and thus, themes of artifice and authenticity are common in fashion literature.[13] The iconic presence of puffed sleeves in the text presented both Montgomery and her readers with a rare opportunity to collapse seemingly contradictory categories of beauty in fashionable dress, since at the time of the novel's completion, such sleeves were associated with mainstream modishness as well as artistic dressing.

By the time *Anne of Green Gables* was being written, the discourses of artistic dress and some of the features of Aesthetic dress from the 1880s and 1890s had been absorbed into the mainstream fashion literature that influenced Montgomery. One could be artistic, pastoral, imaginative, and unique while also tapping into mainstream fashion which, though conformist and often lacking in uniqueness, was nonetheless progressive, provocative, and socially empowering. Elizabeth Wilson has argued that fashion, similar to other facets of aesthetic culture, must be understood as primarily ideological, where it 'functions to resolve formally, at the imaginary level, social contradictions that cannot be resolved.'[14] The tension between distinction and belonging, or between artifice and authenticity, is highly relevant for Anne, who seeks both to define herself and to find acceptance within the wider community of Avonlea.

The Multiple Meanings of 'Puffed Sleeves'

If fashion is a social cipher in the novel, as we have suggested above, what exactly is the meaning of puffed sleeves? At the turn of the twentieth century in Canada and the United States, corsets and overall silhouettes changed more slowly than sleeve styles, which were a good barometer of how up to date and fashion-forward an individual woman was.[15] During the 1880s, erotic attention was focused on the lower half of a woman's body. Skirts and various styles of bustles or ornamentation drew attention to and emphasized the posterior, whereas plain, tightly fitting sleeves sheathed the arms. Starting in the 1890s, however, there was a radical shift of interest to the upper body. Fashion focused on the torso and contrasted with slim, tailored skirts. As this visual and decorative emphasis shifted upwards, the most striking element of women's dress was the exaggerated gigot or leg-o'-mutton sleeve, which reached its apogee between 1895 and 1896. Joan Severa, in her account of everyday fashion in nineteenth-century America, argued that this sleeve and its changing shape provided the best dating tool for fashions of the 1890s: 'The leg-o'-mutton sleeve was for some time the shape of choice, sometimes thought of as the only choice, which it certainly was not.'[16]

This contrast between fashionable and outdated sleeve styles is reflected in the attitudes of Avonlea's female inhabitants. Mrs Lynde, Mrs Allan, and Diana are up to date and knowledgeable about fashion. By contrast, Marilla's puritanical attitude towards dress and vanity causes conflicts with her young charge. When Anne receives her three plain new dresses from Marilla with the tight, outmoded sleeves of the 1880s, she can't help but express how much more thrilling it would be to wear gowns with puffed sleeves. Marilla replies: 'Well, you'll have to do without your thrill. I hadn't any material to waste on puffed sleeves. I think they are ridiculous-looking things anyhow. I prefer the plain, sensible ones.' 'But I'd rather look ridiculous when everybody else does than plain and sensible all by myself.'[17] This quotation encapsulates both Anne's (and the author's) ambivalent attitude towards fashion, capturing its emotional appeal and 'thrilling' qualities while simultaneously maintaining an intellectual distance by satirizing and rationalizing fashion as a set of completely arbitrary rules. However, most female readers would have immediately felt empathy with Anne's desire to fit in with her peers. Despite what Marilla may have thought, puffed sleeves were not simply a frivolous luxury or a waste of fabric, but a necessary part of conforming to Victorian social codes, even if, as Anne puts it, these codes meant looking as 'ridiculous' as everyone else.

Upon receiving a puffed-sleeved dress as a gift not from Marilla but from Matthew, Anne expresses her gratitude that she has been given a dress with sleeves that are 'still fashionable.'[18] However, despite the seeming historical specificity of her desire for puffed sleeves, they function in the novel as a general cipher for fashionability rather than as a tool for determining historical dates. While tight sleeves were typical of the 1880s and puffed sleeves of the 1890s, dresses with some form of puffed sleeve were almost constantly in fashion from 1890 to 1905, the period in which Montgomery herself came of age, conceived of, and wrote the novel. While the features of Anne's dress lack historical specificity for both period and contemporary readers, the same is not true of the textiles and culture of home dressmaking in the novel, which are less familiar to us now. When examined in the light of the relatively new discipline of material culture, the social and historical connotations of the actual fabrics used in Anne's wardrobe are revealing. While contemporary readers may enjoy the quaint image of rural women garbed in dresses of wincey, calico, and Gloria, female readers of the period would have had a more complex understanding of fashion's socioeconomic and aesthetic implications grounded in their own experience as consumers and home dressmakers. Describing a dress colour or the type of cloth it was made from was not merely an empty narrative device, since details of cut and fabric illuminated the more personal transformative narrative of Anne's coming of age as a stylish young aesthete for a largely female readership interested in fashion themselves. On a larger level, the changing materials of Anne's wardrobe tell a more elusive story about class and consumption in late nineteenth- and early twentieth-century Canada.

Throughout this period, North America saw major changes in the ways that clothing was marketed, retailed, and acquired. While Montgomery prided herself on her own fashionable flair and ordered her elegant trousseau from Toronto and Montreal,[19] her novel strangely elides many of the consumer practices that were becoming common even in rural Canada. While many provincial women would still have obtained fabric from local dry-goods stores, the period from roughly 1890 to 1910 saw the blossoming of mass-marketing techniques in Canada. Department stores like Eaton's and Simpson's expanded their operations during the 1890s and increasingly moved into the mail-order business.[20] This expansion made a wide range of fabrics and ready-made garments available across the country. While dresses for special occasions would most often have been made up by a home or a professional dressmaker, Eaton's did offer this service to its customers, who could send in their personal measurements. In the traditional rural world of Avonlea, most clothing is made by home dressmakers and fabric is always purchased through the local dry-goods store. No hint is made of more modern methods of making or acquiring fashionable textiles and dress. Even more unusual is the fact that despite her evident interest in fashion, Anne is never framed as an active consumer. From her first appearance in a yellow wincey dress to her apotheosis in Matthew's puffed-sleeved gown, Anne's wardrobe is not actively acquired but given to her as a charitable donation, a practical necessity, or a loving gift.

One might be tempted to attribute Anne's passive role in fashion consumption to either a lack of money or her youth. From a practical point of view, she has no personal fortune nor has she ever had nice clothing. While children and adolescents of this period would have been dressed by parents and relatives, leaving them little agency in their choice of clothing, Anne's situation was much more extreme. At the beginning of the novel, Anne tells Matthew: 'This morning when I left the asylum I felt so ashamed because I had to wear this horrid old wincey dress.' She then admits that the ill-fitting, yellowish-white dress was something of a uniform for orphans: a well-meaning merchant had donated three hundred yards of the wincey to her orphanage the previous winter.[21] In terms of her wardrobe, she is literally a poor charity case and would have been understood and pitied for her 'horrid' clothing. Wincey is the Scottish-English term for linsey-woolsey, a coarse textile valued for its warmth and durability but not for its appearance.[22] In her autobiographical narrative *Incidents in the Life of a Slave Girl* (1861), Harriet Jacobs recalls the dresses her mistress gave her as an adolescent: 'I have a vivid recollection of the linsey-woolsey dress given me every winter by Mrs Flint. How I hated it! It was one of the badges of slavery.'[23] Clothed in fabric worn by slaves and the poor, Anne nonetheless imagines herself in a 'beautiful pale blue silk dress ... and a big hat all flowers and nodding plumes, and a gold watch, and kid gloves and boots.'[24]

While most adolescents would not have had a personal budget for dress, documents such as diaries, inventories, and Montgomery's own journals and scrapbooks reveal that stylish wardrobes were already important to a young woman's identity. An actual thirteen-year-old's diary entry demonstrates that even rural, working women had access to fashion. Mary Louise Pickering-Thompson was the daughter of a carpenter whose family moved from Ontario to Portage la Prairie, Manitoba. At fifteen, she was a schoolteacher like Anne and later became a farm wife.[25] Mary-Louise's inventory of her wardrobe in 1893 reveals how sparse thirteen-year-old Anne's wardrobe of simply cut calico cotton frocks was by comparison: 'Dresses: Navy Blue Cheviot, Ribbon Trimmed, Red Blouse Waist, Grey Gored Skirt, Pink Shambra Dress, Cream Blouse, Honey Suckle Print, Lace, White Muslin, Embroidery, Fawn Cashmere, Silk, Nunsveiling, Poplin, Pink Flannellette, Blouse, Cream and Red Sailor Blouse.' She also lists four coats to Anne's one, several items of jewelry, handkerchiefs, eight hats, kid gloves, two pairs of boots, undergarments, and 'Hair Ribbons, Bows and Laces without number.'[26]

The items in Mary Louise's closet reflect up-to-the-minute fashions, including items worn by adult women of the early 1890s such as gored skirts and colourful shirtwaists.[27] Mary-Louise's wardrobe seems typical of the clothing of other Avonlea girls like Diana that Matthew observes at close range: 'he was quite sure that Anne's sleeves did not look at all like the sleeves the other girls wore. He recalled the cluster of little girls he had seen around her that evening – all gay in waists of red and blue and pink and white – and he wondered why Marilla always kept her so plainly and soberly gowned.'[28] This encounter with more gaily dressed girls convinces Matthew to acquire Anne's Christmas gift, whose 'lovely soft brown gloria with all the gloss of silk' is a marked step up in the world from the rough, serviceable wincey of her first dress.[29]

The dress itself and in particular the fabric that Mrs Lynde selects for it merit further analysis. While the puffed sleeves broadcast its fashionability, the luxuriousness of its lace trim, lavish use of fabric for extra ruffles and pin tucks, and the connotations of the Gloria material itself would have resonated with readers alive to the nuances of textile trade names. Also called zanella cloth, Gloria is a closely woven fabric of silk and wool or cotton in a diagonal twill weave and most often used to cover umbrellas at the time.[30] While it was not nearly as expensive as pure silk taffetas or crepes-de-chine, it first appears in the Eaton's catalogue as a cream-coloured dress fabric in fall–winter 1907–1908. It is listed under the heading for cloth for 'High-Class Fancy Evening, Receptions, Wedding or Street Costumes' and marketed as 'Cream sublime or Gloria, a rich, brilliant satin-finished silk and wool fabric. Will not cut easily. Elegant and dressy in costumes, shirtwaists; also a serviceable lining fabric.'[31]

Both the terms 'sublime' and 'Gloria' advertise the fabric as capable of effecting an almost religious transformation. Perhaps the author was even hinting at the transfiguration of its starry-eyed young recipient, who upon receiving the dress looks at it 'in reverent silence.'[32] On a more material level, the very cloth she wears initiates Anne into a social realm in which she is appropriately dressed to participate in 'High-Class' and 'Fancy' public occasions such as the Avonlea recital, an arena in which she acquits herself admirably, 'living up' literally to her newly stylish apparel. Ultimately, the linking of the luxuriousness of the fabric Gloria with the drama of puffed sleeves proves to be an irresistible combination for Anne, underlining the narrative importance of such garments in the transaction and negotiation of social power.

Anxieties Surrounding Fashion

Examining the visual culture and ideological markers inherent in the motif of the puffed-sleeved fashion-figure at the time the novel was written supplies important clues about the mindset and motivation of both Montgomery and her readers. Montgomery herself was a collector of fashionable images and memorabilia, keeping scrapbooks and notebooks that contained contemporary and historical references to fashions, textiles, celebrities, and events connected with the fashion world. She reminisced about her days as a Dalhousie girl in July 1905 while looking at her old scrapbooks: 'An old-time fashion plate with big sleeves! The big puffed sleeves are in again now.'[33] Anne's quest for puffed sleeves appealed to different age groups: for teenagers they were a symbol of current trends and modes, but for older readers who came of age in the 1890s, including Montgomery, they revived nostalgic memories. More importantly, they would have called to mind both contemporary and historical images of fashionable women throughout the pages of magazines, billboards, and literary papers. An equally important theme in the text aligns Anne's sense of her self physically, with the standards of artistic dress. As the cover of the September 1903 issue of *The Delineator* attests, artistic dress was a viable alternative to mainstream fashions worn by the likes of the iconic Gibson Girl.

As Gammel points out in *Looking for Anne*, the first book cover was not original art but a 'recycled' Gibson Girl from the 1905 cover of *The Delineator*. As a bust portrait, drawn by George Gibbs, it does not show clothing at all, but emphasizes the timeless, sculptural qualities of this noble head. At the same time, the Gibson Girl embodied the ideal young woman, a fashion plate whose dress and hairstyles were emulated by the 'rising' classes in the early twentieth century.[34] This entirely mainstream model of femininity presumably depicts Anne at the end of the novel, when her transformation into a polished young lady is complete. By contrast, most subsequent cover art, including the 1964 Ryerson Press edition illustrated by Hilton Hassell, chooses to focus on Anne as wide-eyed orphan child, clad in her ill-fitting linsey-woolsey dress. Instead of the sophisticated updo of the original, she sports the girlish braids topped with a straw boater which have become visual icons in and of themselves. While the original cover would ensure the book's appeal to aspirational younger readers and more mature readers alike, subsequent covers underline the novel's appeal as juvenile literature.

Montgomery's interest in fashion was a significant factor in the writing of *Anne of Green Gables*, both in terms of themes and visual material. It marks Anne's transformation in economic status and her acquisition of social skills, education, and a prominent place in her community. In Montgomery's scrapbooks, important events and news clippings are mixed in with fashion imagery in a way that visually links modern fashion with contemporary life. Of particular importance is a page in her Blue Scrapbook where Montgomery's excellent examination results of the Prince of Wales College and Normal School from July 1893 are pasted on a page with a clipping of a carefully chosen fashion figure. Dressed neatly and fashionably all in white, the figure stands assertively upright and stares determinedly out at the viewer.[35] In fact, clippings, cartoons, and other references to the debate on women and education abound in her scrapbooks, never far from the fashionable images. Montgomery herself placed fifth out of 264, and one is tempted to wonder if for Montgomery, social empowerment through fashion was linked with education and erudition.

Yet, despite the fact that fashion informs pivotal moments in Anne's development, it is mediated by several key elements and narrative strategies. First of all, there is a curious lack of any mention of mainstream fashion sources vital to a fashionable consciousness. Anne seems aware of what is fashionable, and yet there is a marked lack of any kind of material associated with mass or popular culture in the novel. We read of no fashion publications or indeed of any kind of visual culture reading material that a young girl of Anne's age would likely be drawn to. There are no scenes of Anne and Diana window-shopping in town or poring over the latest fabrics available to them, either at local stores or from mail order catalogues. Anne's education and home life are curiously remote, isolated, and very nearly cloistered. The elements that influence her world view are directly or indirectly drawn from the natural world that surrounds her, her imagination acting as a filtering mechanism that transforms this raw material into the narratives and stories that inform her life.

Also crucial is the fact that Anne's access to fashion is both restricted and enabled by those around her. Although fashionable dress is a powerful social and ideological marker, it is also indicative of uniformity, excess, and a spoiled or tainted obsession with vanity and appearances. Much of the anxiety surrounding fashionable dress revolved around cultural stereotypes of the New Woman, who was viewed as carelessly breaking acceptable rules of feminine behaviour and presentation, dressing in ways that suited herself rather than her family or her community. Efforts to reinforce traditional feminine roles and by extension acceptable modes of dressing existed in the advice and lifestyle journal literature alongside fashion plates and contemporary discussions of the latest fashions.[36] Anne achieves her access to the positive associations of fashion in the form of gifts, and is therefore a passive consumer, neither shopping for dresses and fabrics nor making her own clothing based on patterns or fashion plates. Her agency is expressive; she communicates her desire for puffed sleeves to those closest to her with varying levels of success. Anne's obsession is rooted in the same social codes and conventions influencing other individuals within Avonlea, and, importantly, it is they who bequeath her fashionable status upon her.

Marilla initially dismisses Anne's request for puffed sleeves, but ultimately gives in when Matthew and Mrs Lynde conspire to bring Anne her puffed sleeve dress, pointing out the importance of 'fitting in.' Later, Diana becomes the taste-maker by helping her dress for the hotel concert at White Sands. Diana suggests that her friend wear her white organdy gown, to which Anne anxiously replies that her pretty blue-flowered muslin is more fashionable: 'But it suits you ever so much better,' said Diana. 'It's so soft and frilly and clinging. The muslin is stiff, and makes you look too dressed up. But the organdy seems as if it grew on you.' Thus, Anne is positioned as 'naturally' stylish in the flowing organdy. She does not make this wardrobe selection herself. Rather, she is enabled and given permission to be unique and artistic by Diana, who has become 'notable' for her taste in dressing.[37] Crucially, it is the active intervention of others and their function as intermediaries that allow Anne to access the symbolic codes defining fashionable and ambitious women at the turn of the twentieth century.

Finally, as an emblem of modernity, femininity, and empowerment, fashion is a structuring narrative device that is at once pervasive and yet curiously absent in *Anne of Green Gables*. It should be said that social reform and artistic reform, which are often clearly linked, lay behind the Aesthetic reframing of the self and one's environment. Anne clearly engages with this process of refining and reforming the self, physically as well as intellectually and morally. Fashion appears to be a comforting and reifying presence in the novel – the girlhood rituals, the wreaths of flowers, the shared moments of dressing, Diana and Anne preparing for the social rituals and events of daily life. The pastoral and rural setting is emphasized, as is Anne's inherent naturalness. Yet fashion in the novel serves a more subversive purpose as well, alluding to the modern world of ambition, evolution, and physical and intellectual transformation. So pervasive is the influence and power of modern fashion that it must be mediated for Anne in the text. This chapter has outlined the ways in which various intermediary figures in the novel provide access and eventually sanction the presence of 'modern' fashion in Anne's world. Through this indirect use of the codes of fashionability, Anne is allowed to have modern desires but remain untainted by the more disturbing elements of the New Woman as she is positioned in late nineteenth-century literary and visual culture. Instead, Anne stays in a safe pastoral space, removed from the modern world, close to home, hearth, and nature, and yet at the same time ambitious, educated, and ultimately fashionable.

NOTES

1 LMM, *Anne of Green Gables* (hereafter in the notes as *AGG*), 88. Throughout this volume, all quotations from *Anne of Green Gables* are taken from the New Canadian Library edition published by McClelland and Stewart in 1992.

2 Emilie Benson Knipe (1870–1958), an American illustrator and co-author of many early twentieth-century children's books with her husband, college football star and coach Arthur Alden Knipe, was only twenty-three years old when she drew the image.

3 Recent publications with a national or geographical focus include Goodrum, *The National Fabric*; Breward, Conekin, and Cox, *The Englishness of English Dress*; Welters and Cunningham, *Twentieth Century American Fashion*; Steele, *The Corset*; Steele, *Paris Fashion*; Gilbert and Breward, *Fashion's World Cities*. Some notable publications on specifically Canadian fashion are Palmer, *Couture and Commerce*; Palmer, *Fashion*; Cooper, *Magnificent Entertainments*.

4 Some examples of work on fashion and literature include C. Hughes, *Dressed in Fiction*; Boucher, *Le vêtement chez Balzac*.

5 For discussions of fashion in *Anne of Green Gables*, in particular the complex meanings inherent in Anne's puffed-sleeved dress, see Careless, 'The Highjacking of Anne'; Gammel, *Looking for Anne*, 169–84.

6 Lears, *No Place of Grace*, xiii.

7 'Fitness and Fashion,' 339.

8 Wahl, 'Fashioning the Female Artistic Self,' 73.

9 Haweis, *The Art of Beauty*, 273–4.

10 Entwistle, *The Fashioned Body*, 108.

11 Gammel, *Looking for Anne*, 171. Gammel adds that 'Wilde, the Irish pope of aestheticism (the pursuit of beauty for its own sake), stopped in Charlottetown, Prince Edward Island, on his tour to America, on October 11, 1882' (ibid.).

12 Ibid., 180–1.

13 Entwistle, *The Fashioned Body*, 108–9.

14 E. Wilson, *Adorned in Dreams*, 9.

15 Severa, *Dressed for the Photographer*, 589.
16 Ibid., 458.
17 LMM, *AGG*, 88.
18 Ibid., 218.
19 LMM, 23 May 1911, in *SJ*, 2: 64–7.
20 Monod, *Store Wars*, 122–3.
21 LMM, *AGG*, 21.
22 Consider the following definition: 'Coarse fabric of linen and wool or cotton and wool, originally made at Lindsey, England. Very popular in American colonies.' Picken, *A Dictionary of Costume*, 214.
23 Harriet Jacobs, *Incidents in the Life of a Slave Girl*, Project Gutenberg, http://www.gutenberg.org/files/11030/11030.txt.
24 LMM, *AGG*, 21.
25 Archives of Manitoba, 'Biography of Pickering-Thomson, Mary Louise, 1879–1967,' Manitobia: Life and Times, http://manitobia.ca/cocoon/launch/en/biographies/MPT/en/MPT.xml.
26 William, 'The Diary of Mary Louise Pickering-Thomson,' 42.
27 Fabric, technique (embroidery, lace), and colour or print (honeysuckle) are the shorthand used by both marketers and consumers of dress at the period, partly because the fabric was one of the most important determinants of how much a garment cost.
28 LMM, *AGG*, 212.
29 Ibid., 217.
30 Picken, *A Dictionary of Costume*, 150.
31 *Fall and Winter Catalogue, 1907–1908*, 175. Prior to this catalogue, the fabric is listed only as an umbrella covering. In the catalogue from four years earlier, umbrellas covered with Gloria cost from $1 to $1.50 coming in at the middle end of the price range. Pure silk taffeta cost between $1.50 and $4, while a simple wool poplin was cheapest at $.50. *Fall and Winter Catalogue, 1903–1904*, 121.
32 LMM, *AGG*, 217. A historical reconstruction of the Gloria dress was made by Katelyn van Massenhoven in 2008 and is housed in the Modern Literature and Culture Research Centre at Ryerson University.
33 LMM, 30 July 1905, in *SJ*, 1: 309.
34 Kitch, *The Girl on the Magazine Cover*, 41.
35 Epperly, *Imagining Anne: The Island Scrapbooks*, 20.
36 For details of L.M. Montgomery's putting great stock in advice and etiquette columns, see Gammel, *Looking for Anne*, 99.
37 LMM, *AGG*, 257.

3 'I'll Never Be Angelically Good': Feminist Narrative Ethics in *Anne of Green Gables*

MARY JEANETTE MORAN

'Which would you rather be if you had the choice -- divinely beautiful or dazzlingly clever or angelically good?'

'Well now, I -- I don't know exactly.'

'Neither do I. I can never decide. But it doesn't make much real difference for it isn't likely I'll ever be either. It's certain I'll never be angelically good.'

– Anne Shirley in conversation with Matthew Cuthbert[1]

Anne's conviction that she can never be 'angelically good' reads like a parody of Coventry Patmore's well-known poem *The Angel in the House* (1858), which came to describe the popular Victorian image of the woman as morally superior and yet at the same time submissive to the man. Underlying this gender stereotype was the ideological belief that wives, who did not participate in the morally ambiguous public sphere, could maintain a kind of instinctive purity that would make the home a safe place to raise children and provide a refuge for their world-weary husbands. As Anne Shirley ponders her want of the ideal wifely qualities (most notably her lack of beauty and moral perfection), she concludes that she would make, at best, a suitable wife for a missionary, since missionaries are not so particular in their choice of wives.[2]

Satirical and funny as it is, Anne's question in the epigraph signals the novel's critical and serious engagement with gender issues, issues that have preoccupied a generation of feminist L.M. Montgomery scholars. Indeed, Anne's ambivalent (or perhaps bidirectional) answer to her own question can be seen as a reflection of the conflict between, on the one hand, her desire to conform to her community's idealized expectations of feminine morality and, on the other hand, her sharp, matter-of-fact critiques of a society that relegates women to the private sphere. Thus it comes as no surprise that feminist critics have had varied interpretations of Montgomery's 1908 novel, as they have claimed it as a feminist text, yet have also wrangled over its scope as such.[3] Taken in its own context, Anne's question to Matthew foregrounds one of the practical dilemmas that faced adolescent women of the early twentieth century as they tried to establish their identities within the options available to their gender: following the model of feminine morality that says women must disavow all thought of self even though this ideal may contradict their own intellectual pursuits.[4] Anne despairs of ever reaching such heights of 'angelic goodness,' largely because she sees this particular type of morality as an inborn quality, one that is socially desirable in women but not present in her own personality.

In 1905, when Montgomery wrote *Anne of Green Gables*, the legacy of 'the angel in the house' lingered despite the emergence of the New Woman and the mischievous gamine in Victorian and Edwardian literature. In turn, literature for girls and young women often depicted this self-abnegating feminine ideal with explicit or implicit approval. Although *Anne of Green Gables* avoids the more straightforward didacticism of earlier novels for girls, such as Charlotte Yonge's *Countess Kate* (1862) and Hesba Stretton's *Jessica's First Prayer* (1867),[5] it does present an ethical model for its readers to follow. According to Shirley Foster and Judy Simons in *What Katy Read* (1995), '*Anne of Green Gables* certainly has lessons to teach, but they are neither the narrowly religious ones of Warner and Cummins, nor the more secularized but still Puritan-oriented ones of Alcott and Coolidge.' Compared with these earlier authors, the lessons of Anne certainly offer a more 'transcendental and organic spiritualism,' as Foster and Simons suggest,[6] but also do more in suggesting a secular, feminist ethics of care. In fact, as I propose, the novel offers valuation for ethical choices that preserve or nurture relationships while at the same time challenging essentialist assumptions that women *naturally* care for others and that they alone bear this responsibility. Montgomery's view of feminist ethical care is by no means one-dimensional, however, as she also makes her readers aware of the darker sides of story-telling – which occasionally appear to threaten rather than enhance community.

More specifically, as I argue below, the feminist ethic of the novel arises from narrative – the stories that Anne tells and to which she listens as well as the way the novel addresses its implied reader. Like all narratives, the stories of *Anne of Green Gables* do not work in a simple or straightforward manner. These stories need the active participation of both teller and listener in order to foster ethically responsible relationships; moreover, inequitable power dynamics can enable those participants to use the narrative situation in a controlling, manipulative, or otherwise unethical fashion. But these very complications reinforce the idea that ethical decision-making requires careful consideration, a paradigm that furthers the autonomy of the novel's young protagonist (and potentially its young readers as well). Articulating the moral lessons of *Anne of Green Gables* through a combination of feminist ethical and narrative ethical theories allows us to see that the novel moves away from a model of angelic, passive, self-sacrificing morality, instead offering its readers across gender boundaries a model of ethical acting, being, and living that ultimately anticipates more recent feminist ethical thought.

Relational Ethics and Story-telling

In her book *In a Different Voice* (1984), Carol Gilligan argues that in addition to the types of ethics that rely on universal principles, there exists an alternative but equally legitimate way of making ethical decisions based on people's emotional connections to each other. Gilligan recognized this alternative paradigm when she tried to understand why existing ethical models consistently rated girls as less ethically mature than boys, and her study explains some of the connections between gender roles and the ways that people make and judge ethical decisions.[7] Since Gilligan, feminist ethics has developed into a multifaceted field, but most feminist forms of ethics share the two components on which Gilligan's study centres: a focus on women's concerns that have been ignored or neglected by more male-centred philosophies and an attempt to develop new ethical theories either arising from these issues or from reconceptualizations of what a system of ethics should be. Feminist ethicists such as Claudia Card and Virginia Held suggest that philosophers should devise guidelines for behaviour based on the theory that relationships with others constitute all human identities, and that as relational beings humans owe various levels of responsibility to particular others and to the communities in which they exist.[8] According to Eve Browning Cole and Susan Coultrap-McQuin, 'many thinkers in feminist ethics argue that moral decision-making should not focus narrowly on the mechanical application of abstract principles but must be sensitive to the ways in which various specific human relationships generate different varieties of responsibility. Finding the desirable moral response requires an assessment of role responsibility.'[9] When making ethical decisions, people should therefore make choices that will construct and maintain relationships and communities.[10] In other words, since my sense of identity depends in part on my relationships as daughter, sister, friend, and teacher, among others, it is ethically right for me to consider the effect of my decisions on these relationships and the people within them.

Many feminist philosophers have found the concept of an ethic of care to be useful in structuring a relational response to moral dilemmas. According to Cole and Coultrap-McQuin, these philosophers 'have turned to women's experiences with care-giving … for concrete demonstrations of feminist ethics. They view the willingness to nurture and a ready capacity for emotional involvement as essential to a humane moral stance in a world of injustice and alienation. They also argue that those values can be expressed in ways that are liberating to women.'[11] Consequently, feminist ethics seek not to replicate the patriarchal (or popular Victorian) model of self-sacrificing, self-abnegating female morality in which women have been encouraged to privilege the good of others in all cases, even when that good conflicts with their own needs (think of Leslie Moore in Montgomery's 1917 novel *Anne's House of Dreams*, who married a man she despises simply to save her mother's house). Instead, feminist ethics hold that caregivers must be given the same kind of consideration granted to those for whom they care, as Nel Noddings observes: 'An ethic of caring strives to maintain the caring attitude. That means that the one-caring must be maintained [as] the immediate source of caring. The one-caring, then, properly pays heed to her own condition … To go on sacrificing bitterly, grudgingly, is not to be one-caring.'[12] In other words, those enacting a caring ethic must also care for themselves in order to maintain the 'ethical ideal' that guides their actions; in addition, it is important to recognize the self as not just a means to enact a caring ethic, but a person who deserves and needs care as much as others do.

Feminist relational ethics, then, prioritize responsibility for others as well as care of the self, as seen in the highly debated example in the final chapter of the novel, when Anne turns down the Avery scholarship so that she can support the ailing Marilla and thus save Green Gables from being sold: 'I can't let you sacrifice yourself so for me. It would be terrible,' Marilla protests, trying to prevent what she assumes is a self-denying decision, but she can only devise a similarly self-sacrificing solution in response.[13] Anne, however, manages to move beyond the angel-in-the-house mentality; her decision 'is no sacrifice,' not because it privileges the needs of others before her own, but because it allows her to strengthen the caring relationship between herself and Marilla, while maintaining their community at Green Gables, and studying Latin and Greek on the side – thereby keeping her options open.[14] With this decision, Anne nurtures the relationships that have always supported her without neglecting her need for intellectual stimulation.

But *Anne of Green Gables* supports a feminist, relational model of ethics not simply through the actions of its characters, but also through the way that those characters – and the novel itself – spin narrative to weave connections among people. Of course, this impulse is not utopian; just as Michel Foucault reminds us of the constant shiftiness of discourse, suggesting that the same discourse can be used as both a discourse of power and a discourse of resistance, so narrative can be spun to different ends; it is because people's stories *can* be used unethically that the implied motivations and consequences of narrative processes must always be carefully considered. Although the moral aspect of narrative has always been of great interest to both critics and readers, in particular with regard to children's literature, late twentieth- and early twenty-first-century scholars of narrative ethics have moved away from placing a value judgment on the morality of the author or the message a text conveys.

Instead, critics such as Wayne Booth, Adam Zachary Newton, and James Phelan analyse the ways in which narrative functions as an ethical process: that is, a process that raises moral dilemmas and necessitates decisions about them. In other words, every time Anne tells a story, she not only brings characters and places to life but also creates an opportunity for ethical recognition between herself and her audience. Phelan describes narrative ethics as arising from the 'principle that literature in general and narrative in particular, through their attention to the concrete particularities of human situations and their capacity to engage our emotions, provide an especially rich arena for the exploration of ethical issues.'[15] Thus, ethics and stories are inherently intertwined because of the human connections created by the narrative process; ultimately, story-telling constructs a triangular relationship among teller, listener, and tale, in which the teller and listener bear an ethical responsibility to each other as well as to the story being told.

Anne invents stories as naturally as she breathes, weaving the people and events of her daily life into fantastical romances that have a real effect for her family, friends, and community. Although Anne's stories are sometimes, as we shall see, antithetical to the ethics of care, their effects are generally positive for herself and others, revealing Anne's empathy and ability to recruit kindred spirits through narration. More often, Anne's tales illustrate the ethical and nurturing function that Newton and Phelan describe, her narratives aligning her with a feminist ethic of care, as seen, for example, in 'Anne's History,' the stories Anne tells about her life before arriving at Green Gables, when her imagination provides her with companions and a source of hope in a life otherwise filled with drudgery. In Anne's first foster home, the Thomas household, the bookcase provides the lonely little girl with a 'narrative friend,' despite the fact that its door is smashed from when Mr Thomas was 'slightly intoxicated.'[16] By fantasizing that her reflection in the remaining bookcase door is a friend named Katie Maurice, Anne creates a community from the only material she has: herself. In imagining this narrative dynamic, Anne also constructs the ethical responsibility entailed by the act of story-telling. Anne would talk to Katie Maurice 'and tell her everything,' pretending that, if she could, her friend 'would have taken [Anne] by the hand and led [her] out into a wonderful place, all flowers and sunshine and fairies.'[17] Anne repeats this narrative pattern at her next foster home, this time with an echo that she can imagine is talking back to her. Both Katie Maurice and Violetta, the imaginary echo-girl, appear to give Anne the emotional response that stories should elicit from real listeners, for, as she recounts to Marilla, Katie Maurice 'was crying when she kissed me good-bye' and Violetta's 'good-bye came back to me in such sad, sad tones.'[18] Though imaginary, Anne's earliest narrative relationships provide a necessary training ground for her emotional and ethical development, as she treats the imaginary friends with care and sensitivity and fairness.

Still, sometimes there are clear power differentials being sketched through story-telling in *Anne of Green Gables*, and on occasion, there is a darker dimension to the story-telling, one that is ultimately crucial to Anne's ethical development, and which opens up fascinating spaces of ethical ambivalence. Consider, for example, the apology scene with Mrs Lynde, after Anne calls Mrs Lynde a rude, impolite woman. In that instance, it is difficult not to read Anne's discourse as performed and simulated. In fact, the apology scene is a delicate moral situation, for as the narrator tells us, Mrs Lynde is 'not ... overburdened with perception,' while quick-witted Anne clearly holds the upper hand in being able to deceive Mrs Lynde.[19] Anne has a twofold goal in this encounter: to follow Marilla's instructions that she apologize, and to get as much enjoyment as she can out of playing the role of the penitent. As Irene Gammel notes in *Looking for Anne*, 'overly dramatic Anne is unconscious of the force of her rebellion and unaware that she is playing her role too well.'[20] In other words, Anne's expert play-acting is a tool that allows her to retain a sense of self and triumph while satisfying the needs of her benefactors, as the narrator emphasizes: 'There was no mistaking her sincerity – it breathed in every tone of her voice.'[21] Thus paving the way for Mrs Lynde's forgiveness, this scene of story-telling presents one of the more complex ethical situations in the novel, one that relies on a convenient handicap as well as on a great deal of dramatic irony, and one in which the reader and Marilla are asked to side with Anne's 'innocent' success in quietly duping Mrs Lynde.

There are times when Anne's stories are incompatible with an ethic of care, as during her disastrous tea with Diana Barry, when Anne entertains her guest with two of her imaginative creations (and the domestic catastrophes they cause). In one of the stories Anne tells, she imagines herself nursing Diana's smallpox only to die herself, and in another story she is a nun 'taking the veil to bury a broken heart in cloistered seclusion.'[22] In the first story, Anne plays a stereotypically self-sacrificing role, caring for Diana with no thought of herself. In the second, she reaffirms the idea that a woman without her love has nothing else in life; having lost one relationship, Anne's nun cuts herself off from all other connections by shutting herself away from the world. While Anne romanticizes both versions of herself, describing the smallpox creation as 'the loveliest story,' Montgomery makes clear the futility of these subject positions, eliminating any thread of seriousness by connecting the stories with their real-world consequences. Self-involved Anne does not realize that her story-telling has detached her from rather than connected her to Diana, so that by the time she thinks to ask, 'Why, Diana, what is the matter?' her friend is already 'awful sick' from greedily gulping currant wine.[23] The episode also satirically exposes the problematic nature of self-sacrificing goodness, since these self-sacrifice stories are shown to lessen bonds of responsibility between teller and listener.

Anne also oversteps the boundaries of narrative ethics by employing narrative manipulation, as when she falsely confesses that she has lost Marilla's amethyst brooch. Her deceptive story nonetheless fails to win Anne forgiveness – and the longed-for trip to the Sunday-school picnic.

Here, Anne tries to create a narrative reality that will get her what she wants, yet ends up inducing its opposite: 'Marilla felt hot anger surge up into her heart again. This child had taken and lost her treasured amethyst brooch and now sat there calmly reciting the details thereof without the least apparent compunction or repentance.' Anne's lack of affect in this fraudulent use of story-telling contradicts her usually passionate personality and threatens to derail the growing connection between her and her caretaker. For the first time, Marilla begins to doubt Anne's sense of ethical responsibility, saying, 'she doesn't appear to realize how wicked she's been at all – that's what worries me most. If she'd really felt sorry it wouldn't be so bad.'[24] Once Marilla finds the brooch caught in her shawl, she apologizes to Anne for encouraging the falsehood, thus repairing their relationship.

By no means always positive, then, story-telling can have a darker side, as Montgomery also illustrates in a chapter titled 'A Good Imagination Gone Wrong.' Usually, Anne maintains a sense of the reality behind her fantasies. No matter how effectively she might pretend to have hair 'black as the raven's wing' or be named Cordelia Fitzgerald, she does understand that these delightful prospects are the productions of her own mind. However, once Anne and Diana imagine the Haunted Wood into existence, Anne fully convinces herself that the ghosts of the 'white lady,' the 'headless man,' and the 'little murdered child' really do exist. It is her own stories that distort her perception of reality and disturb her mind just as effectively as she had with Marilla in the matter of the brooch: 'her terror was very real. Her imagination had run away with her and she held the spruce grove in mortal dread after nightfall.'[25] By teaching Anne to treat external and internal audiences with the same sensitivity, the novel not only reveals the complex nature of narrative ethical relationships, but also links narrative ethics to the feminist ethical precept that care for the self is just as important as care for others.

Weaving Webs of Relationship

Having learned the ethical demands of her position as story-teller, Anne uses narrative to challenge others to meet their relational responsibilities as well, putting story-telling in the service of community building. This occurs, for example, when she encounters Diana's redoubtable Aunt Josephine, who exerts the power of her wealth and position to keep the rest of the Barrys in a constant state of anxiety. When Anne apologizes for jumping into the spare-room bed, Aunt Josephine emphasizes the separation between them by claiming: 'You don't know what it is to be awakened out of a sound sleep, after a long and arduous journey, by two great girls coming bounce down on you.' 'I don't *know*, but I can *imagine*,' Anne replies, displaying an intuitive understanding of how imaginative narratives can forge equitable relationships by expressing empathy and connection with her listener. She then continues: 'I'm sure it must have been very disturbing. But then, there is our side of it too. Have you any imagination, Miss Barry? If you have, just put yourself in our place. We didn't know there was anybody in that bed and you nearly scared us to death. It was simply awful the way we felt.'[26] Happily, Miss Barry *does* have an imagination, so that imaginative identification on both sides, prompted by Anne's engaging story of her experience, forges an ethical bond that stays strong throughout the novel and its sequels. Despite being a self-centred old woman, Aunt Josephine becomes a kindred spirit.

On the level of metanarrative, *Anne of Green Gables* reflects its heroine's realization of the feminist ethical responsibilities created by the bonds among tellers of tales, their audiences, and the stories themselves. Anne expresses a desire to recognize the subjectivity of girls – '"when I am grown up," said Anne decidedly, "I'm always going to talk to little girls as if they were, too, and I'll never laugh when they use big words"' – and the novel similarly treats its implied reader and its protagonist with respect rather than condescension, using an equalizing tone that reveals the faults, idiosyncrasies, and inner lives of adult characters along with those of the supposedly less mature heroine. The novel alerts young readers to the trials of maturity, for example, when Marilla responds '"I don't know about that" ... with a brief sigh' to Anne's expectation that being an adult 'must be lovely' – an exchange that must surely increase in poignancy for older readers returning to the novel. As Anne grows more and more dear to Marilla, the narrator includes deeper insights into her mind; on the night after Anne leaves for Queen's, for example, Marilla 'buried her face in her pillow, and wept for her girl in a passion of sobs that appalled her when she grew calm enough to reflect how very wicked it must be to take on so about a sinful fellow creature.'[27] The novel thus encourages its audience to accept the ethical responsibility entailed by the narrative process in the same way that its heroine eventually does. Just as Anne had asked Aunt Josephine to use her imagination to lessen the distance between them, the narrative here calls its readers to exercise their creative faculties in order to empathize with Marilla's need for outward control, her intense love for Anne, and her growing realization of the ways that relationships with others structure her own identity.

The novel further models and encourages the narrative development of ethical interpersonal connections by allowing Anne a measure of control over her own story. Anne herself narrates many of the events that are most important to her, describing these experiences in long speeches that have an intratextual narratee but that also provide readers with the only direct account of incidents such as the Sunday-school picnic, how Anne extracts herself from the sinking Lily Maid flat, and the first day of the Queen's entrance exams.[28] Without these sections, the narrator's total control of the narrative would represent a power imbalance that seems antithetical to an awareness of ethical responsibility. Anne's portions of the narrative disrupt this potential and simultaneously allow her numerous opportunities to form an intimate connection with her Avonlea audience and her readers. By attending to Anne's need to express her ideas and her creativity while also constructing a direct narrative relationship between Anne and the reader, these moments both enact an ethic of care towards Anne and encourage readers to recognize their ethical responsibility to her – and, by extension, to all story-tellers.

The stories that Anne tells and those to which she listens often counteract the idea that the ability to care for others is innate or determined by gender, thus making a relational ethic available across gender boundaries, not limited to (and therefore limiting of) women. Feminist philosophers have expressed concern over the potential for this kind of limitation in ethics of care; Patricia Ward Scaltas, for example, worries that 'stressing the values of empathy and nurturance or care and contextual thinking as distinctly female and arising out of a distinctly female reality is potentially dangerous to the feminist cause if these can be seen in any way to imply that they are sex-linked or biologically rooted.'[29] The community of Avonlea divides its daily responsibilities according to conventional gender roles, with the duty of nurturing others falling largely to women.[30] We might expect, then, that *Anne of Green Gables* would blunt any feminist ethical message by suggesting that women care for others because they are biologically fated to do so. Within the context of late nineteenth-century gender roles, however, Matthew's identity as a nurturing listener and Anne's musings about how to be a 'good girl' both reframe caring as an ethical activity and challenge the idea that only women have the inclination or the responsibility to care.

Admittedly, Matthew Cuthbert differs from many of the other men in his society, but his ability to care for Anne by actively listening to her stories nevertheless disrupts the notion that only women sense the ethical imperative to nurture others. After he gets over his initial fear of her, Matthew responds to Anne with a level of understanding and sympathy unmatched by anyone else save, possibly, Diana. Matthew's enjoyment of Anne's stories represents a gift in return to the girl who hungers for kindred spirits to appreciate her; moreover, whenever one of Anne's stories gives an indication of self-doubt or insecurity, Matthew provides support. At the same time, Matthew's own habitual taciturnity is powerful in its own way, as on a number of occasions he manages to make Marilla yield not through speech but through silence. Still, he also participates in a 'narrative situation' that functions as profoundly ethical because it simultaneously nurtures Anne's ideas and strengthens the relationship between himself, Marilla, and the love-starved girl (as his interventions are also designed to mediate between Marilla's somewhat rigid rule and Anne's desire for freedom and pleasure). While Matthew's nurturing warm-heartedness helps dissolve the Victorian essentialism of women as *natural* caregivers and supportive angels, Anne's reflective process of self-improvement – which often involves her own ethical response to narrative – challenges the idea that anyone, male or female, has an inborn sense of morality, thus also deconstructing the 'Angel in the House.' Rather than being motivated by some innate moral compass, Anne finds that she must make a conscious effort to act compassionately and ethically in the same way that she has learned to deliberately craft her stories so that they strengthen interpersonal connections. Anne attempts to model her sense of virtue upon Avonlea exemplars of feminine goodness: Marilla, the minister's wife Mrs Allan, and the beloved teacher Miss Stacy, all of whom play nurturing roles (although Miss Stacy is also a modern, independent woman with her own principles and mind). As Anne works to improve herself, she assumes that these role models possess a quality of 'natural' goodness that she can never attain. For instance, Anne admits that she finds it 'easier to be good if [her] clothes are fashionable,' but she supposes 'it doesn't make such a difference to naturally good people.' This statement suggests Anne's internalization of the theory that 'naturally good people' exist on a supreme level of morality inherently unattainable by people who have to work to be good. According to feminist ethics, though, this idea of natural goodness actually limits our perceptions of morality.

One of the goals of feminist ethics, Held observes, should be to investigate how moral decisions that might have appeared 'merely natural' are actually the result of careful consideration. Indeed, when Anne thinks about morality in the context of the narratives told by others, she demonstrates her awareness that a theory of learned rather than natural goodness offers more hope to the individual and the community. Disagreeing with Mrs Lynde's lack of respect for a minister who had confessed to a childhood theft, Anne says, 'I'd have thought what an encouraging thing it would be for small boys nowadays who do naughty things and are sorry for them to know that perhaps they may grow up to be ministers in spite of it.'[31] Anne's sympathetic analysis of the clergyman's story reflects her own struggles to behave more ethically towards those in her community, both through her stories and her actions. The effort that Anne expends in trying to be good, as well as the encouragement she gleans from the narratives of others, emphasize that the development of an ethical perspective is a choice and an ongoing intellectual struggle.

Ulitmately, many popular adolescent heroines of the nineteenth and twentieth centuries appear to lose the qualities that modern readers admire – originality, intelligence, and initiative, to name a few – when the novels introduce situations that require the traditionally female role of nurturing: Jo March becomes Mother Bhaer and cedes the focus of the narrative to her children in *Little Women*; Mary Lennox helps her cousin Colin recover his health, then nearly disappears from the last few pages of Burnett's *The Secret Garden* (1911); the protagonist of Brink's *Caddie Woodlawn* (1935) agrees that she must leave her tomboy ways behind in order to fit herself for the morally purifying role of an adult woman; the rebellious Lyra Silvertongue both defers to and cares for Will Parry in Philip Pullman's *The Subtle Knife* (1997), the second volume in the His Dark Materials series. However, an awareness of the relationship between gender roles and definitions of ethics opens up greater options for both characters and readers than these apparent regressions would seem to imply. Considering feminist narrative ethics in *Anne of Green Gables* provides a vocabulary with which we can analyse critically instances of nurturing behaviour, not only in Montgomery's novel but in other girls' fiction as well.

Both Anne's story-telling methods and those of the novel show how an individual's intellectual effort, rather than detracting from her goodness, can help to maintain relationships and strengthen community. Although the narrative ethical dynamic can be turned towards destructive as well as nurturing ends, this very ambiguity makes goodness even more of a choice and even more of a mental challenge. In fact, as the novel suggests, intellectual effort might even be integral to relational moral action. If that is the case, then one of the messages of *Anne of Green Gables* is that young women should no longer find it necessary to choose between the pursuit of individual achievement and the responsibility of maintaining relationships, for a carefully trained mind enables one to behave ethically towards others as well as oneself.

NOTES

Work on this chapter was supported in part by a grant from the City University of New York PSC-CUNY Research Award Program. I am also indebted to the insightful editing of Irene Gammel, Benjamin Lefebvre, and Saeed Teebi, which contributed greatly to the final version of this chapter.

1 LMM, *AGG*, 24.
2 Ibid., 24.
3 Julia McQuillan and Julie Pfeiffer ('Why Anne Makes Us Dizzy,' 22–4) claim that the novel both challenges and reinscribes specific gender roles and boundaries. Marah Gubar ('"Where Is the Boy?"') argues that in Montgomery's fiction excessively long courtships and postponements of marriage create a feminist space in which single women form communities with each other; similarly, Temma F. Berg ('*Anne of Green Gables*,' 155) notes the 'subtle pervasiveness of [the novel's] feminism.' K.L. Poe ('The Whole of the Moon,' 16) claims that Avonlea represents a matriarchal and 'womanist,' if not precisely feminist, society, an interpretation with which Erica Rothwell ('Knitting Up the World') concurs. Angela E. Hubler ('Can Anne Shirley Help') discovers that Anne is among the characters most likely to inspire preteen girls to think critically about gender roles.
4 In this chapter, I concentrate on the tensions between the 'dazzlingly clever' and 'angelically good' elements of the dilemma. For a discussion that considers the appeal of the 'divinely beautiful,' see McMaster, 'Taking Control.'
5 For a discussion of periodical stories from the *Girl's Own Paper* that 'profiled self-sacrificing heroines in fact and fiction,' see Nelson, *Boys Will Be Girls*, 23–4.
6 Foster and Simons, *What Katy Read*, 157–8. They include *Anne of Green Gables* in a discussion of the ways in which Warner's *The Wide, Wide World*

(1850), Cummins's *The Lamplighter* (1854), Alcott's *Little Women* (1868), and Coolidge's *What Katy Did* (1872) simultaneously conform to and challenge gendered expectations of their times.

7 Gilligan, *In a Different Voice*, 1–2, 9–13, 18–23, 25–32, 62–3.

8 See Card, *Feminist Ethics*; Held, *Feminist Morality*. For an application of feminist ethical theory to issues such as rape, pornography, and pluralism, see Card, *On Feminist Ethics and Politics*. For a feminist ethical analysis of nineteenth-century British literature, see M.J. Moran, 'Telling Relationships.'

9 Cole and Coultrap-McQuin, 'Toward a Feminist Conception,' 2.

10 Of course, relationships between human beings do not necessarily reflect feminist ideals. Laura M. Robinson ('"A Born Canadian,"' 29) examines the potentially exclusionary side of community building.

11 Cole and Coultrap-McQuin, 'Toward a Feminist Conception,' 2.

12 Noddings, *Caring*, 105.

13 LMM, *AGG*, 324.

14 Much of the decision about whether *Anne of Green Gables* is a feminist text turns on the interpretation of this choice. For example, Cecily Devereux ('"not one of those,"' 122) describes Anne's refusal of her scholarship in this way: 'she chooses home and domestic duty over education and independence.' A feminist ethical viewpoint would counter that the notion of independence is an illusory idea, and that in reality, all people define themselves at least partially through their relationships with others, so to prioritize those relationships does not necessarily mean denying the self. See also Drain, 'Community and the Individual,' 129; Gammel, *Looking for Anne*, 186–9.

15 Phelan, *Living to Tell about It*, 21.

16 LMM, *AGG*, 66; see also Booth, *The Company We Keep*, 181.

17 LMM, *AGG*, 67. These elements of Anne's imagination are also woven in Budge Wilson's prequel, *Before Green Gables* (2008).

18 Ibid., 67.

19 Ibid., 72, 83.

20 Gammel, *Looking for Anne*, 127.

21 LMM, *AGG*, 83.

22 Ibid., 139.

23 Ibid., 105, 104, 106.

24 Ibid., 111, 113. Helen Hoy returns to this scene in her chapter in this volume.

25 Ibid., 24, 179, 180.

26 Ibid., 173–4.

27 Ibid., 162, 297.

28 Ibid., 115, 241–2, 277–9. Elizabeth Rollins Epperly (*The Fragrance of Sweet-Grass*, 18) comments that 'the whole of *Anne of Green Gables* is charged with the rhythm and energy of Anne's voice and personality,' while Trinna S. Frever ('Anne Shirley, Storyteller,' 121) states that the narratives told in Anne's voice '[affect] her characterization and her impact on the reader [because] many of the key episodes of the novel are presented by Anne's narration, rendered through her perspective and speaking style.'

29 Scaltsas, 'Do Feminist Ethics,' 23.

30 See McQuillan and Pfeiffer, 'Why Anne Makes Us Dizzy,' 21–4; Rothwell, 'Knitting Up the World,' 135–6; Gammel, *Looking for Anne*, 123.

31 LMM, *AGG*, 250; Held, *Feminist Morality*, 36, 45; LMM, *AGG*, 229.

4 'Too Heedless and Impulsive': Re-reading *Anne of Green Gables* through a Clinical Approach

HELEN HOY

'And there's one thing certain, no house will ever be dull that she's in.'
– Marilla Cuthbert about Anne[1]

When my partner Thomas King was writing the Dead Dog Café Comedy Hour for the International Indigenous Authors' Tour in Vancouver in October 2002, he decided to have character Jasper Friendly Bear, in his usual ebullient and enterprising fashion, write a novel called *Dan of Green Gables*. Jasper's novel, about a young orphaned Native boy sent to live with an elderly brother and sister who own a farm on an island, was, of course, a tribute to and revision of L.M. Montgomery's *Anne of Green Gables*. In a similar vein, my chapter revises this beloved classic of Canadian literature, and in doing so I risk impertinence for challenging standard readings of this popular character. In particular, the many women readers whom Catherine Sheldrick Ross identifies, readers who return repeatedly to *Anne* when stressed or in need of reassurance, may find this reading disturbing – even though, as Mary Henley Rubio notes in her introduction to the collection of essays in which Ross's work appears, critics have recognized that Montgomery has written about 'a deeply flawed world.'[2] The challenge my reading poses, though, only underscores the contingent, provisional nature of both literary hermeneutics and social constructions of behaviour.

Anne acknowledges herself a 'troublesome person,' and Rachel Lynde concurs in a later remembrance of Anne's early years at Green Gables: '"for an odder, unexpecteder witch of a child there never was in this world, that's what."'[3] A *New York Times* book review of 18 July 1908 also dubbed Anne 'altogether too queer.'[4] 'Feather-brained,' 'addle-pated,' 'abstracted,' 'mooning and imagining,'[5] Anne exemplifies inattentive unpredictability. She pours milk in the yarn, walks off the side of a bridge, uses liniment for vanilla, and forgets to fold clothes, to make tea, to put flour in cake, often despite fervid intentions to attend and almost always because of 'daydreaming.' There is ample evidence of empty chatter, black-and-white thinking, poor social skills, impaired judgment, perseveration (persistence), uncontrolled passion, and impulsiveness. At the same time, Anne also exhibits a number of the characteristic strengths that are the flip side of these vulnerabilities: creative intelligence, verbal skill, a strong sense of fairness, generosity, trusting friendliness, energy, curiosity, perseverance, visual acuity and memory, a talent for kinaesthetic learning, a flair for the dramatic, a rich fantasy life, and story-telling ability. I probably need not illustrate these, as this is the mischievous but lovable Anne most readers know.

What may be surprising, perhaps even unacceptable, is the thought that the particular pattern of strengths and deficits exhibited by irrepressible Anne (at least, until chapter 30) creates the behavioural matrix or phenotype of a disorder that has been recognized as such only since 1973: Fetal Alcohol Spectrum Disorder (or FASD).[6] I begin by exploring the striking yet unacknowledged pattern of the heroine's behaviour, but I hasten to add that my clinical reading of Anne's memorable character does not detract from her charm. Rather, my goal is to challenge assumptions both about the novel and about the line between simply wild and irreverent behaviour and behaviour that has clinical implications. Interpreting Anne Shirley as a character with behaviour suggestive of FASD produces a revised appreciation of both characterization and plot. And reading one of Canada's most beloved heroines as developmentally challenged, with her impairments the source of some of her charm, destabilizes the bifurcation of normal and abnormal. Politically, it works to disrupt the stereotypic association of fetal-alcohol damage primarily with marginalized communities, specifically impoverished and First Nations populations, an association produced by differential rates of surveillance and diagnosis.[7] Such an approach may also help explain why people with disability find strength and encouragement in this particular novel.

Reading Behaviour, Rereading Anne

FASD, which currently affects at least 1 per cent of the population,[8] is one of the most prevalent developmental disabilities; sadly, it is also one of the most preventable. It describes brain damage produced by maternal alcohol consumption during pregnancy, damage marked by irreversible cognitive and behavioural disabilities. Of course, applying this term to a child heroine repeatedly characterized as 'bright' and 'sweet' may be perceived by some as involving deliberate, even mischievous perversity. But in the twenty-first century, with an explosion of diagnoses of Asperger Syndrome, autism more generally, attention deficit, and other disorders, it makes sense to reread the novel through the diagnostic tools available today. FASD, a largely invisible disability, produces children whose misfortune is to have an apparent ability that exceeds their actual ability, a chronological age that exceeds their social and psychological age, and an intelligence quotient that exceeds their adaptive quotient (or daily functioning ability). Textual evidence does not give Anne the facial dysmorphia of what is sometimes called full FAS (the thin upper lip, absence of a philtrum, flat midface, and small eye sockets or palpebral fissures), but it does provide the growth deficiency (and reduced adipose tissue) in her foster mother Mrs Thomas's description of Anne as 'the homeliest baby she ever saw, ... so scrawny and tiny and nothing but eyes,' and in reiterations of Anne's 'small face.'[9] In fact, 90 per cent of those with FASD lack the distinctive facial features – produced by alcohol consumed between days eighteen and twenty-one of pregnancy[10] – and ironically have a less promising prognosis, because more is expected of them.

Since fetal-alcohol problems with communication and social skills include empty chatter, 'talking too much and too quickly, but having little to say,'[11] let's begin where Montgomery does, with Anne's talkativeness: '"Oh, she can talk fast enough. I saw that at once,"' says her adoptive mother Marilla Cuthbert. '"It's nothing in her favour, either."'[12] I don't need to belabour this argument. The 'incessant chatter' can include 'asking "nonsense questions,"' and Anne's fifth sentence in the novel – and to a complete stranger, Matthew Cuthbert, who has come to pick her up at the train station – is a query about the appeal of sleeping in cherry trees in the moonlight.[13] The comic incongruity of many of Anne's questions is of course heightened initially by context and by the stolidity of her interlocutor, Matthew, whose response to a query about thrills is to consider grubs. Matthew's eventual dizziness may arise less from the 'nonsense' of Anne's questions, though, than from the darting transitions of what Matthew experiences as her 'brisk mental processes.'[14] These can take Anne from her red hair to a heroine's alabaster brow via 'lifelong sorrow,' or from 'depths of despair' to a digression on chocolate caramels.[15] Diane Malbin indicates that children with FASD 'may be off topic in conversation, respond to a heard word but miss the context.'[16] Anne's susceptibility to tangents provoked by word association is evident even within her own monologues. In this, as elsewhere, she illustrates another characteristic: disorganized narration. Montgomery shows Anne shifting from patchwork to playhouse to fairies to heroines to fainting to dimples to elbow sleeves to the Sunday-school picnic, all in one paragraph.[17] The entertaining disorder of the narration hints at the shallowness accompanying the liveliness of Anne's mental and verbal activity. And fetal-alcohol speech entails frequent and poorly timed interruptions, illustrated as Marilla thrice attempts to report on Miss Stacy's visit, explicitly trying '"to get a word in edgewise"' and noting Anne's preference for '"the sound of your own tongue."'[18]

Given the degree to which Anne's comic mishaps stem from her extreme distractibility, one might want to argue that she is simply a recognizable instance of what would now be seen as a child with attention-deficit/hyperactivity disorder, or ADHD. The two forms of inattention can have different mechanisms, though, and the distinction Barry Stanley makes between ADHD and FASD inattention is one between under-habituation and over-habituation, between filtering out too little and filtering out too much, between lack of focus and excess of focus. Anne is shown to fixate or perseverate on beauty and romance. Her ten-minute delay in fetching the illustrated card of the Lord's Prayer for Marilla results not from aimlessness but from perseveration in an extended reverie before an affecting painting. Stanley describes such children as 'prisoners of the moment,' and descriptions of Anne often involve scenes of stasis, images of her in 'silent rapture,' 'lost to everything,' 'big eyes fixed unswervingly and unseeingly,' 'motionless [and] rapt,' sometimes in the context of her failure to pay attention to her tasks.[19] Having established this visual motif early in the novel, Montgomery thereafter relies more on Anne's extended verbal accounts of her distractions of the imagination. Along with difficulty 'shifting' (changing direction or stopping), Claire D. Coles associates FASD inattention with difficulty 'encoding' (integrating and generalizing information) – as opposed to ADHD difficulty focusing and sustaining attention.[20] In Anne's recurrent 'little mistakes' of absent-mindedness, fancifulness may displace and conceal fundamental challenges in processing information.

Lack of emotional regulation is equally Anne's nature, as Montgomery shows, from the child's initial outburst with Mrs Lynde to the slate over Gilbert's head to the narrator's later conclusion that 'for Anne to take things calmly would have been to change her nature.'[21] Impulsivity, resulting low frustration tolerance, and quickness to anger reflect prenatal alcohol damage to the corpus callosum connecting right and left sides of the brain, nerve fibres that should permit reflection to act upon impulse.[22] Poor habituation to stimuli, resulting from FASD brain damage, means that the alcohol-affected child 'overreacts to situations with surprisingly strong emotional reactions' and 'displays rapid mood swings set off by seemingly small events.'[23] Anne is shown to react excessively and instantly, experiencing '"deeps of affliction"' or 'dizzy realms of delight' and, as Rachel Lynde observes of her quick temper, likely to '"blaze up and cool down."' She is shown, moreover, to react to minor provocations. Even before Marilla's retraction of permission to attend the Sunday-school picnic has Anne 'crying and writhing in an utter abandonment of disappointment and despair,' mere fear of bad weather produces 'a frantic state.'[24] It is no accident that Montgomery selects, as the word proving Anne's spelling proficiency, 'ebullition,' meaning boiling or sudden outburst.[25]

Perhaps equally prominent are Anne's poor judgment and reckless risk-taking, associated with FASD developmental dysmaturity.[26] These are signalled immediately upon Anne's appearance in the novel by her easy contemplation of a prospective overnight spent in the cherry tree and her account of Mrs Spencer's efforts to keep her from falling overboard as she prowls the ferry. Walking the ridge-pole, at the risk of breaking her neck and with the result of breaking her ankle, and floating prone down the river without oars, at the risk of drowning, when the other girls are too frightened to play the Lily Maid, are two central examples of Anne's imprudent fearlessness. In the latter case, as earlier when she and Diana jump onto a sleeping houseguest, Miss Josephine Barry, Anne recognizes her relentless propensity for getting herself and her friends into 'scrapes' but blames her poor luck. In this, she demonstrates the FASD difficulty with connecting cause and effect or actions and consequences.[27] Admittedly, in both these incidents, chance does play a part – the unannounced presence of Miss Barry in the spare room, the damage to the bottom of the rowboat. But Mrs Lynde in the first instance and Marilla in the second also implicate Anne's judgment: '"It's because you're too heedless and impulsive, child, that's what. You never stop to think"' and '"Will you *ever* have any sense, Anne?"' Anne's response to Mrs Lynde – '"Something just flashes into your mind, so exciting, and you must out with it. If you stop to think it over you spoil it all"' – confirms the impulsivity that is also part of this recklessness.[28]

Verbal superficiality and disorganization, distractibility and inattention, impulsiveness and emotional volatility, poor judgment and recklessness are central behaviours of the alcohol-affected child and of Anne Shirley until almost the end of the novel. Along with these, Montgomery represents perspicaciously in her heroine most of the cluster of other fetal-alcohol behaviours, some more peripherally: sensory-integration difficulties, problems with time, social naïveté, susceptibility to peer influence, difficulty distinguishing fantasy from reality, black-and-white thinking, perseveration, concrete or literal thinking, failures to generalize, and lying or confabulation. Sensory-integration dysfunction describes over- and under-sensitivity to sensory stimuli, including pain and temperature.[29] When Marilla exclaims at Anne's running out into the January snow without hat or wrap, risking 'her death of cold,' impulsiveness may be augmented by insensitivity to cold, a frequent challenge to caregivers of FASD children. What Marilla interprets as a failure to obey, Anne's return from Diana's forty-five minutes late, may well reflect symptomatic difficulties with conceptualizing and managing time, the absence of an 'internal time clock.'[30]

Like her absence of stranger anxiety with the stationmaster and with Matthew at first meeting, Anne's initial encounter with bosom friend Diana Barry is a fine example of social inappropriateness, a tendency to be 'overly friendly, highly social,' and 'indiscriminate with relationships.'[31] Caregivers of alcohol-affected children note their children's difficulty grasping the progressive stages of friendship and intimacy, becoming instead instant best friends. Within moments of their first meeting, Anne gallops from asking whether Diana can 'like [her] a little' to asking the poor child to swear to be her 'bosom friend' for 'as long as the sun and moon shall endure.'[32] Given the norms of the day, her impetuous embrace of Miss Barry could be perceived too as an alcohol-affected lack of personal and physical boundaries.[33] Susceptibility to peer influence for good and ill, including victimization and scapegoating, is another social effect of fetal-alcohol exposure and mental-representation problems,[34] one we see in Anne's inability to resist Josie Pye's goading to walk the ridge-pole. The more positive side of this is seen when Anne perhaps 'caught something of the "model" spirit from Minnie Andrews' when paired with that good influence on her return to school.[35]

Confabulation and 'lying,' whether out of memory gaps and failures or desire to please and appease, are characteristic of children with
FASD, with false confession, especially in legal situations, being augmented by a failure to understand the ramifications of that admission.[36]
Here, of course, Anne's 'confession' over the missing amethyst brooch,
with her innocent request to have punishment meted out at once so that
she can go to the picnic carefree, is a case in point. The brain disorganization that underlies many of these behaviours, Malbin observes, 'requires greater effort and causes fatigue, requiring greater need for rest.'
Positron Emission Tomography or PET scans show the entire brain of
an FASD child working on a task that engages only a small part of another child's brain.[37] The concerned Spencervale doctor's prescription
for Anne, then, of a summer of fresh air and a break from books, before
her final year at the Avonlea school, could be read as recognition of this
global kind of fatigue.

The Context: A Baby in Every Bottle

My reading above, though, hinges necessarily on the possibility, for
Anne, of alcohol exposure before birth. Although alcoholism is present
in the novel in the figure of Mrs Thomas's husband and although even
Marilla persists in producing her own potent-enough wine despite mild
community disapprobation, the novel provides no indication of alcohol
consumption by Anne's birth mother, let alone during pregnancy. What
little we hear of Anne's deceased, young, school-teaching parents suggests impoverished respectability. At the same time, even in 'dry' communities, as an annotation to the Norton edition of the novel points out,
'brandy, rye whiskey, and wines were kept and used as remedies for
many ailments.'[38] An array of affordable herbal patent medicines was
being sold in the period, moreover, some as 'women's tonics' targeting
female consumers. Alcohol was the solvent and preservative and a central component of these patent medicines. Lydia Pinkham's Vegetable
Compound, one of the most popular of these, was sold from 1875 on
and was registered in Canada as No. 4155 under the 'Proprietary or
Patent Medicine Act' as an 'appetite stimulant' and 'general tonic.'[39]
Along with black cohosh and other herbal remedies, it contained 19
per cent ethyl alcohol, making it 38 proof (wine is 13 per cent alcohol,
rum usually 40 per cent).[40] Such tonics provided an opportunity for innocent, even commendable dosing with what might not be recognized
as alcohol, however agreeable the effects. Early marketing even linked

the compound with increased fertility, in the claim, 'There's a Baby in Every Bottle.'[41] Under current medical protocols, in the absence of the distinctive facial dysmorphia (a combination of features unique to FASD), evidence of alcohol consumption during pregnancy is a requisite for diagnosis of FASD. Anne exhibits many of the cognitive and behavioural signs of fetal-alcohol damage, but without confirmed alcohol exposure. So, like many alcohol-affected adopted children, she would technically only qualify for a diagnosis of static (i.e., permanent) encephalopathy, essentially the same disability with an unverifiable cause.

A novel, of course, is not a case study, and Montgomery makes entrancing, comic, and endearing what my discussion threatens to pathologize. Also, youth, temperament, and an early lack of proper 'bringing up' could account for much of Anne's behaviour. And yes, all of these traits can be found in neurotypicals (a term popular in the autism community) – though given the current (low) estimates of at least one case of FASD per one hundred births in North America, some of the counter instances may well be themselves undiagnosed examples of the disorder. Most of us have been distracted, lost our tempers, forgotten to do something, behaved recklessly, held a grudge, or been badly disappointed. What distinguishes children with the disability, however, is the intensity, frequency, inappropriateness, and intractability of the behaviour: 'These characteristics may appear to be typical behaviour in a normal person, but in individuals who have been disabled by prenatal exposure to alcohol, these traits occur in grossly exaggerated form and do not respond to typical interventions.'[42] The concatenation and extremes of the behaviours and deficiencies, few of them unique in themselves, mark out the child with FASD as unusual, and that is precisely how Anne is perceived in Avonlea.

But what about Anne's ability to learn from her mistakes – given that inability to learn from experience is a hallmark of FASD[43] – not to mention her intelligence and her articulateness? Anne's position tied for top place in the province's college entrance exams and winning of the Avery Scholarship do testify to her mental ability. Even today some doctors will use intelligence pre-emptively to dismiss the possibility of FASD. In fact, though, 90 per cent of those children with FASD but without all the facial anomalies have average or above-average IQs, as Streissguth cautions: 'IQ scores alone often fail to give an adequate picture of either organic brain damage or dysfunctional and maladaptive behaviors.'[44] More significant to me as a counterargument is Anne's ability to *use* her intelligence successfully, to apply herself and follow through on her studies, evidence of good executive functioning. Alcohol damage to the frontal lobes means that 'many individuals with FAS/FAE have impairments in "executive function" tasks, involving forming, planning, and carrying out goal-directed behaviors.'[45] Anne's late adolescence, by contrast, testifies to her ability to pursue goals, including academic ones that so challenge the FASD brain. Earlier, too, in saving Minnie May Barry from the croup, Anne strikes the doctor not just as '"smart as they make 'em,"' but as displaying '"a skill and presence of mind perfectly wonderful in a child of her age."'[46]

To this I respond with two considerations. More than today, much of Anne's education requires rote and formulaic learning, whether committing poetry to heart, performing recitations (where Anne's kinaesthetic learning skills come into play), memorizing historical dates and events, or 'hard work and patient grubbing among unimaginative equations and conjugations,' rather than complex conceptualizing.[47] (Miss Stacy's enlightened addition of field trips and 'physical culture exercises'[48] plays to the FASD need for large-muscle activity, physical breaks, and multi-sensory, hands-on, contextual learning, as well as narration and story-telling.) Second, the perseveration that taints her relationship with Gilbert Blythe serves Anne well academically, with her rivalry leaving her 'inflexibly determined on learning.' As with Anne's struggle in geometry, mathematics is typically the bane of the FASD student. The description of Anne's having 'wrestled wildly with decimals the entire evening before' in order to best Gilbert conveys something of the cognitive and emotional cost this persistence extracts.[49] 'Repeat, repeat, repeat' is one of the formulas for training or teaching alcohol-affected children, given memory difficulties. Anne testifies to its efficacy when she states, '"I've pored over that geometry until I know every proposition in the first book off by heart, even when the letters *are* changed."'[50] Similarly, with Minnie May, as Anne herself points out, three pairs of twins with regular croup provide plenty of preparatory practice (and this would be visual and manual, rather than conceptual learning).

Alcohol-affected children have been described as verbal 'savants,' who, because they talk well, are mistakenly assumed to think well, to their great detriment.[51] What is notable in the novel is the degree to which the author draws the reader's attention to the process of Anne's verbal development and the limits of her competence. '"My life is a perfect graveyard of buried hopes. That's a sentence I read in a book once,"' Anne allows. The child with FASD, says Malbin, 'may rely on stereotypic words, phrases ... may borrow words, stories heard from someone else or from TV.'[52] Critics have readily identified the popular literary sources of Anne's elevated phrases, and the text itself often highlights, especially initially, her incomprehension of the incongruous vocabulary and metaphors she adopts. 'Alabaster,' 'mahogany,' and 'squadrons' are all words she luxuriates in, while simultaneously puzzling over their meaning. Similarly, she accompanies figures of speech – that wild horses cannot drag a secret from her or that she can be led to the block for her honesty – with overt acknowledgment of her bewilderment over the phrases.[53]

Montgomery also captures well Anne's misapplication of formulas she has picked up, most notably in concluding her prayer, 'I remain, / Yours respectfully' (with the epistolary typography itself highlighting the inaptness of her formulation). Her parroting of others is made less explicit, though we see her eagerly echoing 'handsome auburn' twice within moments of first hearing it. The repetition of '"Mrs Lynde says"' five times in one paragraph, on the subject of a suitable minister, draws our attention to this verbal echoing and mental apprenticeship.[54] On a larger scale, Frank Davey explores Anne's anxious 'learning of other people's scripts' of apology, confession, and so on, arguing that the narrative endorsement of this mastery 'masks the extent to which the scripts are coming to control her disruptive and "imaginative" aspects.'[55] The anxiety he documents so well can be read as the anxiety produced by neurological difference and by the need to mimic deliberately and consciously what comes more inferentially and intuitively to others. The scripts Anne learns can be seen as the FASD ability to 'pass,' but as Malbin notes, 'the illusion of competency and attempts to "fit in" may also mask the disability.'[56]

But Anne is shown to find success in spite of what I would argue is a presumably inadvertent portrait of a neurocognitive handicap. Apart from an early school refusal, she is presented as headed for none of the usual 'secondary disabilities' resulting from societal failures to accommodate the disability: disrupted schooling, addictions, sexual misbehaviour, trouble with the law, mental health disorders, confinement, and difficulty with employment and independent living.[57] Certainly, in her reiterated conviction that she is not naturally good, Anne could be interpreted as at risk for a common effect of fetal-alcohol exposure, a damaged sense of self. But that outcome fails to materialize. Children with FASD are sometimes described as the children who pass their tests but fail at life, whereas Anne's story here concludes with what, in fetal-alcohol terms at least, would have to be read as a triumph. But Barbara Morse points out that 'only ten to twenty percent of children with FAS may have effects as severe as those represented in the medical litera- ture. Most have subtler effects, and improvement is seen over time.'[58] A number succeed in college or university, in jobs, and with families. In fact, *Anne of Green Gables* offers a hopeful and promising model of possibilities as well as a positive resource in the growing field of biblio- therapy to families dealing with FASD.

A Stable and Nurturing Home

In the course of Anne's story, Montgomery not only illustrates but often also articulates a number of strategies for creating the supportive en- vironment needed by those neurologically challenged, strategies now being spelled out in the field. 'Living in a stable and nurturing home of good quality,' 'not having frequent changes of household,' and 'not being a victim of violence' are three of five protective factors identified by Streissguth, all of which the novel illustrates, at least once Anne ar- rives at Avonlea.[59] The FASD literature stresses simplifying the physical environment as a means of reducing sensory overstimulation, and taci- turn Matthew exemplifies the comfort of silence welcome to those with auditory-processing delays. The tranquil natural setting of Avonlea, to which Anne returns with passionate commitment at the novel's end, is a similarly conducive environment. Marilla illustrates what we now know to work well, the use of strong, exact, and short instructions.[60] (Montgomery is specific too about the predictable futility, by contrast, of Marilla's well-meaning and more extended moralizing.) Critics have discussed the novel's place in negotiating traditional and emergent theories of child development and child-rearing in the culture of Mont- gomery's day. In addition, I suggest, the narrative here models (and in some cases articulates) principles and conditions fostering the well- being of children with neurological challenges that would not be identi- fied for another three-quarters of a century.

Living with a child affected by prenatal alcohol exposure has often been compared to a rollercoaster ride between calms and crises, de- light and distress.[61] In the single scene of the missing amethyst brooch, Montgomery explores in Marilla the range and turbulence of emotions produced by a neurologically damaged (or, admittedly, otherwise non- compliant) child: anxiety, pity, estrangement ('Marilla felt deserted by every one'), emotional exhaustion ('By night she was, as she expressed it, "beat out'"), bitter triumph, 'hot anger,' bewilderment ('"If she isn't [crazy] she's utterly bad'"), misgivings ('"I'm afraid Rachel was right from the first'"), resolve ('"But I've put my hand to the plough and I won't look back'"), redirected frustration ('Marilla worked fiercely ... Neither the shelves nor the porch needed it – but Marilla did'), exasperation, amusement, self-recrimination, and relief.[62] Several times later in the text, Montgomery shows Marilla familiar enough with the rollercoaster to expect 'more trouble,' or 'something queer' when things have been 'too smooth,' recognizing: '"You haven't got into any scrape for over two months, and I was sure another one was due."'[63]

As an alternative to nervous collapse, FASD offers challenged caregivers the opportunity for unanticipated emotional growth. Of the novel, Margaret Atwood argues: 'The only character who goes through any sort of essential transformation is Marilla ... in her battles of will with Anne, Marilla is forced to confront herself, and to regain what she has lost or repressed: her capacity to love, the full range of her emotions.' While stressing Anne's growth too in maternalism, Cecily Devereux supports this reading of Marilla, with her assumption that 'Anne's work has been to awaken "mother-love" in Marilla Cuthbert.'[64] *Anne of Green Gables* provides a narrative not only of the trials and delights of a disabled child, but also of the taxing and transformative course of parenting children with impairments.

My proposed interpretation of Anne as potentially fetal-alcohol affected produces a fresh reading of the novel's debated ending, 'The Bend in the Road.' Devereux writes that 'Gillian Thomas has not been alone in seeing Anne's rejection of a literary career in favour of domesticity as an indication of the heroine's "decline,"' while Elizabeth Epperly concludes that 'Anne's quieting down, two-thirds of the way through the book, suggests her tentative leanings towards the stereotypical image of womanhood that favors reserve, tolerance, self-sacrifice, domesticity, and dreamy-eyed abstraction.'[65] In light of FASD strategies advocating interdependence in place of independence, though, Anne's decision to remain in Avonlea, to surrender her studies in order to support an ailing Marilla, need not be read as either the womanly self-sacrifice or feminist defeat of early and later readings of the novel, and it is here that my essay briefly converges with Mary Jeanette Moran's in the preceding chapter. The reduced cognitive and organizational challenges of the role Anne adopts as local schoolteacher and Marilla's caregiver may represent a better fit with her proclivities and capabilities than college would have. Even as an adult, a person with FASD is likely to need external human supports, familiar structures, and a simplified environment, features of the future Anne chooses in selecting Avonlea and Marilla over Redmond. In the words of one parent of an alcohol-affected child, 'My child's biggest handicap is society's insistence on autonomy.'[66] Read within a disability framework, a positive ending to the novel may call for new definitions of success.

A Final Bend in the Road

I have been arguing that Anne has been read for a hundred years without recognition of what could be seen as a central, though presumably unintentional, organizing structure of her characterization. Within the context of my clinical reading, I will end with a caveat. As disability theory would point out, by simply applying a label, we diagnose and discipline the subject. The medical model of disability, described sardonically by Robert McRuer as 'designed to proffer advice on how to help your kids turn out pathologized,'[67] is at odds with Disability Studies' focus on how the very categories of ability and disability are constructed and what purposes they serve. Whereas the medical model concentrates on how to assist people with disabilities (and is produced by those without disabilities), disability theory (produced primarily by those with disabilities) challenges the assumptions and comparisons that produce the category 'disabled' in the first place. In a now-commonplace formulation, disability theory exposes the social norms that turn impairment (a physical condition) into disability (a social condition). More recently, indeed, theorists have gone on to argue that impairment in itself is already a socially mediated and constructed condition.[68] And so, rather than consolidating Anne's identity as a fictional exemplum of FASD, I would prefer that my reading highlight the contingency of such temporally located understandings.

When *Anne of Green Gables* was written and initially read, the same dialogue and behaviour that I have drawn on to illustrate my hypothesis about Anne were read through quite different lenses. Particular templates of class, breeding, and morality helped organize judgments and emotional responses to the character, her initial actions, and her subsequent development. More recently, issues of national and regional values, of cultural change, and of gendered and sexual identity have been more to the forefront.[69] Reading Anne as intelligible within a disability framework is the application of yet another interpretive paradigm, one currently being lived – and being challenged – just as were the assumptions of class and breeding and morality in Montgomery's day. Readers and the world from which they form their understandings will presumably continue to shift and affect reception of this work, and the text itself provides the fictional ground for such varying interpretations. As Devereux points out concerning tensions between controversial and more conventional readings of *Anne*, 'those ideas and values, while they inhere in the community of readers, are not projected upon the work; they are always textually encoded.'[70]

Even if the textual specifics of *Anne of Green Gables* produce a character with neurocognitive characteristics that can now be read as potentially fetal-alcohol affected, the world within the novel receives them otherwise. Rather than othered as damaged and deficient, Anne Shirley is thoroughly embraced by the end of the novel, as figured in Miss Barry's valuing of Anne's rainbow hues over the 'provoking and eternal sameness' of other girls.[71] Both the characters of fictional Avonlea and Montgomery's readers, until now, have learned to appreciate the differences setting Anne apart, without finally needing to stigmatize them as abnormal. Whether read as 'brisk mental processes' or disordered narration, 'fresh enthusiasms' or impulsivity, courage or recklessness, 'transparent emotions' or impaired emotional regulation, honest passion or poor tolerance of frustration, imagination or distractibility, what matters less are the characteristics themselves than their fit with their social environment. Arguably, diagnoses such as FASD have emerged as we have moved further from a world like Avonlea, where the peculiarities of a brain such as Anne's can find a comfortable home. As Gary Kiger points out, '"disability" has no inherent meaning ... [It] is relational and is not inherent in the individual.'[72] If most of us could fly, those few with mere arms and legs would be disabled, and cars would be special-needs vehicles.

Robert McRuer writes that 'a system of compulsory able-bodiedness repeatedly demands that people with disabilities embody for others an affirmative answer to the unspoken question, "Yes, but in the end, wouldn't you rather be more like me?"'[73] Anne, however, is a character who invites and rewards identification, as the history of the novel's reception over the last hundred years amply testifies. In her adult years, when Anne becomes more 'normalized' just as her flaming red hair becomes more conventionally 'auburn,' my argument becomes admittedly more tenuous, but this is not surprising, given L.M. Montgomery's habit of superimposing conventional endings on her otherwise subversive fiction. Interestingly, it is the heedless Anne – the one who cannot help but get into mischief and who works so hard to endear herself in Avonlea by mimicking its scripts – who captures the reader's imagination more than a century later. In raising the possibility that this iconic character can also be read as impaired, I see *Anne of Green Gables* as confounding the all-too-familiar distinction between fully human people and deficient people, between able and disabled. Even more, though, this reading highlights the degree to which the meaning of disability is a product of the social imagination, as evidenced by our capacity to read the characteristics and behaviours of the same fictional character in such strikingly different ways.

NOTES

1 LMM, *AGG*, 116. A longer version of this chapter, with more detailed evidence of Anne's FASD tendencies, is available from the author.
2 Ross, 'Readers Reading L.M. Montgomery,' 31; Rubio, 'Harvesting Thistles,' 12.
3 LMM, *AGG*, 176, 268.
4 'A Heroine from an Asylum,' 404.
5 LMM, *AGG*, 103, 135, 41, 65.
6 FASD is an umbrella term for diagnoses including Fetal Alcohol Syndrome (including the distinctive facial dysmorphia) and Alcohol-Related Neurodevelopmental Disorder (formerly known as Fetal Alcohol Effect, and lacking the face but including the cognitive and developmental damage). Streissguth, *Fetal Alcohol Syndrome*, 38–9.
7 Malbin, *Trying Differently but Not Harder*, 64.
8 Sampson et al., 'Incidence of Fetal Alcohol Syndrome,' 317.
9 LMM, *AGG*, 47, 130; see also Streissguth, *Fetal Alcohol Syndrome*, 26.
10 Malbin, *Fetal Alcohol Spectrum Disorders*, 143.
11 *Parenting Children*, 11.
12 LMM, *AGG*, 37.
13 Malbin, *Fetal Alcohol Spectrum Disorders*, 31; LMM, *AGG*, 19.
14 LMM, *AGG*, 22.
15 Ibid., 24, 34.
16 Malbin, *Fetal Alcohol Spectrum Disorders*, 14.
17 LMM, *AGG*, 103–4.
18 Malbin, *Fetal Alcohol Spectrum Disorders*, 31; Streissguth, *Fetal Alcohol Syndrome*, 127; LMM, *AGG*, 259, 261.
19 B. Stanley, 'Attention Deficits and FASD'; LMM, *AGG*, 49, 39, 41, 64.

20 Coles, 'Fetal Alcohol Exposure and Attention,' 199–203.

21 LMM, *AGG*, 193.

22 Streissguth, *Fetal Alcohol Syndrome*, 98.

23 Ibid., 126.

24 LMM, *AGG*, 194, 84, 112, 104.

25 Ibid., 122.

26 Malbin, *Fetal Alcohol Spectrum Disorders*, 32.

27 Ibid., 30; LMM, *AGG*, 171.

28 LMM, *AGG*, 171, 246, 171.

29 Malbin, *Fetal Alcohol Spectrum Disorders*, 35.

30 LMM, *AGG*, 161, 102; *Parenting Children*, 9.

31 *Parenting Children*, 8.

32 LMM, *AGG*, 97–8.

33 Ibid., 255.

34 Streissguth, *Fetal Alcohol Syndrome*, 155; 'Appendix: Central Nervous System Abnormalities Associated with Fetal Alcohol Syndrome (FAS),' U.S. Centers for Disease Control and Prevention, http://www.cdc.gov/mmwr/preview/mmwrhtml/rr5411a2.htm.

35 LMM, *AGG*, 151.

36 Malbin, *Trying Differently but Not Harder*, 43; 'Fetal Alcohol Spectrum Disorders and the Justice System,' http://fasdjustice.on.ca/investigation.pdf.

37 Malbin, *Fetal Alcohol Spectrum Disorders*, 31; Malbin, *Trying Differently but Not Harder*, 20.

38 LMM, *AGG*, ed. Rubio and Waterston, 107n4.

39 Doris B. Linden, '"A Baby in Every Bottle?" The Story of Lydia Pinkham,' http://glswrk-auction.com/025.htm.

40 According to Sarah Stage, the label claimed 18 per cent. Even the prescribed dose would apparently equal more than a pint of whiskey a month. Some tonics were as high as 44 per cent alcohol or 88 proof. Stage, *Female Complaints*, 32, 183, 170, 194, 167.

41 Ibid., 127.

42 McKinney, La Fever, and DeVries, *Nurture*, 13.

43 Streissguth, *Fetal Alcohol Syndrome*, 106, 152.

44 Ibid., 31; see also 103.

45 Ibid., 102.

46 LMM, *AGG*, 159.

47 Ibid., 281.

48 Ibid., 205.

49 Ibid., 152, 151.

50 Ibid., 266. Note the FASD difficulty with generalizing here.

51 Jan Lutke and Tina Antrobus, 'Fighting for a Future: FASD and "the System": Adolescents, Adults and Their Families and the State of Affairs,' Proceedings from a Two-Day Forum, 19–20 June 2004, http://www.fasdconnections.ca/HTMLobj-1807/fighting_for_a_future.pdf, 63.

52 LMM, *AGG*, 45; Malbin, *Fetal Alcohol Spectrum Disorders*, 31.

53 LMM, *AGG*, 24, 68, 92, 81, 108.

54 Ibid., 59, 83–4, 184–5.

55 Davey, 'The Hard-Won Power,' 179.

56 Malbin, *Fetal Alcohol Spectrum Disorders*, 33.

57 Streissguth, *Fetal Alcohol Syndrome*, 105, 108–10.

58 Morse, 'Information Processing,' 28.

59 Streissguth, *Fetal Alcohol Syndrome*, 111. The other two factors, involving diagnosis and developmental services, would not apply in the time of the novel.

60 Streissguth, *Fetal Alcohol Syndrome*, 127; Malbin, *Fetal Alcohol Spectrum Disorders*, 49.

61 Buxton, *Damaged Angels*, 260, 264.

62 LMM, *AGG*, 110–12. Characteristics of FASD caregivers include grief, frustration, resistance to suggestions, conflict with other adults, and apparent craziness. Debolt, 'Fetal Alcohol Spectrum Disorder.'

63 LMM, *AGG*, 151, 131, 233.

64 M. Atwood, Afterword, 335–6; Devereux, '"not one of those,"' 124.

65 Devereux, '"not one of those,"' 125; Epperly, *The Fragrance of Sweet-Grass*, 37.

66 Lutke and Antrobus, 'Fighting for a Future,' 11 (see n51, above).

67 McRuer, *Crip Theory*, 151.

68 See, e.g., McRuer, *Crip Theory*; R.G. Thomson, *Extra-ordinary Bodies*; Tremain, 'On the Government of Disability'; and Wendell, *The Rejected Body*.

69 Gammel and Epperly, 'L.M. Montgomery,' 6–9; Robinson, 'Bosom Friends.'

70 Devereux, 'Anatomy of a National Icon,' 41.

71 LMM, *AGG*, 306.

72 Kiger, Introduction, 1.

73 McRuer, *Crip Theory*, 9.

5 Reading to Heal: *Anne of Green Gables* as Bibliotherapy

IRENE GAMMEL

> I used bibliotherapy for years without ever knowing it. There was a time when I practiced domestic law. My clients were constantly coming to me with problems that could not be resolved in a courtroom. The only way I knew to assist them was by recommending books that had helped me through difficult times.
>
> – Jacqueline Stanley, *Reading to Heal*[1]

It was September 2005, in front of our apartment building at Yonge and Wellesley in Toronto. On the warm and sunny fall evening, the rush-hour traffic had subsided, and the evening shift of panhandlers, shoppers, and strollers heading to cafés and restaurants was already humming along on the sidewalks. A middle-aged tourist couple was standing at the corner, immersed in a large map – static in the moving throng. We stepped up to them and asked if we could help. They were looking for the Distillery District, a popular Toronto tourist site known for its Victorian industrial architecture. 'Where are you from?' we asked, and it turned out that they were from New Orleans. Hurricane Katrina had made their neighbourhood unsafe and they had decided to travel through Canada. The woman had a silkscreen printing shop in New Orleans, and after ensuring that their property was secure, they'd flown to Halifax, slated for a cross-Canada tour. Already they'd been to Prince Edward Island. They'd been to Cavendish and had seen Green Gables. It turned out that their son, who was in Grade 8, was reading *Anne of Green Gables* in his Louisiana Junior High School. Is it surprising that Green Gables was the first 'refuge' for two people who had temporarily lost their home in a historic disaster?

Maybe not. Adrienne Clarkson, Canada's governor general from 1999 to 2005, came to Canada as a refugee from Hong Kong, thrust out of her home and into Ottawa in the cold winter of 1942. In a personal essay she recounts that she found an extended family in L.M. Montgomery's fiction. Being orphaned or losing a parent was the stuff of *Anne of Green Gables*, but it was also her situation: 'And Matthew and Marilla were like the safe haven that Canada was for me.'[2] Four decades earlier, in 1912, Anne had arrived in Poland, a country torn between three hostile world powers: Russia, Prussia, and Austria. The Polish Underground Army soldier and poet Jerzy Wyszomirski noted in *Tydzie* magazine in 1948 that in times of stress, Anne brought joy and cheerfulness and comfort to afflicted and traumatized readers in Poland. In fact, during the Second World War, 'the Publishing section of the Polish Army in Palestine issued *Anne of the Island* among other world's classics' (and today there is an L.M. Montgomery School in Warsaw).[3] After the Second World War, Japanese readers similarly connected with the novel when Hanako Muraoka's translation *Akage no An* (Red-haired Anne) hit the bookstore shelves and became part of the school curriculum in 1952. The war had sensitized the Japanese to the plight of orphans, and readers were drawn to the uplifting story, whose power has not abated; today Japanese fans continue to read Anne for inspiration, using it as a guidebook for life.[4]

'I recognize in her nearly all my faults and deficiencies, most of my moods, impulses and secret thoughts,' said thirty-two-year-old Helen Keller about Anne after borrowing the book in Braille from the Congressional Library in Washington in 1912: 'She is a great trial to others in the same way that I am, speaking in large terms. Like me she takes the joys and sorrows of life tremendously and like me she has a passion for everything which "gives scope for imagination."'[5] Deaf and blind at nineteen months of age, Helen Keller also shared Anne's perseverance and ambition to triumph over adversity, as she went on to become an inspirational figure for the visually and hearing impaired. But what is behind the therapeutic benefits reported anecdotally by readers? What is it in *Anne of Green Gables* that would prompt a woman just diagnosed with breast cancer to reread the novel, as reported by Margaret Steffler in this volume, or that would help alleviate the pains of confinement? (Montgomery, who reports the story of a husband who read the text to his wife to distract her in the delivery room, thought the husband was a hero.[6])

Others have preceded me in noting that there may be psychological benefits in reading *Anne of Green Gables*. 'There is psychological therapy in the reading of a book that helps externalize hidden parts and conflicting parts of the self,' writes Elizabeth Waterston in *Kindling Spirit* (1993),[7] while Catherine Sheldrick Ross finds that readers of the Anne and Emily series respond to a 'common set of satisfying elements in Montgomery's books' that provide a 'safe place' for readers and that link readers with their parents and grandparents. In fact, it is the text's very ability to make people 'feel good' that was used by earlier critics to denigrate Montgomery's fiction as passive escapism,[8] a charge debunked by Angela Hubler, whose study identifies the ways in which female readers enter into Anne's struggles psychologically, extrapolating from the text experiences of gender competition or disenfranchisement that mirrored those in their own lives.[9] Meanwhile, Clarence Karr has shown that Montgomery herself used books to fill different psychological needs, picking up a garden book when the snow stormed outside, a girls' book when she felt old, and a boys' adventure book when she was tired of mundane household chores.[10] We now also know that her voracious appetite for books helped her ward off feelings of loneliness and depression, especially during the period that preceded the writing of *Anne of Green Gables*.[11] Collectively these studies have established two important points that will serve as a foundation for this essay: that Montgomery herself was highly familiar with the use of books as therapeutic tools, and that, contrary to what earlier critics claimed, a great deal of agency may be involved for readers who pick up a book to make themselves feel better. Still, we know little about the cognitive processes involved when fans draw therapeutic benefits from Montgomery's fiction. Are there any textual signposts in *Anne* that invite such therapeutic readings? What is the relationship between our aesthetic appreciation of literature and our experience of therapeutic benefits? And how effective is bibliotherapy as an everyday strategy for warding off depression or overcoming anxiety or trauma?

Such questions regarding Anne's therapeutic value are timely and important given the revelation made by Montgomery's granddaughter Kate Macdonald Butler on 20 September 2008: 'What has never been revealed is that L.M. Montgomery took her own life at the age of 67 through a drug overdose.'[12] Published in response to the *Globe and Mail*'s 'Breakdown' series devoted to the mental health crisis in Canada, and following a 2006 national call to end the silence surrounding depression (the so-called Kirby report *Out of the Shadows at Last*[13]), Butler's frank article regarding her grandmother's lifelong struggle with

depression was intended to lift the taboo regarding mental health problems, which had plagued her own family for years. For readers, this is
an important window into finding our own connections to the work.
Within weeks, the Charlottetown *Guardian* noted that the revelation
about Montgomery's suicide 'prompted a deluge of response, the con-
sensus of which seemed to be: it's time to get rid of the veil of secrecy,
it's time to take mental illness completely out of the closet.'[14] In fact,
Montgomery's descent into her final depression began in 1940, two
years before her death, when she fell and injured her right arm, making
it impossible for her to write for many months. The accident severely
unsettled her coping routine, and, with the news of the Second World
War, she spiralled into a mental breakdown from which she never re-
covered. The help of two physicians (her son Stuart, an obstetrician,
and Dr Richard Lane, her family doctor and neighbour on Riverside
Drive in Toronto) was not enough to save her.

It is within this context of Montgomery's own depression and the fact
that she wrote the exuberant *Anne of Green Gables* in the upswing of a
manic-depressive cycle that followed a particularly dark period of depression[15] that the questions regarding the novel's inherent psychological benefits become crucially relevant for twenty-first-century readers.
Of course, there is a distinctive difference between writing as a coping
mechanism and reading as a coping mechanism. Montgomery *wrote*
Anne, while her readers *consumed* it, and those are very different activities, although of course related in achieving much the same ends in
the way of therapy. As I shall argue, Montgomery's own struggle with
depression and recourse to self-help literature not only had sensitized
her to the power and limits of bibliotherapy, but enabled her to embed
strategies that allowed readers in need to decode her text for therapeutic benefits. Moreover, far from being invited into a passive experience,
I propose, the reader of *Anne of Green Gables* is hailed to see reading as
an active tool in identity construction that posits multiple and changing
selves instead of a uni-dimensional or essential self.

Consequently, this essay is a first consistent argument for reading
Montgomery's fiction within the important context of bibliotherapy, or
the use of books in the treatment of personal and mental problems, a
field with long roots in library science (beginning during the 1930s),
but whose efficacy has only begun to be documented in scientific research. At the intersection of literary studies and cognitive behavioural
psychology, bibliotherapy offers methodologies for studying books
that provide interventions into the minds of readers struggling with

loneliness, low self-esteem, body image, or with more serious mental problems such as depression or obsessive compulsive disorders. While it would be naïve to suggest that the reading of a book could offer a lasting cure for severe mental or physical illness, the story of Anne has generated comfort, confidence, pleasure, laughter, and – yes – tears, benefiting readers in pain or in crisis. In contrast to Jungian and Freudian (or neo-Freudian) models of psychological analysis, which focus on bringing to the fore subconscious forces, bibliotherapy belongs to an area of cognitive psychology that emphasizes more pragmatic interventions into the reader's cognitive structure. By shining a light on how Anne effectively models powerful strategies of bibliotherapy, this chapter pursues a line of inquiry about how the novel functions as a tool in cognitive intervention and self-help. By no means the final word on this topic, this chapter hopes to raise questions and to lay the foundation for future research exploring Montgomery's fiction within the context of cognitive psychology, affect theory, and bibliotherapy. This line of inquiry hopes to yield insight into what exactly is involved when we read for our own pleasure and well-being, and in doing so become agents in managing our psyches. Ultimately, these insights are relevant not only for L.M. Montgomery scholars but also for clinical psychologists, clinical social workers, and mental health practitioners.

Bibliotherapy and Everyday Trauma

The idea that reading literature can improve our psychological, emotional, and physiological make-up has a long history. Plato asserted that the muses gave us the arts not 'for mindless pleasure' but 'as an aid to bringing our soul-circuit, when it has got out of tune, into order and harmony with itself,' or as D.H. Lawrence put it more recently, 'One sheds one's sicknesses in books.'[16] Pattie Lou Watkins and George A. Clum's *Handbook of Self-Help Therapies* (2008) cites studies that list the Bible 'as perhaps the most long-lived form of motivational bibliotherapy.'[17] Stories about Abraham, Ruth, and Job show how obstacles can be overcome, while the biblical directives correspond to the prescriptive style of self-help books, as in the following quotation from Philippians 4:8: 'Whatsoever things are true, whatsoever things are honest, whatsoever things are just … ; if there be any virtue, and if there be any praise, think on these things.'[18] Thus bibliotherapy includes fiction and poetry and autobiography – indeed all writings that readers experience as motivating, encouraging, and inspiring.

Psychotherapists and cognitive psychologists define bibliotherapy, more specifically, as the use of self-help non-fiction books to treat personal problems and alleviate psychological distress. Such didactic or prescriptive bibliotherapy can be found in such best-selling literature as David Burns's *Feeling Good: The New Mood Therapy* (1980) and one of my personal favourites, Martin M. Antony and Richard P. Swinson's *When Perfect Isn't Good Enough: Strategies for Coping with Perfectionism* (1988). With step-by-step suggestions for exercises and new behaviours targeting particular disorders such as obsessive compulsive behaviour, social phobias, panic attacks, insomnia, and so on, bibliotherapy employs methods of cognitive behavioural therapy (CBT), in which patients are encouraged to modify negative thoughts and undesirable behaviour. In *Ending the Depression Cycle* (2003), for example, Peter J. Bieling and Martin M. Antony suggest a balanced combination of activities of 'mastery' and activities of 'pleasure' as an effective way to ward off depression through self-help.[19] Moreover, as a self-administered therapy, bibliotherapy has the advantage of providing privacy, significantly reducing shame and humiliation that often comes with having to disclose mental illness or personal failing to a third party.

So why is *Anne of Green Gables*, more so than other books, such an excellent outlet for bibliotherapy? Part of the answer lies in Anne Shirley's very own exuberant personality, which encodes a passion for life, a positive, pleasant energy that is as resilient as nature itself, as psychiatrist Kay Redfield Jamison describes this psychological state in her book *Exuberance: The Passion for Life* (2006). Not only is the exuberant temperament infectious, transfusing hope and joy in others and expanding the horizon of positive energy, but it also presents a powerful antidote against hopelessness and discouragement, and as such is a catalyst for action and self-help. The exuberant temperament activates engagement with the world and others, as Jamison writes: 'It makes both physical and intellectual exploration more likely, and it provides reward for problems solved or risks taken. Through its positive energies, it heals, as well.'[20] In fact, clinical trials have shown that unpleasant pictures stimulate 'the primitive-subcortical' parts of the brain, while pleasant pictures 'activate a phylogenetically much younger part of the brain, the prefrontal cortex';[21] so it is perhaps fitting that Anne Shirley's exuberance is brought out in the novel through an emphatic focus on her youthfulness. Montgomery also depicts exuberance as an innate, irrepressible force, best seen in the blooming of nature and the regeneration of life in spring. Most important, exuberance is a powerful force of healing, as Jamison observes: 'However dreadful the circumstances – death or madness, war, betrayal – the passion for life will surge back. For these [exuberant] individuals, it is an innate and irrepressible force; they are, in every true sense, exuberant by nature.' While for others, recovery after psychological trauma may arrive at a much slower pace, for exuberant individuals the healing process is quicker because it is less passive, as Jamison continues: 'Exuberance defies in strange and powerful ways; it asserts a future that others contrive to deny.'[22] The exuberant person does not merely respond to circumstances, but vigorously *acts* upon them, and since agency is a core principle in any form of self-help, exuberance is ultimately an important catalyst in self-help activities.

Psychiatrist Hagop Akiskal has coined the term 'hyperthymia' to describe the 'cheerful, overly optimistic individual, more often male than female, who is talkative, extraverted, self-assured, and filled with plans and ideas,' but this temperament is also frequently associated with an underside, particularly 'an instability of mood that can lead to intemperate behavior.'[23] Nowhere is this pattern better illustrated than in *Anne of Green Gables*, whose tomboyish heroine is brimming with the self-assurance of her imagination and verbal dexterity, on the one hand, while suffering from intemperate behaviour and mood swings, on the other ('The downfall of some dear hope or plan plunged Anne into "deeps of affliction." The fulfillment thereof exalted her to dizzy realms of delight.'[24]) By turning to literature as a coping strategy, Anne is subject and object, therapist and patient in engaging with the irritable, restless, and tempestuous underside of her character. An introvert who is richly endowed with Montgomery's own power of losing herself in a book, and an extrovert who acts upon the world and transforms it, Anne's dual personality is perhaps the perfect metaphor for the way bibliotherapy functions.

In *Lost in a Book: The Psychology of Reading for Pleasure* (1988), a major cognitive psychological study of reading involving 300 subjects, Victor Nell identifies some of the functions of 'ludic reading,' or reading for pleasure, documenting the complex ways in which pleasure reading relieves tension by letting the reader escape to a make-believe world, thus 'changing the content of consciousness and mediating mood changes.' A book can bring about the 'catharsis of a good cry (though not all crying is pleasurable).'[25] Since reading leads to arousal (which is often misperceived by readers themselves as relaxation), Nell hypothesizes that 'as in hypnosis, the reader's concentrated attention transfigures both the self and the object of attention,' filling him or her 'with the wonder and flavor of alternative worlds.' Consequently, reading is akin to daydreaming, a process that fully occupies consciousness, and it is especially pleasant because threatening experiences are held at bay 'by continually reassuring the reader that the imagined experience is only make-believe'; in fact, readers choose books based on their 'trance potential.'[26]

In this way, Anne Shirley enjoys her favourite books' 'trance potential,' modelling the powerfully positive effects of immersive reading (much like Montgomery herself, who often laughed or cried over a scene in a book). In the beginning of chapter 30, for example, we witness Anne sitting in front of the fire in the Green Gables kitchen, a book having slipped from her hands, and 'now she was dreaming, a smile on her parted lips. Glittering castles of Spain were shaping themselves out of the mists and rainbows of her lively fancies.' More than a passive letting go, it is a scene of vivid abandon that vibrates with lively imagery and 'adventures that always turned out triumphantly.'[27] The realm of fantasy itself is validated as a realm of agency in which the heroine rules supreme. Montgomery's characters are avid readers (think of Emily Byrd Starr and Valancy Stirling) who claim intense moments of pleasure through reading (like the eight- to sixteen-year-old girl readers in Holly Blackford's study who preferred literature 'to take them "off-world" rather then embed them in what they feel to be their real world'[28]). Considering that activities of pleasure are powerful enough to help ward off depression when properly balanced with activities of mastery, as suggested earlier by Bieling and Antony, Anne's modelling of reading as pleasure and empowerment is crucial in inviting readers to do the same. Throughout the novel, she resorts to her exuberance and hope to escape the stark reality of her past and make herself feel better when she feels anxious or overly excited.

In *Reading to Heal: How to Use Bibliotherapy to Improve Your Life* (1999), Jacqueline Stanley lists *Anne of Green Gables* among her favourite childhood books and introduces us to fictional characters who act as inspirational role models, while the aesthetic frame helps control a traumatic experience: 'When the hero/heroine in a novel is undergoing a severe trauma, it has a beginning, a middle and an end.'[29] Consequently, by reliving a traumatic experience vicariously within a safe context, the reader has the opportunity to master it. Throughout the novel Anne gravitates towards dark and sad motifs, finding thrills in melodramatic poetry: 'Don't you just love poetry that gives you a crinkly feeling up and down your back?' she asks Marilla.[30] Sidestepping the trauma of her own early life, paying little attention to the abuse and neglect suffered in the orphanage or in the foster homes, Anne instead has a fascination for poetry such as 'The Battle of Hohenlinden' or 'Edinburgh after Flodden,' poems that 'reflect the happy state of a homeless expatriate,' as the editors of *The Annotated Anne of Green Gables* (1997) have noted.[31] Since this poetry also corresponds directly to Anne's own expatriate status as a homeless and friendless waif all alone in the world, she effectively models the reading strategies of bibliotherapy for her contemporary readers in moments that are filled with added dramatic irony; her readers would have been familiar with these stories of Scottish oppression by the English, recognizing their dark undertones, of which Anne is seemingly ignorant. Reliving her own expatriation in aesthetic form is a cognitive event that allows Anne to distance and to control her dark past by turning it into a moment of aesthetic pleasure. Adrienne Clarkson, for one, would identify with Anne's reading method, likening the emotional tenor of her own personal story as a refugee to the fictional life of expatriate Anne. In both cases, mastering trauma is also a profound assertion of self-reliant identity.

'I read of a girl once in a novel who had a life-long sorrow, but it wasn't red hair,'[32] Anne tells Matthew early in the novel, thereby framing and romanticizing her own worldly sorrow through reference to the literary world. The example may be trivial, but it illuminates the process in which she negotiates and masters negative feelings about her history and body-image through literature, while the comic nature of her well-worn phrases signals an ironic caveat: that literature as self-help is an active, quotidian way of managing negative feelings, though not a magical cure. Conversely, when Anne first meets Diana, Diana is chastised by her mother for poring too much over books, yet it is the girls' fascination with books that provides them with paradigms for their loyal 'kindred spirits' friendship. The template for overcoming loneliness by swearing eternal friendship and the romantic model of the 'bosom friendship' in which Anne becomes wedded to Diana was found in books. In turn, the dynamics of this emotionally charged bond are re-enacted by twenty-first-century readers in book clubs and in various 'kindred spirits' organizations (including the L.M. Montgomery Society of Ontario or the Norval women dedicated to maintaining her legacy), whose members liberally quote from the novel to revivify Anne's spirit, speaking the words both with irony and a belief in their inspirational power.

Likewise, Anne's enactment of the tragic death of Tennyson's mythological Elaine, lying down in the barge and floating down the river, has been read critically by scholars as a parody of popular romance, in which Montgomery signals the need for the heroine to outgrow her juvenile mimicry of book romance.[33] What has been overlooked is the fact that at the age of thirteen going onto fourteen, leaving behind childhood and embarking on adolescence, Anne effectively replays the death of a part of herself using literature as bibliotherapy. Indeed, the threshold age is emphasized, its very repetition suggesting the need for cognitive work in dealing with the loss of childhood at the cusp of adolescence: 'big girls of thirteen, going on fourteen, were too old for such childish amusements as play-houses, and there were more fascinating sports to be found about the pond.'[34] That the putative 'tragic' death is in fact a comic rebirth in the water after Anne's boat springs a leak makes it a perfect metaphor for her traversing a threshold in her developmental journey towards adulthood. The attempt at emotional mastery and the fact that the heroine almost drowns (and needs to be rescued by archenemy Gilbert Blythe) signals the extent to which adolescence is a maelstrom of new cognitive, emotional, and social expectations that require complex social negotiation and mental mastery. Anne's modelling of bibliotherapy thus affirms the reader as an agent and the book as an important tool in managing the vicissitudes of life.

Cheer Up: From Christian Gospel to Modern Self-Help

When Anne tries to convince Marilla to let her go to Diana's birthday party, she recites the exhortative content of the literary entertainment program: 'Prissy Andrews is going to recite "Curfew Must Not Ring To-night." That is such a good moral piece, Marilla. I'm sure it would do me lots of good to hear it. And the choir are going to sing four lovely pathetic songs that are pretty near as good as hymns. And oh, Marilla, the minister is going to take part; yes, indeed, he is; he's going to give an address. That will be just about the same thing as a sermon. Please, mayn't I go, Marilla?'[35] 'There is a lot of Sunday School – and "Pansy" – about Anne,' Cecily Devereux writes, referring to the popular Pansy novels by Isabella Alden who wrote books to 'make things come out alright.'[36] In fact, what may be surprising for readers is that Montgomery found the roots for psychological mood enhancement and self-therapy not in psychology but in theology, and more specifically, in her lifelong schooling in the Christian self-help tradition found in the myriad of ephemeral Sunday school magazines and social gospel newspapers available today only in archives.

Exhortative stories, advice columns, and proverbs were offered along with sage practical lessons by reverends and writers in Chicago's *Ram's Horn*, New York's *The Sunday School Advocate for Boys and Girls*, Toronto's *East and West*, and Boston's *Zion's Herald*. These were some of the important Methodist and Presbyterian magazines that Montgomery read and published in during the years preceding the writing of *Anne*. The 29 July 1903 issue of *Zion's Herald* contained a slew of uplifting exhortations: 'We grow most under burdens. We get strength in struggle.' The Reverend J.R. Miller's motto is echoed in the same column by the Reverend Ozora S. Davis: 'A hopeless Christian, a discouraged Christian, is a blind man complaining at darkness in the ears of men who see the world radiant in sunshine.' Similar exhortation is proffered by James Reed: 'Every day that dawn brings something to do, which can never be done as well again. We should, therefore, try to do it ungrudgingly and cheerfully.' This in turn is followed by the Reverend Mark Guy Pearse's admonishment to avoid fear ('that sulphuric acid which eats into the vitals of a man').[37]

Much of the advice proffered here falls into the category of exhortative instructions for mood enhancement, not unlike the highly effective self-help instructions of modern cognitive behavioural therapy, which work to effect mood change by pragmatically setting about to change the subject's way of thinking, or the pragmatic Mrs Lynde and Marilla in the novel, who seem to have a ready-made proverb for every situation imaginable. Underlying both religious and behavioural self-help practices is the premise that the subject, as the agent of change, is responsible for controlling his or her undesirable thoughts and behaviours. 'Cheer Up' is the command and title of an unsigned poem (published on the same page as Montgomery's short story 'Polly Patterson's Autograph Square' in the 3 February 1904 issue of *Zion's Herald*): 'We were made to be glad, / Not sad.'[38] Mood enhancement through a heavy dose of guilt is the moral of J.L. Harbour's didactic story '"Saddeners of Life"' (in the 7 September 1904 issue of *Zion's Herald*): 'There are people in the world who are never quite so happy as when they are miserable themselves or are making some one else miserable. They know nothing at all of what we sometimes call "delight in life."' The story culminates with the religious moral: 'Keep your windows open toward Jerusalem, and remember that "he who climbs above the cares of this world, and turns his face to his God, has found the sunny side of life.'"[39] Coincidentally, Harbour is the same writer who penned 'Lucy Ann,' the story of the freckled redheaded orphan who provided one of the long-lost and unacknowledged models for Anne Shirley.[40]

Just as Montgomery began writing *Anne of Green Gables*, the 21 June 1905 issue of *Zion's Herald* hailed the ideal of perfect living in an obituary for a preacher, Dr William Clark, who never lost the 'sweetness and hopefulness of his spirit,' and despite his total blindness in later years, showed 'no disappointment, gloom or pessimism.' Sublime in thought, with a 'sunny, spiritual aroma,' the eulogized preacher embodied the spirit of Browning: '"God's in His heaven, / All's right with the world"'[41] – the very lines that Montgomery would use to close her novel, while attaching the spirit of hope to a much more imperfect denizen ('"God's in his heaven, all's right with the World," whispered Anne softly'[42]). Besides focusing on spiritual health, the magazine was equally concerned with physical health, as seen in advertisements for Grape-Nuts (which Montgomery loved), for the nerves and brain, Postum (a coffee replacement) as a cure for headaches, nervousness, and other muscle pains, along with home treatments for 'painful or irregular menstruation in young ladies.'[43]

It was in these Christian writings that Montgomery found the drive to bring exuberance and sunshine into the greyness that is the existence of Matthew and Marilla (and it's noteworthy that the Cuthberts' desire for change is sparked by a health problem: Matthew's bad heart). The sunshine radiated by Anne, her refusal to be thwarted by calamities and setbacks, and her ability to waken love in thwarted characters all belong to the Sunday-school magazine tradition of transforming darkness into light, pessimism into optimism, despair into hope. But there is no doubt that exuberant Anne was also born out of Montgomery's own experience with depression, and out of her personal frustration with the limits of Christian gospel and didacticism.[44] In her journals, Montgomery frequently bemoaned the lack of medical and spiritual help for her own predicament when she felt overwhelmed by feelings of sadness and loneliness so strong she couldn't express them in words. The red-haired little witch Anne Shirley was Montgomery's literary answer to all readers in need of cheering up: Anne was an exuberant motivator and a perfect catalyst for hope in Montgomery's new psychological century.

In fact, with Anne Shirley as the champion for a new form of secularized healing, Montgomery significantly repackaged the theological healing mandate by making it palatable for the twentieth (and the twenty-first) century. For example, Anne's very imperfections and the irony with which they are treated open a space for the reader's own imaginative transformation of self. But Montgomery had also created a character whose ailment is invisible (consisting of emotional scars), but particularly appealing to readers suffering from similar anxieties or emotional imbalance. Experimental studies have shown that early institutionalization has a profound effect on children including socio-emotional difficulties such as 'deficits in joint attention' (the child is not socially linked with others), 'attachment problems' (the child is not securely attached to a caregiver), and 'indiscriminate friendliness' (approaching strangers without fear).[45] All of these traits can be found in abundance in Anne Shirley. Directly correlated with a history of neglect in foster homes and in an orphanage, Anne's excessive friendliness resonates with the novel's lonely characters (such as Matthew, whose social phobia is the reverse mirror image of her indiscriminate friendliness). Yet Matthew's pity is tempered with Marilla's (and the narrator's) irony. The novel focuses on the wounding of Anne's hypersensitive psyche in everyday situations, traumas to which she responds with intense emotionality and excessive rage, as seen in her explosive response to being called 'carrots' in several scenes. Her answers to crises are mediated through the power of melodrama that never fails to capture the attention of viewers who find these scenes simultaneously hilarious and compelling.

Narrative irony is crucial in this reading for therapy, not only because of the healing power of laughter, but because emotional distance is as important to the cure as empathy. A counter-balance to the exuberant temperament is essential, as Jamison notes: 'Exuberant ideas benefit from skepticism and leadshot. Whether the ballast comes from melancholy, from law or social sanction, from an astringent intellect or the incredulity of others, discipline and qualm are conducive to getting the best yield from high mood and energy.'[46] Thus Marilla's deft, pragmatic intervention when she confronts Anne with the fact that the latter's fear of the haunted woods is self-induced anticipates a tenet of behavioural therapy, namely, the idea that anxiety disorders can be treated through exposure in which the subject unlearns the fear through dishabituation. Meanwhile Marilla herself is undergoing an emotional (healing) transformation, as Blackford observes: 'Although the narrator is often aligned with Anne's point of view, we continually glimpse Marilla as a split self whose repressed feelings this Providential child, as if an analyst, can bring to the surface.'[47] In this process, it matters little that Anne relapses, or perseverates, a failing known by all those suffering from emotional disorders, from social phobias and anxieties to depression. Even though Anne claims never to make the same mistake twice, the novel's cathartic comedy relies on narrative repetition of scenes that show Anne relapse and replay similar errors. The oversensitivity about her red hair, her impulsivity and temper, her tendency to jump to negative conclusions and worry excessively, the rapid-fire discourse with which she overwhelms people – each of these 'flaws' is played out in multiple variants that reveal her behavioural perseveration. Anne's hard-to-cure but endearing behaviour is bound to strike a chord with a patient trying to ward off a recurring illness such as depression. Eagerly participating in her own character improvement, Anne energizes the reader, while her very failings are bound to elicit identification and empathy.

Readers routinely report on reading *Anne of Green Gables* multiple times over the life span, often during times of transition (such as travel or immigration) and trauma (such as death of a loved one or loss of home). 'It seems likely that rereading old favorites renders the formulaic even safer and that readers who do a great deal of rereading have especially high needs for this kind of security,' as Nell writes.[48] Montgomery's adeptness at creating narrative safety zones becomes evident when we contrast *Anne of Green Gables* with the orphan stories that provided the building blocks for Anne, such as Mary Ann Maitland's 'Charity Ann,' which includes elements of graphic abuse nowhere to be found in *Anne of Green Gables*, or Margaret Marshall Saunders's *'Tilda Jane*, the 1901 novel about the rambunctious orphan in search of a home. In contrast to these works, Anne is in a cocoon of protection, shielded from the realistic terrors of farm life such as the terrible squealing of pigs about to be slaughtered, or hard manual work, or abusive brutality – all dramatized in some of the progenitor stories, which are much less reassuring. Even the episodes in which Anne puts herself in harm's way, as when she walks the ridge-pole of the roof, we witness her falling into the safety net of the Virginia creepers before we are informed of the true danger that this adventure had exposed Anne to.

A pleasure reading is further facilitated by the fact that 'Anne's History' is revealed in retroversion, not in real time, allowing readers to enjoy the frisson of past danger without the unsettling fear for the heroine's life. In other words, trauma is strategically embedded so that it can be enjoyed aesthetically, and thereby mastered through step-by-step control. Just as cognitive behavioural therapy endows the subject with a feeling of control that is essential to the cure, so the retroversive narration of traumatic events is a key strategy in the novel's therapeutic objectives. In this context, literary quotations and allusions play an important role in layering the novel for children and adult readers, creating a safety net by filtering unsettling information.[49] For example, adult Edwardian readers were familiar with the wildly popular Victorian stories of orphan neglect and abuse, so that allusions and quotations were enough to conjure them up and to fill in the space of Anne's prior suffering and pain. Today's readers who are no longer familiar with this orphan tradition desire to fill the gaps either by reimagining Anne's story of neglect through fiction (in Budge Wilson's *Before Green Gables* and Kevin Sullivan's *Anne of Green Gables: A New Beginning*) or by reassembling the colourful and surprising cast of orphans that Montgomery distills in Anne (the non-fiction story I told in *Looking for Anne*).

Writing for bibliotherapy was a task Montgomery excelled at. Operating on several levels for diverse groups of readers, she provided the reassurance of happy endings, but also invited readers to decode at their own pace the more unsettling realities embedded in her satire.[50] While young readers identify Anne's 'tragical' language as pleasurable ('"I'm in the depths of despair." How dramatic'),[51] the same words are read by many adults as a reflection of Montgomery's communication of the darker side of life. In this context of exploring the darker side of life, the very real death of Matthew in the penultimate Chapter 37, 'The Reaper Whose Name Is Death,' is crucial, as it confronts the now sixteen-year-old Anne and the reader with the brutal shock of grief, the sorrow that she had only played at and practised before. As she confronts this trauma, which is cloaked under hyperbole ('the Great Presence') for young readers, Mrs Lynde's words give it a shockingly anatomical verisimilitude that is hard to miss for anybody who has encountered death before: 'Look at his face. When you've seen that look as often as I have you'll know what it means.'[52] The reader, along with Anne, undergoes the initial shock, the pain of grieving, and the eventual consolidation of emotions that culminates with the realization that life goes on. Anne survives and recovers, and her bond with Marilla grows even stronger. In this sense, the death of Matthew is crucial as part of the novel's ending, as it allows the reader to share and anticipate what is among the most universal of human experiences: grieving the loss of a parent.

Out of the Shadows at Last

When *Anne of Green Gables* was first published, L.C. Page marketed the story of sensitive girlhood as a mood-enhancing tale for the whole family. The Christmas season ad proclaimed: 'THE MORNING AFTER! Thousands of readers have been made happy by an acquaintance with the delightful *Anne of Green Gables*. And each of these will in turn recommend or present the book to another friend.'[53] Ultimately, *Anne of Green Gables* is a novel that invites readings across the life span, with adult readers returning to the novel not just for nostalgic reasons, but to alleviate distress and consolidate emotions and tap feelings of hope. This process is anything but passive, as I have argued, inviting the reader to be an active agent in a process of self-transformation with exuberant Anne Shirley serving as a high-powered motivator. Avoiding the moralistic tone of Christian gospel, Montgomery's novel offers bibliotherapy in a self-consciously ironic way. *Anne* offers empathy to all those who are lonely and sad (and who hasn't been lonely or sad?), creating a community of special people, of kindred spirits who understand each other and who, like Anne, triumph over the drama of the everyday. At the same time, empathy is tempered with irony; instead of feeling self-pity, readers are invited to laugh at their own intensified emotions (worries, anxieties, fears, and phobias) by laughing at Anne's. Empowered by Anne's exuberance, readers are also invited to find endearing humanity in Anne's (and their own) relapses.

Given Montgomery's lifelong battle with depression, the extent to which bibliotherapy is embedded as a reading strategy in her fiction most certainly requires further investigation. The same holds true for the journals in which Montgomery constructs her own identity as an artist through the rhetoric of depression. Since 'depression is often the ultimate negation,' thwarting efforts at putting the illness in language, as Janice Fiamengo has written in her study of the journals, the therapeutic effects of reading thousands of pages of journal alongside the fiction has only begun to be explored.[54]

NOTES

1 J. Stanley, *Reading to Heal*, 11.
2 Clarkson, Foreword, x.
3 Wachowicz, 'L.M. Montgomery,' 11, 10; 'InfoPEI: Anne of Green

Gables – Quick Facts,' http://www.gov.pe.ca/infopei/index
.php3?number=81411.

4 Akamatsu, 'Japanese Readings,' 209–10.

5 Lash, *Helen and Teacher*, 380–1.

6 LMM, 27 June 1931, in *SJ*, 4: 136.

7 Waterston, *Kindling Spirit*, 47; see also Waterston, *Magic Island*, 207–15.

8 Ross, 'Readers Reading L.M. Montgomery,' 28–30.

9 Hubler, 'Can Anne Shirley Help,' 273.

10 Karr, 'Addicted to Reading,' 307.

11 Gammel, *Looking for Anne*, 50–7.

12 Butler, 'The Heartbreaking Truth,' F1. For full details on Montgomery's death, including the contention that suicide cannot be firmly established, see Rubio, *Lucy Maud Montgomery*, 575–8; see also Gammel, *Looking for Anne*, 259–70.

13 Michael J.L. Kirby, 'Out of the Shadows at Last,' http://www.parl.gc.ca/39/1/parlbus/commbus/senate/Com-e/SOCI-E/rep-e/rep02may06
-e.htm.

14 'Mental Illness: It's Time to Lift the Stigma,' *The Guardian* (Charlottetown), 8 Oct. 2008, http://www.theguardian.pe.ca/index.
cfm?sid=178709&sc=103.

15 Gammel, *Looking for Anne*, 40–73.

16 Quoted in Blake Morrison, 'The Reading Cure,' *The Guardian* (London), 5 Jan. 2008, http://www.guardian.co.uk/books/2008/jan/05/fiction
.scienceandnature.

17 Watkins, 'Self-Help Therapies,' 3. For more on Christian self-help materials, see Johnson, Hillman, and Johnson, 'Toward Guidelines for the Development.'

18 Quoted in J. Stanley, *Reading to Heal*, 82.

19 Bieling and Antony, *Ending the Depression Cycle*, 108–10.

20 Jamison, *Exuberance*, 7.

21 Ibid., 95.

22 Ibid., 303.

23 Ibid., 101.

24 LMM, *AGG*, 194.

25 Nell, *Lost in a Book*, 244.

26 Ibid., 264, 146.

27 LMM, *AGG*, 257.

28 Blackford, *Out of This World*, 39, 133.

29 J. Stanley, *Reading to Heal*, 41.

30 LMM, *AGG*, 49.

31 Doody and Barry, 'Literary Allusion and Quotation,' 457.

32 LMM, *AGG*, 24.

33 Epperly, *The Fragrance of Sweet-Grass*, 26–7; Howey, '"She look'd down to Camelot"'; Lefebvre, 'Stand by Your Man,' 157–61.

34 LMM, *AGG*, 239.

35 Ibid., 164–5.

36 Devereux, Introduction, 19. Isabella Alden, 'Pansy,' http://www .isabellamacdonaldalden.com/about.html.

37 'Thoughts for the Thoughtful,' 954.

38 'Cheer Up,' 146.

39 Harbour, '"Saddeners of Life,"' 1137.

40 Gammel, *Looking for Anne*, 211–13.

41 'Translation of Dr William R. Clark,' 775.

42 LMM, *AGG*, 330.

43 Advertisement for Grape-Nuts, 564; advertisement for menstruation medication, 219; advertisement for Postum, 787.

44 See, in particular, Hilder, '"That Unholy Tendency to Laughter."'

45 Moulson et al., 'Early Adverse Experiences,' 17.

46 Jamison, *Exuberance*, 285.

47 Blackford, Introduction, xiv–xv.

48 Nell, *Lost in a Book*, 251.

49 See Wilmshurst, 'L.M. Montgomery's Use'; Epperly, *The Fragrance of Sweet-Grass*, 17–38; Gammel, *Looking for Anne*, 193; Doody and Barry, 'Literary Allusion and Quotation'; Devereux, Introduction, 33–5.

50 On Montgomery's use of subversive strategies, see Rubio, 'Subverting the Trite.'

51 Original Post-It notes collected at LAC exhibition (4 June 2008 to 31 Mar. 2009), Modern Literature and Culture Research Centre, Ryerson University.

52 LMM, *AGG*, 315.

53 Advertisement for *Anne of Green Gables*, cover.

54 Fiamengo, '… the refuge of my sick spirit …,' 172.

6 Reading with Blitheness: *Anne of Green Gables* in Toronto Public Library's Children's Collections

LESLIE McGRATH

A girl of 13 asked for 'Lorna Doone' for supplementary reading. Other books on the list were 'Peck's bad boy, Anne of Green Gables, Rainbow Valley.' We wonder at the teacher's judgment!
– Daybook of Dovercourt Children's Room, Toronto Public Library, March 1922[1]

Vapid romance heroines and incorrigible rule breakers did not escape the vigilant eye of early children's librarians trained to weed out unsuitable reading for children, as the epigraph to this chapter illustrates. Yet what may sound judgmental or elitist to twenty-first-century ears reflects the mores and library practices of an era with different benchmarks and expectations for children's reading. While the selection criteria have most certainly changed to include reader responses today, librarians continue to make discriminating selections about which titles are placed on library shelves for child patrons. Children's librarians have long negotiated the delicate balance between encouraging literature that is perceived to have literary value and discouraging writing perceived as merely formulaic and entertaining. By assigning a carefully calibrated status to books, libraries also provide a literary barometer that registers the rise of a book to the status of a classic, as was the case with *Anne of Green Gables*.

While Canadian literary critics throughout a century have debated the literary value of *Anne of Green Gables*,[2] one group of professionals that has been quietly promoting the novel to readers almost since its initial publication consists of children's librarians, who treated seriously the kinds of 'sentimental' novels for children or about childhood that critics derided. They established high standards in the selection of books considered to possess literary merit and facilitated access to such books by providing tactful endorsements in print reviews and allowing readers to make their own choices about what would remain on library shelves in the long term. By embracing *Anne of Green Gables* as a book for children, children's librarians successfully sidestepped the kind of negative attention that the novel received from Canadian literature critics and that could very well have prohibited the book from remaining or even appearing on the adult shelves.

This essay is a first attempt to recover the overlooked involvement of librarians in promoting *Anne of Green Gables* to children, to parents, and to teachers since the novel's first publication in 1908. As the head of the Osborne Collection of Early Children's Books at the Toronto Public Library (TPL), I draw on my own experience as a librarian as well as on daybooks, articles, interviews, and listings in major evaluative bibliographies to explore how children's librarians at the Toronto Public Library contributed to the novel's durability. Ultimately, this essay encourages new directions in the study of L.M. Montgomery's work by including the role of librarians and library studies in the considerations and interpretations of how *Anne of Green Gables* became a literary classic. More generally, I hope to open new lines of inquiry into the role of libraries not as strongholds of conservative values but as agents of social change.

Establishing Benchmarks: Lillian H. Smith, 1912–1952

Anne of Green Gables was on the TPL children's shelves by 1912, the year in which Chief Librarian George Locke recruited Lillian H. Smith (1887–1983), a Canadian-born librarian who ran the Children's Room at the New York Public Library's Washington Heights branch, to manage its new Boys' and Girls' Division. In fact, children's services at Toronto Public Library officially began with the hiring of Smith, who lost no time in creating a divisional structure, overhauling the few children's books currently in the system collections, and establishing an ambitious schedule of programming, book clubs, and outreach. Inspired by the mentoring of NYPL children's services head Anne Carroll Moore, Smith taught her staff to choose the 'best' books for children by comparing titles to a list of 'benchmark' classics and by comparing the standards of plot, language, and style to these works by such authors as Dickens, Scott, Thackeray, Kipling, and Stevenson. Her standards later found expression in the literary criticism of C.S. Lewis, whom she quoted: 'no book is really worth reading at the age of ten which is not equally (and often more) worth reading at the age of fifty.'[3] Duplicates of good books were to be bought instead of a wider variety of materials of inconsistent quality. The intent was to uplift and to improve, preparing children to be educated and hard-working citizens. *Anne of Green Gables* survived Smith's initial weeding out of unsuitable materials and has remained on children's shelves ever since. (Librarians later admitted *Anne of Avonlea* to the children's shelves, but during Smith's incumbency they barred the later sequels because they considered them to be for older readers.)

The year of Smith's appointment to the Boys' and Girls' Division marked the beginning of an era in which the children's services at TPL became eminent in the field, both in size and in service, as the Canadian equivalent of NYPL's Children's Services Division. A large urban population, to which waves of immigration contributed major influxes, had created a pressing need for social services. Legislation relating to juvenile factory employment and school attendance resulted in more leisure time for many young people, but there were few friendly indoor places for juvenile recreation. Services for children in public libraries helped meet their social and educational needs in ways that garnered wide support from politicians and philanthropists. They had a proven record of success in the United States as well as in some smaller Canadian libraries, such as Kitchener and Fort William. While Toronto was regarded by many in the Canadian library world as behind the times in providing children's services before 1912,[4] the success of Smith's efforts and those of her colleagues was evident in rising statistics of attendance and can be seen in the numerous photographs showing lines of children waiting to enter Boys and Girls House each Saturday morning, indicating that the high level of attendance was typical.

Throughout Smith's tenure as head of the Boys' and Girls' Division from 1912 to 1952 (during which time it was also known as the 'Boys and Girls Division,' as the use of apostrophes in the Division's name varied over the years) and subsequently when her trainees took over the children's department, the team of children's librarians was empowered to create their own direction within a newly defined professional area of specialization. The librarians aimed in their reviews to evaluate a book, rather than simply to describe, condemn, or praise it. As Smith commented in her 1953 study *The Unreluctant Years*, which sought to establish standards for evaluating reading materials rather than provide a selection guide, 'Children's books do not exist in a vacuum, unrelated to literature as a whole. They are a portion of universal literature and must be subjected to the same standards of criticism as any other form of literature. This basic principle should underlie all good book selection, whatever kind of literature is judged.'[5] Ordinarily, no book would be recommended for selection without explanation, unless it was a classic or part of a series by an established author.

Smith's librarians were not, as described in library literature of and about the era, 'tender technicians' or merely 'hostesses,' a role to which early children's librarians were relegated by some dismissive administrators.[6] Nearly all librarians who joined in the early years of the Division, including Chief Librarian Locke, were Methodists, a denomination that Montgomery's writings gently but persistently parody. They had strong connections to education and publishing in Ontario. Many, including ministers' daughters such as Smith, combined a passion for nurturing the children they served with a homiletic ability to 'reach' and entertain them, even though services and collections were intentionally non-denominational in content and approach.[7] They promoted educational and enrichment opportunities to all children, but especially those who were deprived of a reading environment at home, and girls, whose years of study were often curtailed for economic reasons. (This offset somewhat the librarians' tendency to promote hobby and technical activity books in 'boys' corners' at the expense of access by girls.)

Smith and her colleagues compiled lists of recommended books to library periodicals, but their first independent lists of children's books for distribution to parents and teachers were booklets approximately fifty pages in length. This series, *Books to Read*, published irregularly by the Ryerson Press in Toronto from 1923 on (the 1938 issue is the tenth and last booklet in TPL collections) and distributed gratis, may be seen as an historical development following the Methodist Book Room (forerunner of the Ryerson Press, which took its name after Methodist minister and educator Egerton Ryerson in 1919) as a supplier of high-quality reading materials for the young. Books by other publishers were included, together with prices. All could be ordered from the Ryerson Press on the form attached to the booklet. In 1927, Smith and her colleagues prepared their first lengthy, hardcover list of recommended titles, *Books for Boys and Girls*. As in the booklets, Canadian titles were listed according to perceived merit, and not for nationalistic reasons.

As a domestic comedy set in small-town Canada, sentimental in tone, and written by an author whose work was not yet critically acclaimed and who had produced a large number of sequels, *Anne of Green Gables* was not an immediate candidate for inclusion in the TPL. Throughout Smith's tenure, formulaic 'series' books such as those mass-produced by the Stratemeyer Syndicate including Nancy Drew, the Bobbsey Twins, and the Hardy Boys were banned from TPL children's departments, and any rapid production of books by a contemporary author was viewed with suspicion, although librarians were not so narrow-minded as to overlook an author's need to continue writing and publishing for personal satisfaction as much as for financial gain. Evaluative commentaries about *Anne of Green Gables* in various editions of *Books for Boys and Girls* demonstrate the shifts in the ways in which the novel was treated. The 1927 edition is limited to a descriptive entry ('The setting of this Canadian story is laid in Prince Edward Island'), one that is revised slightly for the 1940 edition ('The setting for this Canadian story is Prince Edward Island').[8] Brief as it is, this entry is a coded endorsement: its inclusion in *Books for Boys and Girls* is itself indicative of the book's quality, but the terse description shows a reluctance to risk more than passing praise, tactfully avoiding a direct confrontation in print with the opinion of recognized literary experts.

The annotation from the 1954 edition of *Books for Boys and Girls*, replicated in the 1966 edition, is equally revealing: 'An orphan girl, instead of the expected boy, is sent for adoption to an elderly couple but wins a place for herself in spite of misadventures. A Prince Edward Island village chronicle of an earlier generation. First published in 1908.'[9] The dust jacket of the 1954 edition also lists *Anne of Green Gables* as one of the books that the resource recommends. Once more, the entry emphasizes the geographical location and summarizes the plot, rather than offering an evaluative comment. The authors of the entry distance themselves further by hinting that the novel is an old-fashioned domestic work and a sentimental favourite. By contrast, Kate Douglas Wiggin's *Rebecca of Sunnybrook Farm* (1903), seen by some critics as an inspiration for *Anne of Green Gables*, receives a similar descriptive entry in the 1927 edition ('the story of a lively little girl who was adopted and brought up by her two prim New England Aunts') but disappears completely in the subsequent three editions.[10] And so, whereas the wording of the later entries implies a critical evaluation, the continued inclusion of *Anne of Green Gables* and exclusion of *Rebecca of Sunnybrook Farm* indicates that the former book succeeded where the latter eventually failed.[11] Similarly, the entry on *Anne of Green Gables* in *Books for Youth* (1966), for older readers, offers a shorter but warmer recommendation, which is indicative of a shift away from evaluating books with inflexibly high standards and towards factoring in whether they constitute enjoyable reading material: 'An orphan girl is adopted by an elderly couple living on a farm in Prince Edward Island. Her romantic imagination and love of mischief involve her in amusing difficulties both at home and at school.'[12]

The consistent inclusion of *Anne of Green Gables* in this evaluative bibliography stands in stark contrast with landmark selection guides for children's literature that precede and follow *Books for Boys and Girls*: in the August 1917 issue of *Ontario Library Review*, an indispensable resource to which TPL children's librarians frequently contributed, Smith includes *Anne of Green Gables* in her 'List of Books for Boys and Girls':

> The books comprised in the following list have been included by reason of their *usefulness* in actual experience with the reading interests of boys and girls in our children's rooms. All the books are not of equal merit, and from a literary standpoint some of the titles are only of mediocre value. These are included through having justified their place on our shelves as stepping-stones to the better kind of books, which are not always immediately appreciated by children who come from bookless homes, or who have been saturated with the vapid reading matter contained in the Alger and Elsie books.[13]

Montgomery's novel is not included in a 1923 list of fifty 'Canadian Titles of *Value* in the Children's Room' compiled by Louise Huffman of Woodstock Public Library.[14] In the same year in which Huffman compiled her list, however, Miss Rorke of the Beaches branch of the TPL is reported as having included *Anne* in one of twelve literary tableaux representing favourite heroines of Canadian fiction in Canadian Book Week celebrations.[15]

Librarians Reading Anne, 1930–1980

What did the TPL children's librarians see in *Anne* that resulted in the book's inclusion and promotion in the branch collections? One answer, I propose, lies in Montgomery's countless literary plays and allusions that she inserted in her writing to establish her claim to a literary text. Librarians knew the books that she alluded to, and thus had the tools to recognize the subtle innovations and parodies (even though they may have had some misgivings about the marketing of Montgomery as a popular writer of sequels). Let us briefly consider, then, the subtle methods by which Montgomery renovated the genre in ways that appeal to sophisticated (and professional) readers.

First, Montgomery's *Anne* departed from traditional orphan stories and family stories, which, as part of the genre of 'moral stories' influential in the nineteenth century, had emphasized the misery of orphaned children, from which they are rescued by a benefactor or liberated by death. Dickens and many less accomplished writers had explored the theme of the lonely orphaned child, 'a rather gloomy stereotype of Victorian fiction and a telling reflection of the high mortality rate in real-life society then.'[16] A popular form was the shorter tale, the traditional 'happy death story' for children, which Montgomery herself admitted to enjoying, and which invited parody, as did the story of the unloved, neglected child, like Martha Finley's *Elsie Dinsmore* (1867), which was also followed by a number of sequels until 1905. Ever since Catherine Sinclair's *Holiday House* appeared in 1839, there had been stories about naughty children who did not necessarily (like one of Montgomery's favourite protagonists) literally have to break their necks and die because they climbed trees to pick cherries on the Sabbath. Yet throughout the 1800s the neck-breaking stories remained more numerous, if not better-loved, than the *Holiday House* type of tale.

The early librarians who read *Anne of Green Gables* as adults had themselves been raised on the *Peep of Day* religious instructional books and on the moral stories of Hesba Stretton, with their stylized views of hunger and drunkenness. Familiar with Elsie Dinsmore's self-righteous moralizing at her elders, for example, they possessed the tools to recognize the contrast offered by Montgomery's playful twists on these worn themes. Anne's first prayer, unlike Jessica's in Stretton's famous *Jessica's First Prayer* (1867), is a common-sense business letter to an unknown correspondent. Most of Anne Shirley's mistakes are in fact based on good intentions and eventually lead to positive results. Her initial refusal to lie about taking the amethyst brooch is sound; allowing herself to be driven to telling a lie about it brings Anne and Marilla to worse conflict, until the brooch is found. The 'affair of honour' on the ridge-pole may literally show pride coming before a fall, but the consequence of her subsequent tumble is that it brings Marilla to realize that she loves Anne. Anne's matter-of-fact account of Mrs Thomas's alcoholic husband, including his death through falling under a train, is less romanticized than a spontaneous and instant cure to alcohol addiction through 'getting religion,' as in Stretton's *Little Meg's Children* (1868) and a host of temperance tales.[17]

A second attractive feature of *Anne* is its sophisticated use of language, not only in Montgomery's numerous quotations from the Bible and classic works, used in amusing juxtapositions with commonplace events, but in the twisting of clichés to give them fresh meanings. Marilla, who, we are told, is as fond of morals as the Duchess in *Alice's Adventures in Wonderland*, nonetheless offers her own variation on a popular saying of the day, 'Be good sweet maid, and let who will be clever' (from Charles Kingsley's 1858 poem 'A Farewell') in her description of Diana: 'she is good and smart, which is better than being pretty.'[18] Throughout the novel, exalted language is punctured by commonplace events and domestic disasters, and yet it is precisely this language that brings consolation and dignity to everyday situations.

Many of the literary allusions within episodes in *Anne* were familiar to the well-read librarians in the children's department in the novel's first decades of publication, allowing them to appreciate the humour of the parroted phrases from the Catechism that Anne repeats without comprehending. Matthew's rash venture on the merry-go-round recollects Tony's in Juliana Horatia Ewing's *Jackanapes* (1883), illustrated by Randolph Caldecott. Miss Stacy's guidance, in contrast to the capricious and vindictive actions of Mr Phillips in the Avonlea schoolroom, contains echoes of Thomas Hughes's *Tom Brown's Schooldays* (1857) and Ralph Connor's *Glengarry Schooldays* (1902). To all familiar with early etiquette books and articles for children, there is a special delight in Marilla's pithy piece of advice for Anne, who is worried about how to behave at the manse: 'you're thinking too much about yourself. You should just think of Mrs Allan and what would be nicest and most agreeable for her.'[19] What a contrast Montgomery's light-hearted take offers compared with the minutiae of table etiquette offered in the instructional books and periodicals of the day![20] In fact, by 1927, humorous instruction had become much more the order of the day, as evinced by the titles included in the *Books for Boys and Girls* lists, although much of this humour consisted of parody of Victorian etiquette. Among the works that offered amusing commentaries, much like *Anne of Green Gables*, were Carroll's *Alice in Wonderland* (published in 1865, recommended in all editions of *BBG*), Hoffman's *Struwwelpeter* or *Slovenly Peter* (published in English in 1848, recommended in *BBG* in 1927, 1940, and 1954), Gelett Burgess's *Goops and How to Be Them* (published in 1900, recommended in 1927), Alcott's *Little Women* (published in 1868, recommended in all editions of *BBG*), and Beatrix Potter's works, notably *The Pie and the Patty-Pan* with its disastrous tea party (published in 1905, recommended in all editions of *BBG*). Put in such context, it becomes easy to identify the particular brand of allusive, subtly humorous language Montgomery offered as a prime reason why librarians of the day were so interested in *Anne*.

A third attractive point is that *Anne* represents a feminized type of adventure tale, a new version of the 'survival' story, a 'social survival' tale set in a Canadian community, in which aggressive, thoughtless, or mean people who by virtue of age (Mrs Lynde) or gender (young Gilbert) are assigned positions of power, must be managed, tamed, and eventually controlled by those they oppress.[21] The librarians' critical measure of a good tale, according to Smith, is the idea behind the story, for even if such an idea is 'obvious or hackneyed,' it is the author's inspiration that gives it new life: 'Authors of second-rate children's stories too often choose an improving theme.'[22] Few such stories were published in early twentieth-century Canada, and even fewer appeared in *Books for Boys and Girls* lists, which makes somewhat more difficult the task of identifying their inclusion in the lists as part of a pattern that includes *Anne*. Missing, for example, is Nellie L. McClung's popular *Sowing Seeds in Danny* (1908), a work with explicit references to drunkenness (as opposed to, in *Anne*, the solitary affair of the currant wine, or the restrained references to Mrs Thomas's drunkard husband). Muriel Denison's 'Susannah' series is included in the 1940 *BBG*, with *Susannah: A Little Girl with the Mounties* (1936), but this and her subsequent adventures, including a stint at boarding school, are left out of subsequent lists. The Pearlie Watson and Susannah books were printed in various editions, which points at an element of selection. Many titles not listed were considered unworthy or were simply not available.[23] The novels of Bessie Marchant, in which poor orphan girls learn they are heiresses or members of the nobility did not meet criteria for inclusion in *Books for Boys and Girls*, just as Horatio Alger's novels, with improbable plots of poor boys suddenly becoming rich, were rejected. The Canadian heroines like Maria Chapdelaine and Anne, found in all editions of *Books for Boys and Girls*, find their rightful place in society not through luck, but by possessing a fine character, shown through selflessness, honesty, and a willingness to work.

In an urban area in which immigration had created numerous social challenges and opportunities, and in which children's librarians took an active part in welcoming new Canadians and helping them adjust to their new home, the characters of Anne and of her adoptive parents offer important exempla not only of the integration of people displaced from a wide variety of cultural and socioeconomic backgrounds, but also of the promotion of religious tolerance. In the context of the stressful amalgamation process that joined three Protestant denominations into the United Church in 1925, the religious education of Marilla and Anne – the first becoming more Methodist (more demonstrative and emotional) and the second becoming more Presbyterian (more restrained in language and behaviour) – is an illustration of the uplifting benefits of empathy and understanding.[24] There is ample evidence in the daybooks and reports of the post–First World War years to suggest that the librarians used their collections and services to help create the sense of welcome and of being home that many children had missed. Ruth Soward, TPL librarian at the University Settlement House, whose clientèle included twenty-five nationalities of children, reported in the 1933 TPL Annual Report that many of these youngsters, whose countries were hereditary enemies, now sat peacefully sharing library books.[25] Canadian novels addressing the concerns of specific immigrant groups are a fairly recent development, but the fictional model of Anne as the orphaned and homeless child, unwanted for being a girl, resonated with readers of every background and offered a common literary frame of reference.

Most importantly, in addition to these useful tie-ins, the librarians appreciated children's enjoyment of reading *Anne*. A comment by the Wychwood branch librarian recorded in the daybook dated 5 December 1917 illustrates this point: 'A little girl said to me, "You know I have *quite despaired* of ever getting Anne of Green Gables."'[26] A book that is not enjoyable to read is doomed to oblivion, as Smith commented in *The Unreluctant Years*: 'No force in the world can compel children to read, for long, what they do not want. They defend their freedom of choice with great skill and persistence. They may not know why they reject one book or cling to another, for their judgement is seldom analytical. It is based on something genuine – pleasure – and "without blithenesse" they read reluctantly if at all.'[27] (Smith's focus on the pleasure of reading is crucial, though Smith may be underestimating children's agency in decoding narrative aesthetics; Holly Virginia Blackford has traced the sophisticated ways in which girls read literature specifically for the aesthetic experience, emphasizing the mental activities of seeing and imagining involved in adolescent girls' reading processes.[28])

In annual reports, the Boys and Girls Division boasted of holding multiple copies of the works of Dickens and Carroll. These did not emphasize that *Anne* was held in sufficient quantity to support book talks (short promotional lectures to classes, after which the book might be borrowed), with at least three copies per regular branch and later in 'great numbers' of the paperback edition, especially after the Kevin Sullivan miniseries aired on television. This is noted by Ruth Osler, who was a TPL children's librarian in the 1950s, eventually becoming head of the Boys and Girls Division.[29] Prominence was also given by red maple leaf spine stickers affixed to Canadian children's library books in the 1970s. There were comparatively few of these books, and among them, *Anne* stood out as a favourite.

Anne of Green Gables was first published in Canada by the Ryerson Press in 1942 with the iconic cover image by Toronto illustrator Hilton Hassell. TPL children's librarians stocked their shelves with the Ryerson edition. By the 1940s, most of these librarians had themselves read *Anne of Green Gables* as children and retained fond memories of the pleasure the book had given them.[30] M.O. Grenby reminds us 'that the popularity of books is affected by a time-lag. Adults buy for their children the books they themselves enjoyed a generation before.'[31] With many young readers requesting suggestions for enjoyable books, the librarians would have greater opportunity than most adults to share their own favourites.

A Canadian Classic: The 1980s to Today

In 1987, *Favourite Books for Boys and Girls, 1912–1987*, the TPL children's services publication in celebration of its seventy-fifth anniversary of children's services, first plainly defined *Anne* as a Canadian classic. 'Instead of the boy they planned to adopt, the orphanage sends Matthew and Marilla Cuthbert impetuous, imaginative, talkative, red-haired Anne Shirley. A classic Canadian story set in Prince Edward Island.'[32] The most recent resource with a link to the TPL, *A Guide to Canadian Children's Books in English* (by Deirdre Baker, lecturer of Children's Literature at the University of Toronto, and Ken Setterington, children's and youth advocate for library services, TPL), echoes this high recommendation: 'despite its age, this classic Canadian novel continues to win readers of all ages.' As did the children's librarians of 1927, Baker and Setterington identify Anne's well-known 'scrapes' as an element of subversive excitement and the book's appeal.[33]

Anne had reached the status of a 'classic' in the collective opinion of children's librarians of the post-Smith era, and they were willing to say so. Earlier librarians acknowledged the importance of other successful books from publication; why did *Anne* have to wait? The answer may lie in *Anne*'s immediate popularity. Popular appeal, as opposed to established critical approval based on literary merit, was not an immediate measure of what was considered 'best,' and the test of time was required for Montgomery's work to prove the enjoyment would endure. Though *Anne* was well written enough to be included in collections and to be promoted through displays, book clubs, and book talks, endorsing any new novel merely for its popularity would have been unthinkable. This would mean the inclusion of the series books that librarians considered worthless, if not immediately harmful, in their collections. Twenty years before *Favourite Books for Boys and Girls, 1912–1987* appeared, praise was qualified. In *The Republic of Childhood* (1967), Sheila Egoff, a TPL children's librarian from 1942 to 1952, states: 'Mrs [*sic*] Montgomery belongs to that breed of writers who give themselves away in their second and succeeding books. Of Anne, we are inclined to say, "Her I can accept," but the increasing sentimental dishonesty of the succeeding books tends to destroy the first … It is sad but true that the Anne books continue to evoke nostalgia from many adults to whom much vastly superior modern Canadian writing is unknown.'[34]

Library historian Lorne Bruce has traced the evolution of Ontario libraries from Victorian didacticism, intended to model behaviour and belief, to a responsive service ethic.[35] This evolution is reflected in the change of government bodies that directed provincial library legislation. Ontario's public libraries began under the aegis of the Bureau of Agriculture, moved to the Department of Education, followed by the Ministry of Colleges and Universities, then to Ministry of Citizenship and Culture, to the Ministry of Culture and Recreation and its succeeding agencies (presently the Ministry of Culture), a change that illustrates an increasingly consultative and interactive approach to policymaking for libraries that found its way into every level of administration and service, including book selection and promotion. However, the children's services staff at TPL were cautious innovators, particularly about book selection. Recognition of Montgomery as an author of international stature came first from abroad. As early as 1934, though many critical reference works then used by American librarians for the selection of children's books omitted any mention of L.M. Montgomery, she was invited to submit a biographical sketch to *The Junior Book of Authors*.[36] While this piece is not an evaluative review, Montgomery's presence in it indicates that her work was familiar and interesting enough to American readers to merit the inclusion of her life in a reference tool.

The respected *Horn Book* magazine for some years contained only brief references to Montgomery's novels, but a 1988 article by children's librarian and author Sarah Ellis in her column 'News from the North' discusses the publication of *The Selected Journals of L.M. Montgomery* in terms that suggest Montgomery's reputation, at least in Canada, is secure: 'Those interested in Canadian children's literature are ruefully aware that *Anne of Green Gables* is the only Canadian children's book ever to have achieved the rarefied heights of a classic. And classic it is, available in numerous editions and languages and regularly appearing on children's own lists of their favourite books from inner-city America to Eastern Europe. The whole business of classics is a mysterious one, a seemingly almost arbitrary filter of the offerings of a particular age.'[37] Two years before that, Norma R. Fryatt had written 'A Second Look: Emily of New Moon' for the same periodical, commenting on Emily as a 'career novel' about writing, in which 'the concentration on writing may account for the warm recollections of *Emily of New Moon* felt by some present-day authors, among them Rosemary Sutcliff.'[38] In *Modern Canadian Children's Books* (1987), Canadian library educator Judith Saltman follows the widespread influence of Anne, 'L.M. Montgomery's unofficial international diplomat,' in contemporary fiction.[39]

Library work with children, so firmly entrenched at TPL in written recommendations of 'only the best,' evolved more slowly than its adult counterpart, but just as surely, towards a more participative model of interaction with the public, and greater confidence in making judgments based in part upon reader response. Smith's retirement in 1952 occurred at the beginning of the change; slowly the rhetoric of a narrowly defined selection process that had never entirely matched the collection and that no longer expressed general library policy was discontinued. With increased competition offered by other media, and greater involvement by parents and teachers in children's reading, the monopoly libraries had held on directing the leisure time of many children began to dwindle. Librarians were strongly motivated to know and to acknowledge in print the books that won child readers away from comics, television, and cinemas to reading, even as the books themselves had begun to infiltrate the new media. Literary historians have commented, 'What differentiates *Alice's Adventures in Wonderland* or *Treasure Island*, for example, from the novels of Henty or Brazil has been their adaptability, the continual reinvention of the text.'[40] *Anne of*

Green Gables was one of these adaptable books, and will continue to be one, when so many authors with whom *Anne*'s was disparagingly compared are forgotten, or, like Austen, Brontë, and Dickens, have largely migrated to the adult department.

Today, the TPL offers numerous editions of *Anne of Green Gables*, in hardcover and in paperback, a search listing fifty-nine catalogue entries: retellings of *Anne* in picture books, videos of the television adaptations, books on tape, audio books, CD-ROMs, DVDs, and multiple languages; its special collections hold first editions of all Montgomery's novels, literary curios, choice handwritten literary letters by Montgomery, and a good number of her early magazine articles, together with scholarly research on every aspect of her influence on Canadian culture. Books inspired by Montgomery's work are found in adults' and children's departments; magazine article databases can be searched on every aspect of Montgomery's life and work; websites in English and in Japanese connect *Anne* enthusiasts in an interactive Internet environment. It is a pleasant reflection that TPL children's librarians helped to assure Montgomery's place today by keeping *Anne* in sight, available, and recommended, regardless of mainstream critical trends, and that Anne's history in becoming a 'classic' is a reflection of their trust in children's discernment, no less than a measure of their own.

There are other reasons why L.M. Montgomery Studies and Library Studies should be especially compatible in future research. A voracious reader, Montgomery loved books and collected them with passion; her personal library is available for scholarly exploration at the University of Guelph Library Archives and Special Collections, and while it has been catalogued has yet to be fully examined. Moreover, what few readers know is that Montgomery herself was a local librarian who joined the Book Committee of the Cavendish Literary Society in 1903, as Irene Gammel has documented; here she assumed responsibility for book purchases for the community's lending library in the Cavendish Hall. In this role Montgomery helped make selections about which books were purchased, books that she herself also devoured and that influenced her writing.[41] Montgomery also served briefly as a trustee on the local committee for the Swansea Memorial Free Public Library after her move to Toronto in 1935. Gammel has shown that for Montgomery library books were a lifeline in her apprenticeship as an author, but more research is required to explore more fully the complex relationship between libraries and this author who was deeply steeped in the world of books. Montgomery sums it up best when writing about the Literary

Society in Cavendish on 4 April 1899: 'It is a wise ordinance of fate – or Providence? – that I cannot get all the books I want or I should certainly never accomplish much. I am simply a "book drunkard."'[42]

NOTES

I would like to thank Lorne Bruce at the University of Guelph Library, who kindly read this chapter, and Ruth Osler and Lucy Browning, retired librarians, who were interviewed for it.

1 Unsigned entry by a children's librarian, Dovercourt Children's Room Daybook, n.p.
2 For an overview of the novel's early critical reception, see Waterston, *Kindling Spirit*, 19–24. Responses to the novel by E.K. Brown and by William Arthur Deacon are included in Margaret Steffler's contribution to this volume.
3 Quoted in Smith, *The Unreluctant Years*, 17.
4 See McGrath, 'Service to Children,' 83.
5 Smith, *The Unreluctant Years*, 7. Canadian content of any kind is rare in Smith's study, possibly related to its publication in the U.S. for a largely American audience, as well as to the lack of 'benchmark' Canadian classics for children.
6 Bruce, *Free Books for All*, 118.
7 McGrath, 'Service to Children,' 97.
8 *Books for Boys and Girls*, 154; Smith, *Books for Boys and Girls*, 270.
9 J. Thomson, *Books for Boys and Girls*, 217; Bagshaw and Scott, *Books for Boys and Girls*, 68.
10 *Books for Boys and Girls*, 224.
11 In fact, Irene Gammel's *Looking for Anne* reveals that Montgomery and Wiggin's novels were likely influenced by the same formula adoption stories found in magazines, but Montgomery was more successful in creating a more self-consciously playful and parodic text, transcending these formula orphan stories. Gammel, *Looking for Anne*, 207–19.
12 Robertson et al., *Books for Youth*, 24.
13 Smith, 'A List of Books,' 11; emphasis added.
14 Huffman, 'Canadian Titles of Value,' 76; emphasis added.
15 'Library Notes and News,' 40.
16 Cadogan, *Mary Carries On*, 21. Cadogan's book devotes an entire chapter to the 'Anne Shirley Centenary,' describing *Anne of Green Gables*, together

with Grahame's *The Wind in the Willows* and Richards's *The Making of Harry Wharton*, as 'classic-timeless in the truth of its characters and concepts, and in the vitality of its writing' (ibid., 20).

17 LMM, *AGG*, 59–60, 107–8, 111–14, 199–203, 47–8.

18 Kingsley, 'A Farewell,' 9; LMM, *AGG*, 66.

19 LMM, *AGG*, 191.

20 Typical of these is James Pitt's *Instructions in Etiquette* (1830), reprinted three times since published by the author in Manchester. Included in the Osborne Collection, this children's reference text includes a list of most frequently asked questions.

21 Weiss-Townsend, 'Sexism Down on the Farm?' 91; Åhmansson, *A Life and Its Mirrors*, 51–2; Hammill, *Literary Culture and Female Authorship*, 84.

22 Smith, *The Unreluctant Years*, 38.

23 One is an intriguing orphan story, *Betty and Bob* (1903) by Anne Helena Woodruff, which tells of two foster children in St Catharines who encounter cruel, ill-bred children and difficult situations, but succeed in winning the love of their foster-parents, who adopt them. An historical tale, *A Little Girl in Old Quebec* (1906) by Amanda M. Douglas, was, like *Betty and Bob*, published in the United States, and is another orphan story; here an unruly girl learns gentleness and makes her home in the New World.

24 For more on these aspects of the novel, see Rubio, 'L.M. Montgomery'; Hilder, '"That Unholy Tendency to Laughter."'

25 *Fiftieth Annual Report*, 30.

26 Unsigned entry, Wychwood Daybook, n.p.

27 Smith, *The Unreluctant Years*, 13.

28 Blackford, *Out of This World*, 19.

29 Ruth Osler, telephone interview with the author, 10 May 2008.

30 Lucy Browning, retired TPL children's librarian, telephone interview with the author, 10 June 2008. Correspondence archives, Osborne Collection.

31 Grenby, Introduction, 5.

32 Osler, Vincente, and Scott, *Favourite Books for Boys and Girls*, 4.

33 Baker and Setterington, *A Guide to Canadian Children's Books*, 182.

34 Egoff, *The Republic of Childhood*, 252.

35 Bruce, *Free Books for All*, 220.

36 LMM, 'L.M. Montgomery.' Among the selection guidebooks consulted by TPL children's librarians (which are kept in the Marguerite Bagshaw Collection and at the Osborne Collection of Early Children's Books, both located in the Lillian H. Smith branch), *Anne of Green Gables* is mentioned in the following. Of those published in the United States, the most substantial entry is in Sutherland, Monson, and Arbuthnot, *Children & Books* (71):

'L.M. Montgomery's *Anne of Green Gables* (1904) [*sic*], a Canadian story of a lively, independent orphan, was as popular in the United States as it was in Canada.' See also Lipson, *The New York Times*, 266; Cullinan and Galda, *Literature and the Child*, 28. In Britain, the novel is listed in the Library Association's *Books to Read* (492): 'A Canadian story of the school life of a lively child. The setting is laid in Prince Edward Island,' along with a ranking of 3 out of 6. Also in Sayers, *Books for Youth*, 257.

37 Ellis, 'News from the North,' 663.
38 Fryatt, 'A Second Look,' 175.
39 Saltman, *Modern Canadian Children's Books*, 58.
40 Grenby, Introduction, 19.
41 Gammel, *Looking for Anne*, 286, notes 26, 29.
42 LMM, 4 Apr. 1899, in *SJ*, 1: 235. For more on Montgomery and reading, see Karr, 'Addicted to Reading.'

7 Learning with Anne: Early Childhood Education Looks at New Media for Young Girls

JASON NOLAN

> Here, too, the ethical responsibility of the school on the social side must be interpreted in the broadest and freest spirit; it is equivalent to that training of the child which will give him such possession of himself that he may take charge of himself; may not only adapt himself to the changes that are going on, but have power to shape and direct them.
>
> – John Dewey[1]

In L.M. Montgomery's *Anne of Avonlea* (1909), sixteen-year-old Anne Shirley articulates a progressive pedagogical attitude that seems to coincide with Dewey's *Moral Principles in Education*, published the same year: 'No, if I can't get along without whipping I shall not try to teach school. There are better ways of managing. I shall try to win my pupils' affections and then they will *want* to do what I tell them.'[2] Drawing from her own childhood experience depicted in *Anne of Green Gables*, fledgling teacher Anne describes a schooling experience that would treat the student as she once wished to be treated. As a child, Anne embodied the model of a self-directed learner who actively engaged with her physical and social environment, making meaning and constructing her own identity and understanding of the world, indeed creating a world in which she could live. As a student and a teacher growing into adulthood, the older Anne exemplifies both romantic and progressive attitudes towards social relationships and learning that are governed by both her imagination and her determined self-confidence. Many readers who have come to love Anne for who she is, what she does, or how she views the world are inculcated to this perspective, and some even take on the moniker of 'kindred spirits' to signify a covenant among aficionados.

Anne Shirley and Emily Byrd Starr continue to be cited as exemplars of both appropriate conduct and subversive practice by fans involved in the many Anne- and Emily-related popular culture practices of the twenty-first century. Not only how Anne and Emily are seen, but how they see themselves and the codes and rules they try to live by have been leveraged for diverse educational and commercial purposes. Anne's and Emily's stories, primarily in *Anne of Green Gables* and in *Emily of New Moon* (1923), are very much in the tradition of the bildungsroman, as scholars have noted: both are stories of becoming where the narratives follow the heroine's growth and development through her girlhood.[3] As Brenda Weber, a self-confessed 'Anne fan with an academic bent,' notes: 'These two characters offer the reader models comparable to the models my grandmother offered me. Anne and Emily are interested, eager, questioning – the very qualities we try to instill in our students in literature courses.'[4] The desire to become Anne or Emily is as much an educational act with its own peculiar pedagogy and curriculum as it is an act of imaginative (re)creation of self and identity. These educational and imaginative processes are themselves open to manipulation and influence by agents external to the relationship between the reader and the protagonist, in this case, by the new media industries that find the affinity of Montgomery's audience so attractive.

As we enter the second centennial of the publication of the novel *Anne of Green Gables*, several new social networking websites have invited girls to learn with Anne and through Anne. Anne's Diary, located at http://annesdiary.com/, invites girls aged six to fourteen to socialize online and 'keep a top-secret virtual Diary' within a safe environment that they refer to as 'an innovative, fun and educational space in which girls can communicate with their peers and improve their creative writing and reading skills.'[5] New Moon Girls, located at http://www.newmoon.com/, similarly markets itself as 'Safe. Educational. Advertising-Free' by inviting girls to 'develop their full potential through self-discovery, creativity, and community in an environment designed to build self-esteem and promote positive body image in the important tween years.'[6] Also marketed as a learning tool is Sullivan Entertainment's *Anne of Green Gables: The Animated Series*, a twenty-six-episode series for five- to nine-year-old viewers that first aired on PBS and TVO in 2000–01. The back cover of a boxed set of three DVDs comprising six episodes of the series proclaims: 'Anne's out of control imagination leads her through adventures which demonstrate important lessons in loyalty, resolving conflict and problem solving.'[7] Sullivan's animated

Anne, Anne's Diary, and New Moon Girls are three examples of how characters and themes from Montgomery's work have been taken up as loci for formal and informal learning, through the identification of Anne variously as a marketing icon and as an ideal young girl, as well as through the way Montgomery constructed learning environments within her novels.

An exploration of new media through the lens of Early Childhood Education reveals an important interplay and tension: on the one hand is the pull of the curriculum and pedagogy that Montgomery encoded into her fiction; on the other is the powerful push of the educational and business goals of twenty-first-century commercial websites. These new media sites offer legitimate locations where young girls are invited to engage with each other and, in doing so, potentially subvert the commercial and social restrictions placed by adults on these 'safe spaces' for girls to interact, as Sara Grimes suggests in her discussion of online communities for girls.[8] More specifically, this chapter maps the curriculum and pedagogy that Montgomery infused into *Anne of Green Gables* and *Emily of New Moon* in order to explore how the fiction is translated into the educational agendas of Anne- and Emily-inspired new media and social technologies amid the competing goals of media creators, content providers, and the young fans of all things Anne. While Montgomery wrote for both young people *and* adults, the focus of this chapter is specifically on the kinds of pedagogy that these media sites offer through young readers' engagement of Anne and Emily (including readers too young to have read the novels), an area of exploration that has not been considered thoroughly.[9]

This chapter ultimately hopes to open up a new field of investigation at the intersection of Early Childhood Education, New Media Studies, and L.M. Montgomery Studies by beginning to explore the following research questions: What kinds of learning experiences are possible in these commercial networking sites, and what is the educational experience when young fans visit these locations and join these communities? How is *Anne-ness* – Anne's global appeal, her creative, good-natured enthusiasm and vitality, and her embodiment of traditional moral and cultural values – harnessed and packaged into a commodity that can be marketed and leveraged for commercial gain?

Anne of Green Gables social networking sites provide us with a girl's-eye view of the world that is usually shared with kindred spirits and perhaps a locked diary. The content is personal and private, yet involves many very public and social events. As intriguing as it is to peak behind the doors to see exactly what these girls are doing and sharing, how they are co-constructing identity and voice through their writing and shared activities, these sites are not public, in the way that much of the web is. Access is restricted to participants and parents. A research project is presently under way to study the cross-talk between these kinds of environments, and I hope that there will be some discussion about what goes on behind closed doors. For now, the diaries and stories are locked away from our view, and we must search for clues in the margins and by peeking through the cracks, and look to research in other locations that are more public to give us hints as to what might be going on when we learn with Anne online. Fortunately, the locations are themselves learning environments, and we can explore their structure and shape, as well as the ideas behind their design, to unpack the kinds of learning that are implicitly and explicitly presented to participants.

Situating Early Childhood Educational Perspectives

L.M. Montgomery had a keen interest in childhood education, as past scholars have noted. Irene Gammel and Ann Dutton have shed light on formal learning (or schooling), suggesting that Montgomery drew on her own experiences both as a humiliated student and as an idealistic teacher to reveal a complex interplay between pedagogical ideals and practical realities, though they also note that the young teacher Montgomery acknowledged her experience with the 'rod and rule.'[10] Aware of how adults used and abused power in learning contexts, Montgomery's fiction 'argues for a space of imaginative freedom within the disciplinary boundaries of school life, allowing the rebellious child to push against the boundaries of rigid conventions.'[11] As a one-time one-room schoolteacher, a long-time Sunday-school teacher, a writer of fiction about childhood, and a mother of two sons, Montgomery kept herself well informed regarding prevalent trends and theories in child development and learning. In 'Marigold and the Magic of Memory,' Elizabeth Waterston identifies the educational models and theories that influenced the later Montgomery, ranging from Friedrich Froebel's nineteenth-century idealistic philosophy of the 'kindergarten' to the more social and practical notions of twentieth-century education philosophy found in the works of John Dewey and Maria Montessori. In Canada, Dewey's ideas were promoted within the context of eugenics by Helen MacMurchy, chief of the Division of Child Welfare in the Dominion Department of Health and author of the popular *The Almosts: A Study of the Feeble-Minded* (1920). Not only was MacMurchy a friend of Montgomery, but her sister Marjorie MacMurchy's novel *The Child's House* (1923) has marked similarities to Montgomery's novel *Magic for Marigold* (1929).[12] The later Montgomery was also aware of William Blatz's influence on developmental psychology at the Institute of Child Studies at the University of Toronto with its emphasis on children's creativity and self-discovery within a social context, and the general interest in play, emotions, and the imagination, as opposed to heredity. These, along with popular works of fiction for children such as those by A.A. Milne (best known for *Winnie-the-Pooh*, published in 1926), ensured that Montgomery was well versed in the variety of perspectives on child development that surface throughout her fiction.[13] Not only did this understanding make a mark on most of her novels, but it has been incorporated into various adaptations of Montgomery's work for television and new media audiences.

For educational theorists learning is part of our lived experience, a primarily social act that is formally institutionalized in schools. In fact, most of what we learn comes from our interactions with others in our lives, or from various cultural artifacts we encounter such as books, music, film, the arts, *and* online media, as well as through our experiences within cultural and religious communities and sporting events. What is also important to recognize is that shopping malls and public parks, businesses and workplaces, and even the Internet have a curriculum to be learned and a pedagogy that outlines how we interact with and within them. These are often called 'informal learning environments.'[14] In *Life in Classrooms* (1968), Philip Jackson first described the learning that takes place outside the classroom by coining the term 'the hidden curriculum,' initiating an inquiry into the kinds of learning that children were experiencing beyond the formal teacher/student interaction.[15] Elliot Eisner later extended Jackson's thinking when he described 'explicit,' 'hidden,' and 'null' curricula that make up learning.[16] The explicit curriculum is what we are taught while having awareness of being taught, such as school knowledge, whereas the hidden curriculum, or what we learn without that awareness, may include social norms and attitudes as well as skills that we pick up as we interact with others. The null curriculum is that which is not taught because it is pushed aside by the explicit and hidden curricula; while it is often unacknowledged, it is as important for our understanding as the other learning choices and experiences we engage in. The locations of learning themselves represent both hidden and null curricula. Their features and affordances need to be explored and documented as learning environments, before we move on to inquire into the actual activities and interactions participants engage in.

Educational theorists such as John Dewey, Jean Piaget, and Lev Vygotstky have identified what is now generally known as 'social constructivist' aspects of learning – the premise that learning is situated in social interactions and mediated through language and communication.[17] Combining this notion with both the understanding that 'informal learning environments' and opportunities surround us throughout our lives, and that there are explicit, hidden, and null curricula involved at every step, educators quickly realize that the social world that children grow up in is a political arena. Not only do Montgomery's fictional constructions of Anne Shirley and Avonlea or Emily and New Moon draw readers into the narrative, but they claim to teach readers how to live, how to learn, and how to interact with each other. Montgomery's Scottish Presbyterian values, rooted in the island culture of Prince Edward Island and overlaid with Sunday-school values drawn from Canadian and American magazines and newspapers, inform and influence readers' own values thousands of miles away and even decades later. Recognizing this influence, we can now turn our attention to modern re-imaginings of Anne in new media, probing their stated pedagogical agendas. To discover what kinds of learning these environments afford, we probe the explicit, hidden, and null curriculum opportunities they offer.

Anne's Diary and Biometric Scanning

Because young readers of the twenty-first century get to know Anne in all her manifestations, including movies, television series, and new media, their relationship with Anne involves an informal learning environment in which Anne's life and experiences form a heuristic lens through which experience is shaped and new knowledge is constructed in the individual.[18] This learning often results in the shared or co-construction of knowledge when individuals participate in online and face-to-face communities that focus on kindred experiences and activities. Anne's Diary – like New Moon Girls and Sullivan's animated Anne, discussed below – situates itself within the context of informal learning. This online learning site highlights how the shared community experiences and how the identity construction opportunities that are the hallmark of social networking and online learning environments are marketed to young girls and their families as engaging educational sites that are safe and fun.

As a social networking site, Anne's Diary is a form of computer-mediated communication consisting of a series of tools or features that allow girls to interact and share information of interest to them. The main headings are PLAY, DISCOVER, MEMBERS, VIDEO and SHOP, with the following subsections:

- PLAY: GAMES, PET'S CORNER, E-CARDS, FUN HOUSE, WALLPAPER, QUIZZES
- DISCOVER: COMPUTER SAVVY, EMPOWERMENT, HOMEWORK HELP, ONLINE SAFETY, BOOK CLUB
- MEMBERS: PARENTS LOGIN, REGISTER, SAFETY FORUM, HELP, GETTING STARTED
- VIDEO (introductory video of how Anne's Diary operates)
  SHOP: BOOKS, DVDS, MUSIC, ART GALLERY, COLLECTIBLES, SPECIALS

Activities that do not allow communication among members are free. The games (DRESS UP, MAKEOVER, FASHION, DOLL MAKER, ROOM DECORATING, BARBIE) appear to be part of Arcade Dressup.com,[19] as that is where the REGISTER link on the games takes the viewer. Anne's Diary is intended to block access by individuals outside of the intended demographic, and so it is difficult to obtain information as to the discourse of the community and the kinds of activities girls find interesting and which are dormant. In fact, in order to keep the site private, Dolphin Digital Media, which owns the site, uses a biometric scanning (finger printing) to identify members, a controversial new online safety measure.

ANNE'S DIARY VIDEO, found under the registration subsection of the MEMBERS and REGISTER headings, provides the best description of what Anne's Diary offers. A cheery voiced character with red hair, braids, a straw hat, in a brown print dress over a green shirt welcomes the viewer: 'Hi. Welcome to Anne's Diary. Hello. I'm Anne. Wanna see my room? Follow me!' At this point, she places her index finger on a button under the text SCAN FINGER which changes to ACCESS GRANTED. She goes on to point to 'all [her] stuff' and her magical diary, in which she can write but can also talk to her friends around the world in a 'safe chatroom.' She shares pictures taken with her friend Diana and enters her stories into contests. Anne lauds the fact that she can talk to anyone and do anything 'because the room is completely safe,' explaining the identity verification and fingerprinting process, information storage (the depiction of a boy being denied access to the site is shown at this point).[20]

The striking elements of Anne's Diary lie in how it integrates free and commercial external materials and in the rationale and technology for isolating communication and interactions and for how these elements function within the context of the image of Anne in Montgomery's novel. The key issues of Anne's Diary appear to be twofold: first, to identify marketing opportunities and product tie-ins; and second, to test the waters with biometric scanning in social networking contexts. The marketing opportunities and product tie-ins are similar to what Grace Chung and Sara Grimes describe in other online media when they note: 'many popular children's sites are often commercially owned and operated, responding primarily to advertiser demands and other corporate interests ... This relationship is clearly illustrated within popular branded children's online game communities, such as Neopets.com, EverythingGirl.com, and Postopia.com. While these sites provide young users with hours of entertainment and endless online play opportunities, they simultaneously engage them in data mining activities that transform children's play into a way of gathering information.'[21] In this case, the tie-ins are primarily to Sullivan Entertainment media, with the majority of links going to the Sullivan Boutique site, where members can purchase everything from books, CDs, and DVDs to dolls, furniture, and stationery.[22] This is not novel, as Mickey Mouse, Barbie, and My Little Pony all have product-based websites.[23] Anne's Diary's parent company, Dolphin Digital Media, is responsible for the *Zoey 101* and *Ned's Declassified School Survival Guide* brands on Nickelodeon.[24]

Anne's Diary has as its explicit primary focus the facilitation of giving voice to their members and the sharing of ideas, options, and personally constructed narratives within the context of a same-sex, similarly aged community demographic. The premise of the site is that providing a paradigm of youth communication and activity that is based on the familiar Anne narrative will in turn motivate and empower girls to construct and share their own stories, ideas, and interests. In other words, the site provides an example that its users are encouraged to emulate and extend in their own ways. An important feature of Anne's Diary is that it promises to ensure that this kind of personal story-telling takes place within a safe setting.

To do so, however, Anne's Diary has chosen a user authentication system employing biometric scanning as its form of safety, whereby the technological 'fix' abdicates adult participation in the community, leaving little opportunity for the kind of mentoring experiences found in L.M. Montgomery's work. The technology is suited to large-scale deployment for very large communities where it is impossible to watch for inappropriate communication, but it also assumes that children are not capable of inappropriate communication, and that adults are the only risk factors. Opportunities for guidance from more experienced members of the community who have outgrown the intended demographic yet who can now take on mentoring roles are lost.

In fact, the issue of biometric scanning in social networking contexts requires closer investigation. According to the site, 'Anne's Diary has partnered with Fujitsu Microelectronics and 123ID to provide biometric login kits for fingerprint authentication that replaces password authentication.'[25] This partnership appears to be the first to attempt to initiate children into a culture of seeing the use of biometric scanning as part of their lived experience. In a post-9/11 world of global anxiety, with the added fears that every child is at risk from Internet predation that apparently makes even the private home unsafe, some parents may feel that surrendering the most fundamental mark of identity to a commercial media corporation is a reasonable price to pay for the illusion of safety it provides.[26] Anne's Diary appears to be predicated on this two-pronged experiment in social media as a marketing tool.

One cannot help but think that adults monitoring communication would have a much greater chance of identifying inappropriate communication, especially since even the supposedly safe environment provided by the new technology appears to be fallible, as, according to newspaper reports in January 2009, a Korean woman successfully fooled biometric scanners at a Japanese airport.[27] Ultimately, Anne's Diary creates a Panopticon, a system of supervision that is both omnipresent and unknowable.[28] Once the authorities have collected and authorized a girl's identity and it has been stored online, the collected information is used to control access to the community, at which point the invisible hand of authority withdraws. The user has her own private *virtual* bedroom, where she can keep her journal, upload media, and chat with friends, all of whom have been authenticated, fingerprinted, and authorized by one of the listed sponsors.[29] The entire system appears designed to minimize the opportunities for the kind of rebellion that is at the core of Anne's personality in the novel.

In fact, there does not appear to be much inherent allegiance or kinship to Anne herself, beyond her recognition value as a precocious little girl with red hair. While there is passing reference to *Anne of Green Gables* on the site's 'About us' page (which is aimed at adults), Anne's Diary makes few further attempts to connect its users to the literature the site is inspired by. In that sense, Anne is used less as a literary reference point than as a paradigm of the tween 'everygirl,' an easy signpost for expressive and self-referential girls. This detachment from Anne does not diminish any of the putative value Anne's Diary may have as a social networking tool for young girls, but may even enhance it by nullifying potential thematic or conceptual constraints that close adherence to the Montgomery texts may confer.

New Moon Girls and Pedagogical Value

In *Negotiating Critical Literacies with Young Children* (2004), Vivian Mara Vasquez argues that even for the very young there is a need to be engaged in a dialogue on issues that are important to children and in a manner that allows them to start making critical and ethical choices as a foundation for meaning-making and learning. Consequently, there is a need to recognize that playful social interaction among Anne fans is also a pedagogical or learning act with long-term implications on development that may be far from innocent.[30] Although Montgomery did not write exclusively *for* children, her work has been taken up by adults who are interested in children's learning as a model of the kinds of learning communities they envision. The goals and outcomes are distinctly different, as are the technologies or the communities they support. These are intentional learning communities that girls or their parents/caregivers choose to participate in, as seen above in the case of Anne's Diary. The pedagogy of the locations is particularly interesting in terms of the overlapping, and somewhat conflicting, notions of how they promote or support community formation and identity construction, and take up issues of protection of children, learning, and the commodification of Montgomery-related ideas.

As a social networking site launched in 2007, New Moon Girls contains a number of features that position it differently from Anne's Diary. According to its website, the objective of New Moon Girls is 'to help girls, ages 8 to 15, discover their unique voices and express them in the world in ways that matter.' The mission statement continues: 'We fulfill our mission by keeping girls at our center. Through active girl

1   'A Ryerson Showcase: The Centenary of *Anne of Green Gables*,' 7 Apr. 2008.
    Conference poster by Laura Brown, Toronto.

2 Cover image of *Anne's House of Dreams*, by L.M. Montgomery. Toronto: McClelland & Stewart, 1942. Library and Archives Canada, Amicus No. 20991443.

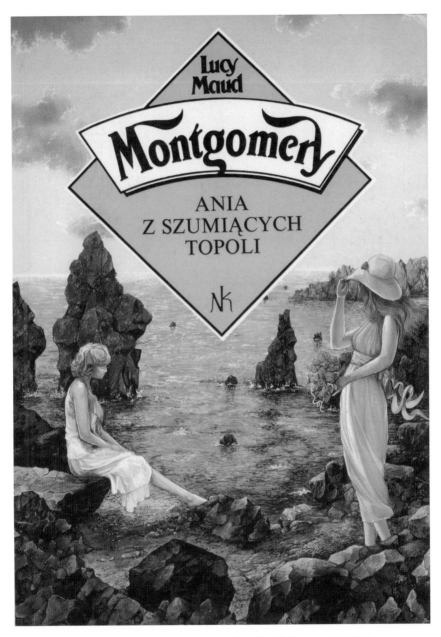

Lucy Maud Montgomery

ANIA
Z SZUMIĄCYCH
TOPOLI

3   Cover of Polish translation of *Anne of Windy Poplars*, by L.M. Montgomery.
Warsaw: B. Nasza Ksiegarnia, 1977. Library and Archives Canada, Amicus
No. 14083342. Cover design by Janusz Oblucki (Kanie, Poland).

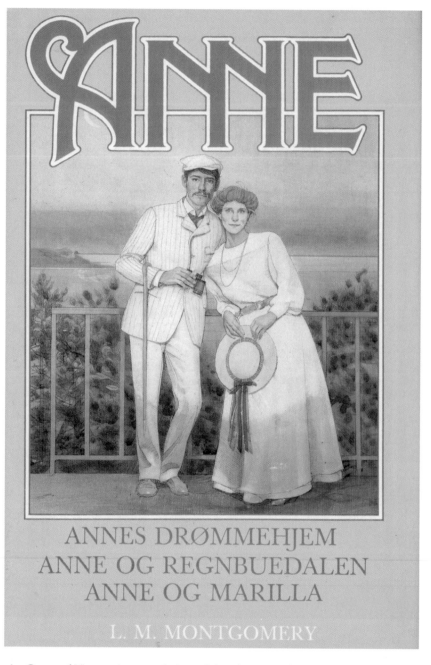

ANNES DRØMMEHJEM
ANNE OG REGNBUEDALEN
ANNE OG MARILLA

L. M. MONTGOMERY

4   Cover of Norwegian translation of *Anne's House of Dreams*, *Rainbow Valley*,
and *Rilla of Ingleside*, by L.M. Montgomery, trans. Jo Tenfjord. Oslo:
Aschehoug, 1989. Library and Archives Canada, Amicus No. 21493870.

세계명작 21
빨간머리앤
몽고메리 지음
이재철 옮김
대일출판사

5   Cover of Korean translation of *Anne of Green Gables*, by L.M.
Montgomery. Seoul: Daeil Publishers, 1972. Library and Archives Canada,
Amicus No. 22190550.

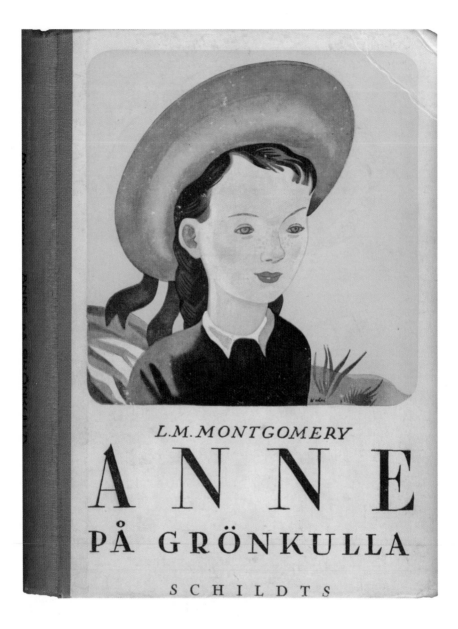

L.M. MONTGOMERY

ANNE
PÅ GRÖNKULLA

SCHILDTS

6 Cover of Swedish translation of *Anne of Green Gables*, by L.M. Montgomery, trans. Karin Lidforss Jensen. Helsingfors: Holger Schildts, 1946. Library and Archives Canada, Amicus No. 26942906.

در گرین گیبلز کتاب اول
آنی شرلی
ال. ام. مونتگمری
ترجمهٔ سارا قدیانی

7   Cover of Iranian translation of *Anne of Green Gables*, book 1, by
L.M. Montgomery, trans. Sara Ghadyani. Tehran: Ghadyani Publishing House,
2007 [1997].

美国学生课外阅读丛书

美国人文学科基金会推荐

ANNE OF GREEN GABLES

绿山墙的安妮

〔加拿大〕露西·蒙哥玛利 著

马爱农 译

人民文学出版社

8 Cover of Chinese translation of *Anne of Green Gables*, by L.M. Montgomery, trans. Ainong Ma. Hangzhou: Zhejiang Art and Literature Press, 2004.

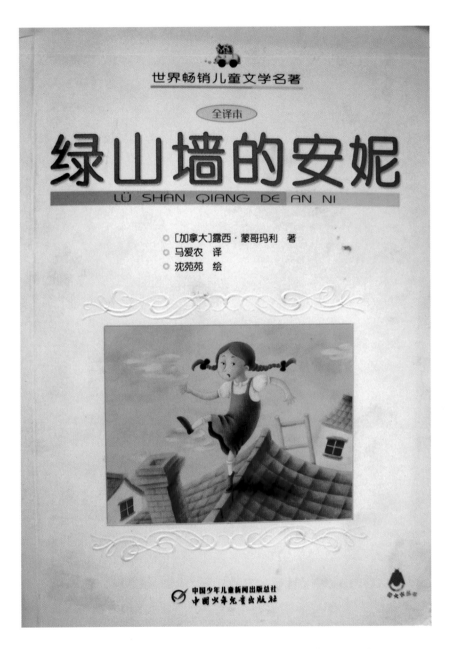

9   Cover of Chinese translation of *Anne of Green Gables*, by L.M. Montgomery, trans. Ainong Ma. Hangzhou: Zhejiang Art and Literature Press, 2006.

【加拿大】 露西·蒙哥玛利 著

花季的安妮

◇马爱农 译◇

Anne of Avonlea

10   Cover of Chinese translation of *Anne of Avonlea*, by L.M. Montgomery, trans. Ainong Ma. Hangzhou: Zhejiang Art and Literature Press, 1997.

The beloved and timeless heroine who has inspired millions of girls

加拿大经典名著安妮系列二

少女
Anne of Avonlea
〔加〕露西·莫德·蒙哥玛利 著

中国Anne Fans 热力推荐

作为一种成长小说，
The Anne Series
畅销西方近百年

绿山墙的Anne
营造世界旅游胜地

安妮

浙江文艺出版社

11   Cover of Chinese translation of *Anne of Avonlea*, by L.M. Montgomery, trans. Ainong Ma. Hangzhou: Zhejiang Art and Literature Press, 2002.

12   'Blackberries.' Cover image, *The Delineator*, Sept. 1903. Illustration by
Emilie Benson Knipe. Toronto Reference Library.

13   Artistic gown for a young girl, Messrs. Stephens and Co. *Home Art Work*,
Apr. 1890, 9. Victoria and Albert Museum, London.

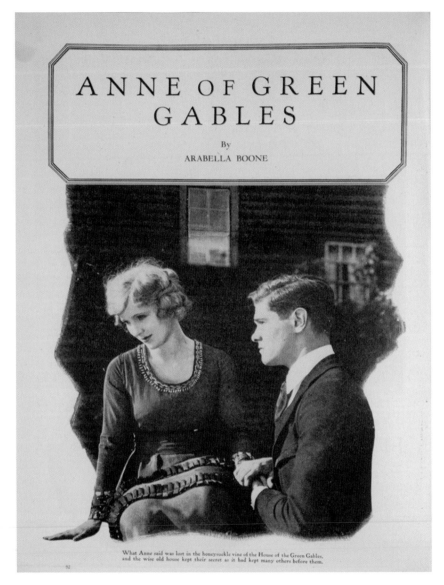

ANNE OF GREEN GABLES

By
ARABELLA BOONE

What Anne said was lost in the honeysuckle vine of the House of the Green Gables, and the wise old house kept their secret as it had kept many others before them.

14   Image from 'Anne of Green Gables,' Arabella Boone's 'film story' of the 1919 silent film appearing in *Photoplay Magazine*, Jan. 1920, 52. With Mary Miles Minter as Anne and Paul Kelly as Gilbert. George Eastman House International Museum of Photography and Film, Rochester, N.Y.

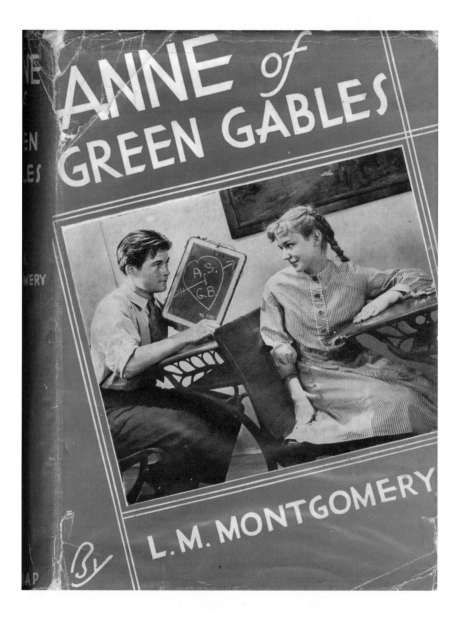

15   Cover of *Anne of Green Gables*, by L.M. Montgomery. London: George G. Harrap & Co., 1934. Library and Archives Canada, Amicus No. 10624791.

16   'Anne Made Me Gay,' 29 Nov. 2008. Cabaret poster by Suzy Malik. Cabaret curated by Moynan King and Rosemary Rowe. Buddies in Bad Times Theatre, Toronto.

involvement and participation in all our business decisions, we provide respectful, creative, energetic and safe communities where girls explore, discover, create, grow and share their voices to make a positive difference in their lives and in the world.'[31] The site is organized into categories that are broken down as follows:

- VOICES: LUNA'S CHATTER BOX, BEAUTIFUL GIRLS, VIDEO AND MUSIC, SHOUT OUT!, ASK A GIRL, DEAR LUNA, MOON GLOW GALLERY, and POETRY
- FEATURES: CHANGING THE WORLD, BODIES AND FEELINGS, FOR THE CURIOUS, ARTS AND CULTURE, SISTER TO SISTER, and SPOTLIGHT

New Moon Girls, which ran for over a decade as a print journal before going online, grew out of founder Nancy Gruver's desire to create a safe and nurturing environment for girls. From its beginning, girls had a voice on the New Moon Girls editorial board, while the advisory board was composed of a group of female academics (such as Professor Deborah Tolman, Dr Harriet S. Mosatche, and Professor Cheryl Dellasega) engaged in issues related to women and girls.[32] There is a strong sense throughout the site that New Moon Girls exists to provide a forum for girls' voices to be heard without interference from commercial media or corporate influence.

New Moon Girls is a commercial venture, however, charging a yearly subscription fee and selling back issues of their print magazine as well as books, T-shirts, and other items emblazoned with messages that celebrate girls' voices and their uniqueness in slogans such as 'Everyone is Beautiful,' 'Be Your Dream,' and 'Listen to Girls.'[33] New Moon Girls features a great deal of content that points to Montgomery, Anne, and Emily, highlighting the kinds of deeds and actions that are associated with these literary characters; in this way, the connection to *Anne of Green Gables* is not at all tenuous. However, the overall thrust of New Moon Girls is not to laud or linger upon Montgomery's creations, but to present the type of girl with whom Anne or Emily would be interacting and discussing things of interest, from teen Hollywood singer/actress Hilary Duff to questions of sexuality and social justice. The site's use of Anne and Emily extends beyond their simple brand values, to encompass a deeper sense of how their inquisitive spirits might manifest themselves in modern-day girls' interests.

Like Anne's Diary, New Moon Girls is a social networking site where girls can communicate with each other, but in contrast to Anne's Diary,

New Moon Girls uses a moderated posting format that involves adults to read and check posts for inappropriate content and mentor members about community expectations. New Moon Girls also stands in contrast with Anne's Diary (and Sullivan's *Animated Series* discussed below) as far as their curriculum and pedagogical aims are concerned. New Moon Girls is less about being a fan of Anne-media than it is about emulating the core traits that Montgomery instilled in characters, such as imagination, creativity, courage, confidence, loyalty, ambition, passion, and affection. New Moon Girls locates the power clearly in the girls who visit their site. The fact that New Moon Girls has a 'Girls Editorial Board' solidifies the interrelationship between the governance of the community and the members participating in it.[34] The community structure itself appears to provide opportunities for growth and nurturing built in, and this structure, in turn, evokes the close-knit social structure of the communities in which Montgomery's characters grow up, but without idealizing them or representing them nostalgically. While the content is not wedded to Emily or to Anne, it is specifically the community context that is the link: focusing on shared relationships and experiences among young girls within a larger social context that promotes the growth and development of specific ethics and values modelled by older girls and women who take leadership within the community. There's a level of continuity that suggests an intentional modelling of what it means to grow up in a women-centred community context. And as we find in Montgomery's texts, there is a discernible male presence, but it is found in supportive and administrative roles that are clearly secondary to issues of identity, governance, and community.

Animated Anne: 'Much Scope for the Imagination'?

With its proven formula of family values, nostalgia, innocence, wholesomeness, and happiness blended with scenes from Montgomery's novel,[35] Sullivan Entertainment's *Anne of Green Gables: The Animated Series* DVD boxed set also makes explicit statements about its educational values: 'There is so much scope for the imagination,' we are told. Couched in the language of 'madcap adventure,' the marketing text directs attention to a core set of learning values and attitudes:

> Welcome to the world of Avonlea, home to the irrepressible Anne Shirley. Avonlea is an exciting place to live especially as Anne's vivid imagination is always causing havoc for her and her friends. Anne is very, very good

at getting herself and others into hot water but always with the best intentions … Join Anne and her friends in each episode as they get into scrapes but recognize the importance of family, friendship and self-confidence.[36]

Due to the inherent limitations of broadcast media, *Anne of Green Gables: The Animated Series* is restricted to more passive observational learning opportunities, though the addition of KIDS COMMENTS and ANNE'S CLUB online shows an attempt to infuse interactive elements into the programs. The DVD identifies features that can be viewed along with the episodes as learning extensions, and points to a website, http://learningwithanne.com/, containing educational information.

A second educational website proclaims Anne a role model because of her 'can-do' attitude, a girl whose adventures and lessons help children to solve everyday problems and to cope with 'life's ups and downs.'[37] Viewers can learn the lessons contained in the episodes, and there are teacher-driven learning materials on the 'Annetoon Teachers Page' website with its teaching guides to all twenty-six episodes.[38] The Educators Guide boasts standard discussion questions (that are not free of spelling errors, however). Its stated educational objectives are to enrich the viewing experience of its young viewers; to manipulate the knowledge of characters; to sharpen critical viewing skills; and to improve collaborative learning (although it's not entirely clear how collaborative the learning is, given the traditional teacher/student set-up).[39] Discussion is possible through a link to the KINDRED SPIRITS CHAT; this chat, however, is not directed to any specific age group and is basically an open bulletin board for all of Sullivan Entertainment's Anne-related media offerings.[40] In this sense, communication is under the umbrella of a commercial agenda to generate discussion about Sullivan Entertainment's products, rather than being a forum for age-appropriate discussion about the series itself, or an autonomous fan site. There is no mention of or specific linkages to the animated series or discussion of the learning materials that would extend the materials from the 'Annetoon Teachers Page.'

Expanding Children's Horizons

Sullivan Entertainment's animated offering explicitly locates learning within a narrative produced by adults, showing the influence of the Disney model of inculcating family values and modelling traditional learning practices of the classroom and teacher. Anne's Diary and New

Moon Girls chart different paths by both locating discourse within the child and encouraging the co-construction of narrative and shared meaning through peer-to-peer communication. The location of the discourse resides primarily with the individual and is tied to her interests and experiences, though it is embedded within the larger cultural context of the online communities she visits.[41] By chatting or posting comments or participating in a threaded discussion where girls only have the opportunity to submit their opinions to discussions of interest to them, members of Anne's Diary and New Moon Girls are invited to create and share their own stories and maintain their own narrative spaces in a sustained and reflective manner, one that places them at the centre of the experience, not on the periphery. This gives them the level of control and autonomy over their own narrative spaces that bloggers, for instance, find so appealing.

On one level, Anne's Diary certainly leverages the iconic appeal of Anne developed by Sullivan Entertainment as the marketing strategy to entice participants into a culture of corporate surveillance and product-driven identity construction, wherein Anne models both acquiescence and consumerism. The New Moon Girls site engages Montgomery's world in ways that resonate more fundamentally with her fiction in general including the *Anne* and *Emily* series. They take, as their model, the very notions of community and informal learning that Montgomery describes her heroines experiencing together, and within a larger social context, inviting participants to explore the world collectively beyond the confines of a single cartoonish identity, very much as Montgomery's characters do. In this context, we should also be mindful of Holly Blackford's insights in *Out of This World: Why Literature Matters to Girls* (2004), in which she argues that girls read *beyond* their experiences, turning to literature to connect with experiences that are not necessarily theirs: 'Believing that they open themselves to the vision of life that a text represents, the girls journey out of this world, a world that, they feel, limits them to one subjective point of view and one realm of experience.' In other words, these Anne-inspired sites ultimately have the potential to expand children's horizons, and like the literature discussed by Blackford, afford child readers the opportunity to move beyond their own experiences and 'to experience something radically different from their everyday lives.'[42]

Ultimately, this essay represents a glimpse at the context and surface features of these three locations in cyberspace, only cracking the surface of examining how all the promised features play themselves out in the hands of the girls who are signing up to share their passions and dreams. Its objective is to explore the foundations and landscapes of these sites in preparation for future research into this virtually unexplored intersection of Childhood Education, New Media Studies, and L.M. Montgomery Studies. More research is required to ascertain not only the diverse ways in which Anne- and Emily-inspired new media provide educational models and life skills for young children, and comprehend more fully how the values that Anne models in the novels work in unison with the technologies in constructing individual and communal identities in the name of Anne. More than this, the goal of future research is also to find out what is really going on inside, the kinds of stories and narratives that are being constructed and shared, the opportunities available and denied, and develop a sense of how participants are maintaining their kindred spirit relationships, if such relationships are in fact possible at all in these mediated spaces.

NOTES

1 Dewey, *Moral Principles in Education*, 8.
2 LMM, *Anne of Avonlea*, 27.
3 See Kornfeld and Jackson, 'The Female *Bildungsroman*'; Poe, 'Who's Got the Power?'
4 Weber, 'Confessions of a Kindred Spirit,' 56. See also Ross, 'Readers Reading L.M. Montgomery,' and the reader responses discussed by Irene Gammel in this volume.
5 'Anne's Diary: Introduction,' http://www.annesdiary.com/corporate/?m=introduction.
6 'New Moon Girls,' http://www.newmoon.com/. Although New Moon Girls does not explicitly associate itself with L.M. Montgomery's work, the combination of its name and its dedication to supporting young girls' 'self-discovery, creativity and community' makes it a kindred spirit enterprise.
7 *Anne of Green Gables: The Animated Series*, DVD boxed set, back cover. For a complete episode guide, see '*Anne of Green Gables: The Animated Series*,' L.M. Montgomery Research Group, http://lmmresearch.org/filmography/aggas-2000/.
8 Grimes, 'Kids' Ad Play.'
9 For earlier studies of Montgomery's spawning of e-mail discussion groups, see Nolan, Lawrence, and Kajihara, 'Montgomery's Island in the

Net'; Nolan and Weiss, 'Learning in Cyberspace'; van der Klei, 'Avonlea in Cyberspace.'

10 Gammel and Dutton, 'Disciplining Development,' 111; see also LMM, 6 Dec. 1894, in *SJ*, 1: 125.

11 Gammel and Dutton, 'Disciplining Development,' 107.

12 For Montgomery's responses to MacMurchy's novel, see LMM, 2 Mar. 1924, in *SJ*, 3: 167.

13 Waterston, 'Marigold and the Magic'; see also Richard Volpe, 'The History of Child Study and Education at the University of Toronto,' http://www.oise.utoronto.ca/ICS/resources/Hist%20of%20ICS.pdf, 4.

14 Nolan and Weiss, 'Learning in Cyberspace,' 293.

15 Jackson, *Life in Classrooms*, 33–5.

16 Eisner, *The Educational Imagination*, 97–103.

17 See, e.g., Piaget, *The Language and Thought*; Vygotstky, *The Mind in Society.*

18 See the Informal Learning Environments Research Group, 'a special interest group within the American Educational Research Association,' http://www.umsl.edu/~sigiler.

19 'Welcome to Arcade Dressup,' http://arcadedressup.com/.

20 'Anne's Diary Video,' http://www.annesdiary.com/diary/demos/video/.

21 Chung and Grimes, 'Data Mining the Kids,' 528.

22 Sullivan Boutique, http://www.sullivanboutique.com/.

23 See http://disney.go.com/mickey/, http://barbie.everythinggirl.com/, and http://www.hasbro.com/mylittlepony/, respectively.

24 Dolphin Digital Media, 'Company Profile,' http://www.dolphindigitalmedia.com/info.php?id=1.

25 Novell User Communities, 'Success Story: Anne's Diary,' http://www.novell.com/communities/node/2986/success-story-annes-diary/.

26 Brad Stone, 'Report Calls Online Threats to Children Overblown.' *New York Times*, 14 Jan. 2009, http://www.nytimes.com/2009/01/14/technology/internet/14cyberweb.html.

27 Yomiuri Shimbun, 'S. Korean Woman "Tricked" Airport Fingerprint,' http://www.yomiuri.co.jp/dy/national/20090101TDY01303.htm.

28 Foucault, *Discipline and Punish*, 84; Nolan, Mann, and Wellman, 'Sousveillance.'

29 Anne's Diary, 'Setting New Standards in Online Safety: Who counts as a sponsor?' http://www.annesdiary.com/?v =help&cc=193#Sponsor.

30 For more on ideology and texts for children and what is taught passively about race, gender roles, the past, community, the family, adult predators, commercial television, and cyberspace, see Nodelman and Reimer, *The Pleasures of Children's Literature.*

31 'New Moon Girls,' http://www.newmoon.com/.

32 New Moon Girls, 'Our Experts,' http://www.newmoon.com/experts/.

33 'New Moon Store: Great Gifts for Girls and Women,' http://www
    .newmooncatalog.com/default.asp.

34 Nolan and Weiss, 'Learning in Cyberspace,' 295.

35 Lefebvre, *Road to Avonlea*,' 177. See also 'Anne of Green Gables: The
    Animated Series,' *Ready to Learn: Wisconsin Public Television* 5, no. 11 (Nov.
    2001), http://www.wpt.org/kids/wipbs/pdf/nov01.pdf. The television
    series was followed by *Anne: Journey to Green Gables* (2005), an animated
    prequel in the style of Walt Disney's *Cinderella*, featuring characters such
    as Madame Poubelle, who owns the Grout Orphanage, her henchmen Wil-
    fred and Tupper, and a trusty red squirrel named Bailey. See '*Anne: Journey
    to Green Gables*,' L.M. Montgomery Research Group, http://lmmresearch
    .org/filmography/ajgg-2005/.

36 *Anne of Green Gables: The Animated Series* DVD, vol. 1, back cover.

37 UNC TV, 'Teachers and Childcare Providers,' http://www.unctv.org/
    education/teachers_childcare/workshops/anne.html.

38 'Annetoon Teachers Page,' http://www.annetoon.com/teachers.html.

39 Also included on this website are guides for Sullivan Entertainment's
    live-action adaptations of Montgomery's work. See, in particular, Chris
    Worsnop and Roberta Bartlett, '*Anne of Green Gables*: Educators' Guide,'
    http://annetoon.com/EducatorsGuides/LiveActionEducatorsGuide.pdf.

40 'Anne of Green Gables Message Boards,' http://www.anneofgreengables
    .com/board/.

41 Haste and Abrahams, 'Morality, Culture and the Dialogic Self,' 381.

42 Blackford, *Out of This World*, 2, 6.

8 On the Road from Bright River: Shifting Social Space in *Anne of Green Gables*

ALEXANDER MACLEOD

> Is it lack of imagination that makes us come to imagined places, not just stay at home?
>
> – Elizabeth Bishop, 'Questions of Travel'[1]

On 23 May 1997, at about four o'clock in the morning, a small, nine-teenth-century farmhouse that once belonged to Margaret and David Macneill of Cavendish, Prince Edward Island, was damaged by a fire that began in a first-floor bedroom before moving quickly to the exterior walls, the upstairs, and the roof. By the time firefighters arrived on the scene, the house was fully engulfed in smoke while flames could be seen flashing through the broken windows of the upper story. For a few tense hours before the blaze was brought under control, the possibility that this house – known throughout the wider world as Green Gables – might burn to the ground was a real and immediate threat. The timing for such an incident could not have been worse. Prince Edward Island's tourist industry was about to swing into high season and the Confederation Bridge, the controversial 'fixed link' that would join Prince Edward Island to mainland New Brunswick permanently, was scheduled to open to public crossings for the first time eight days later, on 31 May. With major celebrations planned to mark the historic event and the entire island gearing up for a record-breaking year of visitors, many feared the Green Gables disaster would cast a dark cloud over what was supposed to be a festive and triumphant summer.

Public response to the fire was dramatic and instantaneous. P.E.I.'s provincial fire marshal called the damage to the house 'a devastating loss.'[2] Patrick Binns, the premier of the province, predicted the fire could have a profound negative effect on the Island's economy and, after surveying the damage, promised to have the house back in shape in time for the Canada Day festivities on 1 July. Immersed in the clamour of a federal election at the time, Sheila Copps, minister for Canadian heritage, made an emergency visit to Cavendish to deliver a cheque for more than $100,000 along with unequivocal support: 'The Government of Canada wants to ensure that this wonderful symbol of our culture and our history continues to inspire all Canadians and people from around the world for many years to come.'[3] Anonymous contributors from across the province, the county, and around the world – with a large proportion of the donations coming from Japan – sent money for the relief and repair efforts. In the weeks that followed, crews worked around the clock, and in the end, the park met its ambitious deadline and reopened to the public on 1 July. For a few years after the fire, there was even a webcam permanently fixed on the house, continuously beaming its reassuring real-time image of Green Gables into cyberspace.

The Green Gables fire, the reaction it triggered, and the frantic repair effort it required are interesting to me for a number of different reasons. As a fan of *Anne of Green Gables*, I was worried when I heard the news about the blaze. I teach courses on Atlantic Canadian literature at St Mary's University in Halifax, and I regularly include the novel along with major excerpts from Montgomery's journals in my syllabi. I have made the trip to the Island, via ferry or bridge, many times, and I have visited the park, bought the souvenirs, and, in my more cynical moments, made all the standard jokes about the Godzilla-like presence of Anne in Prince Edward Island: the way it sometimes seems as though, even as her image is consumed by thousands of tourists, she, in turn, is consuming them and absorbing a whole province into a Disneyfied theme park of rural Victorian farmhouses, horse-drawn carriage rides, and gift shops bursting with mass-produced 'traditional' trinkets. With more than 200,000 visitors travelling to this site every year, it is easy to understand why the fire would have been interpreted as a major disaster for people who work in the local tourist industry and derive their livelihoods from it.

Still, the incident raises more complex issues. We know that Montgomery never lived and never wrote in this house and that, in the years before the publication of the novel, the buildings that make up the Green Gables Heritage Site were simply part of a nearby relative's farm and did not hold any special status (except perhaps for the fact that the author did attend her friend Myrtle Macneill's wedding there

while writing *Anne*).[4] Montgomery's journals tell us that she took inspiration from this particular house, but the same passages provide
even clearer evidence of the 'annoyance' the author felt towards naïve,
misguided visitors to P.E.I. who, just two years after the book's publication, sought to establish clear one-to-one connections between the imaginary settings of her novel and the real world of Cavendish.[5] Scholars
of architecture, tourism, cultural studies, and folklore have examined
the contested status of the Green Gables house and farm as sites that
sometimes successfully and sometimes problematically combine Montgomery's biography with parts of Anne's story. Parks Canada historian
James De Jonge readily admits that 'there will probably always be some
confusion among visitors' between the Macneill-Webb farmhouse that
is now Green Gables and the Macneill homestead where Montgomery
actually lived from 1876 to 1911. *Anne of Green Gables* was written in
the latter in 1905, but this house was demolished in the 1920s by Montgomery's uncongenial Uncle John Franklin Macneill, the legal heir to
the property.[6]

Part of the confusion may lie embedded in the novel itself. Irene
Gammel's *Looking for Anne* reveals just how much Montgomery's novel
mingled personal and local elements with many other cultural texts,
objects, and influences from the nineteenth century and beyond. Effectively blending 'the personal and the borrowed, the literary and the
popular, the local and the global,' the fictional Green Gables is a web
of surprising and unacknowledged influences from the wider world
that lonely and isolated L.M. Montgomery had absorbed vicariously
through her voracious reading of popular magazines.[7] Moreover, after
the publication of *Anne*, Montgomery herself initially encouraged Anne
tourism by identifying local inspirations as the landmarks in *Anne of
Green Gables* in interviews and in her 1917 memoir *The Alpine Path*.
However, by 1929, when the first plans for larger-scale operations were
beginning to circulate, a conflicted Montgomery admitted that she was
glad that her real home had been torn down and would 'never be de-
graded to the uses of a tea-room.'[8]

It is clear that Montgomery, her readers and critics, the designers
of the Parks Canada site, and the legions of tourists who visit Prince
Edward Island every year interpret the north-shore landscape in very
different ways. The mere existence of the Green Gables Heritage Site,
combined with the threat of its destruction, raises questions that may
be difficult to answer. What was it, exactly, that was nearly lost in
that fire? If the Green Gables Heritage Site is ostensibly dedicated to

preserving Montgomery's legacy, what kind of nationally significant cultural resource needed to be rescued, protected, and restored? If we direct our investigation in a different way, we might ask: Why don't we see the same millions of fans making annual pilgrimages to the Manse in Leaskdale, Ontario, where Montgomery lived from 1911 to 1926 and where so many of Anne's further adventures were written? What, exactly, are visitors looking for when they come to Green Gables? Are they trying to forge a closer connection with Montgomery or with the fictional character she created?

In his work on cultural geography, Edward Soja has explored the relationship between real and imagined geographies and the 'perceived' and 'conceived spatial epistemologies' that have normally been used to read, interpret, and understand the linkages between the two.[9] Like many of the other leading figures of the 'spatial-turn' in critical theory (including David Harvey, Doreen Massey, and Derek Gregory), Soja, directed by the ground-breaking example of Henri Lefebvre, suggests that the stark division that once seemed to separate idealist and materialist readings of social space no longer applies and that scholars, especially those concerned with contemporary readings of place, must come to understand that real and imagined models of spatiality not only coexist simultaneously, but are actually interdependent. In his discussions, 'Toward a Spatial Ontology' in *Postmodern Geographies* (1989) and 'The Trialectics of Spatiality' in *Thirdspace* (1996), Soja dismantles the binary that separates real and imagined readings of place and argues instead for a strategically rebalanced combination of the two, a simultaneously 'real-and-imagined (or perhaps realandimagined)' concept of 'lived' or 'experienced social space.'[10] Imaginary geographies are continually being projected into the real world, and in turn, these imagined projections shape our everyday experience of real social space. The same interdependent cycle works in the opposite way: perceived readings of real geography shape our imagined visions of place as well as our lived experiences. Neither epistemology can ever be fully separated from the other; imagined geographies are always producing real places and real places are always producing imagined geographies. For literary scholars, especially those interested in questions of regionalism, place-based identity, and canon formation, spatial theory provides a new set of methodological tools and a critical vocabulary designed to examine the sometimes hard-to-articulate relationship between fictional texts and the outside real worlds they represent and produce.

If we use these analytical tools to study *Anne of Green Gables*, we see that the characters inside Montgomery's novel, like the readers outside the text and the real-world visitors to the Green Gables Heritage Site, are all engaged in an intricate set of socio-spatial negotiations. On both sides of the fictional divide, different ways of coding and decoding (or rereading and rewriting) cultural geography coexist and compete against each other. At the beginning of the novel, when Anne moves through her initial scenes with Matthew and begins her first journey down the road from Bright River, she is already harnessing and purposefully directing her power to remake and imaginatively transform the world that surrounds her. The same process repeats itself outside the novel. Just as Anne, the character, rewrites Avonlea to make the landscape correspond with her pre-existing romantic ideals, so her story initiates an identical and equally problematic cycle of geographical transformations that continue, literally, to 'take place' in the real world of contemporary Cavendish.

Others have preceded me in noting that the Green Gables Heritage Site provides us with a textbook example of Baudrillard's infamous argument for the postmodern 'precession of the simulacra.'[11] Where followers of traditional metaphysics and nineteenth-century realist aesthetics might once have argued that it is the real, physical world that is stable, secure, and unchanging and the literary text that is its fluid, imaginative representation, in Cavendish today we find the exact opposite conditions in effect. As we enter the second centennial of the novel's first publication, it is Montgomery's text that has left a secure and lasting impression on the landscape of Prince Edward Island, and it is the real, physical, and material world outside of the story that has been forcefully restructured in an ongoing effort to maintain or to prop up the real to make it better conform with the pre-existing representation it is trying to copy. In her analysis and historical overview of the public development of the National Park and the private infrastructure of Anne tourism, Shelagh J. Squire surveys the actual government policy documents that directed the creation and maintenance of the Green Gables Heritage Site. She explains that in an effort to 'render the property more "authentic,"' several sets of new, traditional-looking shutters had to be added to the windows of the home and that even the signature gables and dormers of the house had to be painted green because they weren't originally that colour. During the 'extensive site redevelopment' of the 1980s, the Park was remade in accordance with several strictly enforced and clearly stated guidelines: 'The surrounding landscape will be created, where possible, according to the interpretation of features described in ... the ... literary works of Lucy Maud Montgomery. Twentieth-century interferences ... will be removed from the site.'[12]

Although these words are drawn from a policy document, even Baudrillard himself could not have made a more explicit declaration on the material existence of 'created' places and the stubborn 'interferences' of a malleable physical reality. Under these conditions, Montgomery's fiction clearly 'engenders the territory' with a projected set of coded meanings, and the imagined text of the novel guarantees the real existence of the National Park. In Cavendish, where Montgomery's images are continuously made literal and concrete, one of Baudrillard's most controversial and cryptic statements – 'The territory no longer precedes the map, nor survives it' – becomes merely descriptive.[13] Every summer, the provincial government of Prince Edward Island produces tourist highway maps that locate the real village of Cavendish at the centre of a fictional place called 'Anne's Land.'[14]

This dissolving of the border between real and imagined spaces is what makes Cavendish/Avonlea such an important destination for people around the world. Although many visitors to the site have a deep interest in Montgomery's life and work, the vast majority of the people who come to Cavendish are attempting to visit the imaginary Avonlea and to put themselves, temporarily at least, into the same shared place where Anne once 'lived' in the real world. At the Green Gables Heritage Site, two entirely different ways of creating, maintaining, reading, and understanding social space come together. Indeed, in articles about the fire, some reporters referred to the Green Gables floor plan, and explained that the blaze began in 'Matthew's room' before heading up to the second floor.[15] The fact that Matthew, a character in a novel, never had a bedroom in Cavendish, never slept, never ate, and never picked up an orphan child at a local train station, does not matter. The real and imagined geography of this place and, in Soja's terms, the perceived and conceived spatial epistemologies we use to understand these two versions of the site combine. There is a miraculous quality to this kind of linkage, a sort of transubstantiation between materialist and idealist readings of space, and it is this obvious co-presence and co-dependence of real and imagined spatial epistemologies that gives a pilgrimage to Cavendish its pseudo-religious significance and explains why so many people choose this place as the site to stage their weddings or other important events.[16] Green Gables functions as a kind of shrine or as a portal between two ways of understanding social space, making the imagined idea of the place and the fact of its physical existence inseparable.

'There is no meaning in a name like that': The End of the Local in Avonlea

The same relationship between real and imagined spaces and the same competitive rereadings and reinterpretations of cultural geography that we see at work at the Green Gables site also play essential roles in the plot and the iconic characterizations of *Anne of Green Gables*. The opening scenes of the novel have been discussed so many times that it may seem redundant to remind readers that Anne's story actually begins with gossipy Mrs Rachel Lynde being 'surprised' to see Matthew Cuthbert, dressed up in his best clothes, riding 'out of Avonlea' with his buggy and sorrel mare, apparently prepared to cover 'a considerable distance.' The sight of Matthew – 'the shyest man alive' – travelling in such an apparently purposeful way disturbs Mrs Lynde, who concludes that she 'won't know a minute's peace of mind or conscience' until she can uncover an acceptable explanation for his out-of-the-ordinary actions.[17] The novel actually remains in this suspended state of surprise for its first three chapters: first 'Mrs Rachel Lynde is Surprised,' then 'Matthew Cuthbert is Surprised,' and finally 'Marilla Cuthbert is Surprised.' Although all of this excitement seems to be initiated by Matthew's travel, it is significant that once he moves beyond the range of Mrs Lynde's early surveillance he makes that initial journey to the Bright River train station mostly by himself and his trip is largely ignored by the narrator and the reader. While readers follow Marilla and Mrs Lynde as they argue and gossip back and forth about the relative value of Barnardo boys and troubled orphans who have been known to 'set fire to the house' or 'suck the eggs,' we are left to assume that Matthew makes it to Bright River uneventfully. The only reference to the trip comes at the beginning of chapter 2 when we are told that Avonlea and Bright River are linked by 'a pretty road, running along between snug farmsteads,' and that Matthew 'enjoyed the drive after his own fashion.'[18]

The second leg of Matthew's journey, the trip home, is a remarkably different kind of passage. On this ride, Matthew does not go alone. Instead, he is accompanied not only by his new travelling companion – a young 'freckled witch' from Nova Scotia – but he also shares his space in the buggy with the narrator and an accompanying crowd of readers who now seem interested in contemplating every detail of that pretty road between Bright River and Avonlea.[19] Although we would expect that, at least from Matthew's point of view, the sights he sees coming back along the same eight-mile route he travelled up only an hour before would remain relatively unchanged, the narrator of these scenes makes it very clear that something dramatic happened to Matthew while he was at that train station and that the entire cultural geography of his Avonlea home is about to be transformed.

The journey down the road from Bright River serves several different functions within the novel. During that first ride with Matthew, Montgomery introduces her readers to many of Anne's signature qualities. Anne's kind and charismatic personality, her expansive vocabulary, her vivid imagination, her impressive strength and determination, and her mile-a-minute conversation style are all on display. Many of the novel's most lasting and influential lines are uttered during this interval. Stunned by the beauty of the landscape, Anne proclaims at different times that the 'Island is the bloomiest place' and the 'prettiest place in the world.' She tells Matthew that she 'used to imagine' she lived on Prince Edward Island and that it is 'delightful when your imaginations come true.'[20] The chapter is filled with references to Anne's lively dream world and to the protective, romantic fantasies she has developed to insulate herself from the painful facts of her life. Anne's love of language and her precocious, elevated diction are demonstrated, as well as the 'big ideas' her 'big words' must express. Although she is new to this place and has never set foot on the Island before, Anne anticipates that Avonlea, unlike her former home in the asylum, will be a place that allows 'scope for the imagination.'[21] As they move along, Matthew luxuriates in Anne's chatter and allows her to direct the conversation in any way she pleases. The narrator tells us, somewhat dismissively, that although Matthew 'found it rather difficult for his slower intelligence to keep up with [Anne's] brisk mental processes,' he still encourages the girl to 'talk as much as you like.'[22]

As these two characters stage their first conversations, a powerful socio-spatial transition begins. In this pairing, Matthew is the local expert, an elderly man who has lived in the same community his entire life. As he journeys back towards Green Gables, he is retracing his own steps through a familiar cultural geography that, at least for him, has already been inscribed with its own set of coded signifiers and meanings. On the road from Bright River, Matthew knows exactly where he is at all times, and though the narrator may occasionally undercut his intelligence and draw attention to the fact that he appreciates the Island's beauty only 'in his own fashion,' it is important to remember that Matthew does possess his own way of understanding and caring for his local social space. His entire personal history has been lived out in this one place and he certainly does not think of Avonlea as fantasy land or a blank void without a past and without meaning. In fact, whenever he does get a chance to speak during the trip, the few words Matthew says usually transmit some detail of local knowledge about place names, or family histories, or local agriculture. He knows, for example, all about the thrilling and disgusting sight of grubs turned up in the cucumber beds and that the spectacular blooming apple trees that surprise Anne were actually planted 'years ago by an eccentric old farmer.' He knows that the Barry family lives in a house called 'Orchard Slope' and that they have an eleven-year-old daughter named Diana, and that this girl was given her 'dreadful heathenish' name not by her parents but by a romantically inclined visiting schoolmaster who had been boarding with the family the day she was born.[23] Again, in that buggy, there is one person who possesses an intimate local knowledge of Avonlea and another who has never seen this place before. It could be argued that Matthew's guest, the girl he picked up at the train station, was actually the first tourist ever to visit 'Anne's Land.' Before she came along and took possession of the site with her apostrophe, Avonlea was understood as a very different kind of place.

The shift from one dominant reading of Avonlea's cultural geography to another takes place very quickly and, on the surface, it seems like Anne's rewriting of the landscape proceeds without any real resistance from Matthew. Whenever Anne asks him for the name of a place, he quickly provides the information. It is what happens next that is critical. Anne's responses to Matthew initiate a profound socio-spatial transformation. After she politely but resolutely refuses to accept Matthew's bare-boned descriptions and his boring taxonomies, Anne puts forth her own alternative possibilities. Rather than acknowledging and accepting local readings of the landscape or the place names that seemed to function perfectly well on the way to Bright River, Anne re-invents these places and re-invigorates Matthew's bland quotidian landscape with what seems, at least on first glance, like a revitalizing new surge of creative energy. When Matthew points to the dull 'Avenue' and tells his guest that it is 'a kind of pretty place,' Anne totally rejects his reading and tells him that there is 'no meaning in a name like that' and that the lane should be properly rechristened as 'The White

Way of Delight.' The body of water formerly known as 'Barry's Pond' moves through a similar transformation when Anne retitles it as 'The Lake of Shining Waters.' She tells Matthew that she is absolutely sure that this new designation is the 'right name' for the pond because of the familiar 'thrill' she feels when she 'hit[s] on a name that suits exactly.' Every site Anne contemplates is altered by her transformative glance and it is clear that the third-person narrator sees through Anne's eyes and shares her readings. In chapter 2, for example, the first time Anne sees Matthew's house, the narrator describes a beautiful setting of 'blossoming trees in the twilight' and 'a great, crystal white star ... shining like a lamp of guidance and promise' above the farm.[24] As readers, however, we know that none of this natural beauty and none of this religious iconography was there the first time we were presented with the house in chapter 1. The suggestive images that the narrator describes and the florid language that convey them to the reader were absent the first time around. In chapter 1, when Mrs Lynde introduced Green Gables, she saw it as a neat but antisocial homestead that had been constructed too far away from the road. Where Anne sees pastoral splendour and a star of Bethlehem, Mrs Lynde sees nothing but an old, 'rambling' and 'unmysterious' farmhouse, a place unfit for 'living,' and suitable only for '*staying*.'[25]

Critics have interpreted the significance of Anne's geographical transformations in a range of ways. In her analysis of the relationship between natural and cultural readings of the popular landscape of *Anne of Green Gables*, Janice Fiamengo argues that 'one of the key images from the novel is the pleasurable spectacle of a little orphan girl, ugly, unwanted, and destitute, boldly asserting her imaginative connection with and linguistic command of her environment.' As Anne 'names the landscape into her power,' she 'lovingly but authoritatively' launches a 'direct and ongoing challenge to the powers of Avonlea.' Although Fiamengo admits that 'at some level *Anne of Green Gables* is about entering a territory that is not your own and taking possession of it,' and although she sees that Anne's language is 'exuberantly imperialist,' she ultimately endorses rather than critiques Anne's 'inherent right' to the landscape. Unlike colonizers or missionaries, who would restructure cultural geographies to serve their own obvious ideological aims, Anne's 'innocent power' and her 'sheer love of the land – a sense of belonging rooted in centuries of loving cultivation of the natural world' – are accepted as legitimate alternatives because they are so directly linked to the 'complex political and emotional needs' of readers and visitors and their desperate desire for a perfectly apolitical communion with 'a green world of comfort and reassurance.'[26]

The 'Critique of Innocence' and the Other Side of Fantasy

But what do these spatial transitions look like from Matthew's side of the buggy? And how might Anne's 'exuberantly imperialist' challenges be interpreted in a slightly less pleasurable way? In his landmark text *The Tourist Gaze* (1990), John Urry argues that even the most innocuous appreciation for the natural beauty of a foreign locale can never really be considered perfectly innocent or apolitical. The tourist gaze – the lens through which visitors view, interpret, and come to possess exotic foreign destinations – is a politically constructed narrative that has been 'socially organized and systematized' and maintained by years of carefully monitored cultural messaging.[27] As Matthew and Anne demonstrate in their conversation, what is seen during any engagement with landscape depends mostly on who is doing the looking. Anecdotal real-world examples of this kind of exchange between locals and visitors are commonplace. There is that standard tale of the millions of New Yorkers who have lived in the city their entire lives but have never visited the Empire State Building or the Statue of Liberty, and there are countless Atlantic Canadians who, like Matthew Cuthbert, have always lived next to breathtaking vistas that have never taken their breath away. The strange and beautiful sights that attract tourists usually cannot hold the same other-worldly significance for locals who have always lived in these cultural environments. When we focus on how Matthew and Anne interpret the same territory in different ways, we see that the process of socio-spatial redefinition that scholars have traditionally discussed in positive and liberating terms also functions in a more problematic and troubling way. As the full consequences of Anne's transformations radiate into new territory, they raise still more questions: Where does Barry's Pond go after Anne is finished with it? Does her innocent power actually give her an inherent right to this landscape? What kind of world is she erasing and replacing? What is being cast away as Matthew silently acquiesces to his talkative companion? And are we, as readers, required to come along for this ride?

Anne's impressive history as a popular culture force should teach us never to underestimate the power this impoverished orphaned girl actually wields. Although Anne is working from a subject position that is marginalized by gender, appearance, age, and economic status, we must also recognize that the vocabulary, the reading strategies, and the discursive practices this girl carries in her head – as well as the spatial epistemology she relies on and the tourist gaze that fuels her fantastic appreciation for the Avonlea landscape – are anything but marginalized. In fact, although Anne lacks social power, the interpretive framework she references and the cultural material she draws on come from some of the most recognizable aesthetic movements in the history of the Western tradition. The texts that influence Anne come from sources as varied as British, American, and German romanticism, the epic tradition in poetry, Victorian readings of the pastoral, the Bible, popular magazines of the Victorian and Edwardian eras, and many other different philosophical and aesthetic reflections on the sublime. Annotated editions of the novel take care to point out these literary references and to demonstrate that nearly every example of Anne's elevated speech originates from some other part of the novel's literary inheritance. The footnotes start to pile up almost as soon as Anne begins to speak. As readers, we learn very quickly that phrases such as 'scope for the imagination,' which is used twelve times in the novel, are lifted from Laurence Sterne's travel novel *A Sentimental Journey through France and Italy* (1768). References to Tennyson, Shakespeare, Longfellow, Keats, Sir Walter Scott, Thomas Gray, and Hans Christian Andersen, along with many, many others, combined with dozens of scriptural passages, create Anne as a composite character whose readings of landscape – far from being marginalized, weak, and strange – fall directly in line with at least four centuries worth of Western cultural dominance.[28]

When we look back at those first scenes again, and watch as Anne sweeps through her first eight miles of Prince Edward Island, we can begin to appreciate just how influential her interpretations of the territory have become in the real world. It may appear that there is no ideological tension in the buggy, but there is a competition going on between Anne's conceived spatial epistemology and Matthew's lived or experienced spatial epistemology. Although he is a willing participant, as Matthew comfortably yields the conversation to his talkative companion, her discourse takes up more and more room and the scope for her celebrated imagination expands until, as Baudrillard and the postmodern cultural geographers might say, her text takes over the territory and the landscape Matthew once knew is transformed by this newly imagined projection. In twenty-first-century Cavendish, the same process is re-enacted. Montgomery's novel functions as a guidebook encouraging readers to follow Anne's example and to interpret the real Prince Edward Island according to Anne's fictional re-visioning of the place. Tourists are invited to see the place through Anne's enchanted eyes. Matthew's local interpretations of his familiar landscape prior to Anne's arrival, like the readings of the local inhabitants of contemporary Prince Edward Island, who may see a different reality from the one portrayed in the novel, are sometimes understandably overwhelmed by this one fantastic projection. Squire's examination of the 'striking contrasts' of Anne's Land includes excerpts from interviews with several local inhabitants of Cavendish who utterly reject the romantic imprint that has overwritten their own experience of local space and 'spoiled the countryside' with 'offensive' attractions. Because the local, permanent population of Cavendish is so much smaller and less economically powerful than the summer visiting population, it has been difficult for native islanders to regulate their own tourist industry or to resist the development plans of external investors. Squire observes that even that first controversial decision to expropriate long-held farmlands from local Cavendish families in order to establish the park in the 1930s 'sparked hostility in the local community that lingers to the present day.'[29]

The cultural consequences of these kinds of changes are obvious but underappreciated in *Anne of Green Gables*. In Avonlea, Anne's imaginings are revolutionary and they challenge any stable reading of place. Critics have traditionally interpreted these challenges as courageous acts of self-definition and paid close attention to the ways that Anne breaks through the ossified social structures of a hypocritical, Victorian, Anglophile Prince Edward Island.[30] Anne has often been cast, quite correctly, as a liberating figure, a character who demands flexibility in the face of social intransigence and thereby creates a better world for herself and for others. If, however, we think again about Anne's transformations from the point of view of local knowledge, or if we interpret them through the perspective of Ian McKay's passionate 'Critique of Innocence' in *The Quest of the Folk* (1994), we realize that there is nothing politically neutral about the 'anti-modern' desire to 'return' to a state of romantic, pastoral enchantment.'[31] While I am not trying to portray Anne as a malevolent, power-mad character who sets out to destroy Matthew's world, her readings of Avonlea's cultural geography are predicated on a rejection of his social space. And though it may be strange to think about it in these terms, the way Anne reads, writes, and interprets Avonlea could never actually produce an 'Anne

of Green Gables,' and never give us a subjectivity that was environ-
mentally determined or shaped by the external social forces of the
world. Instead, Anne embraces the alternative, a flexible spatial epistemology that harnesses the power of the creative subject and its endless
capacity to remake social space according to its own design. It would
probably be more accurate to describe her story as *Green Gables According to Anne.*

As one reading of social space surpasses another, some traditional
nuances are lost and some new alternatives are developed. As generations of delighted readers know, Anne's creativity and her revolutionary interpretations of place do lead Matthew and Marilla out of the
stultified, bland, and repressed world they once inhabited. On the other
side of the ledger, as the novel continues and Anne ages and matures,
her readings of place change and she gradually sees herself as a capable but slightly less-dramatic local person, an almost regular citizen of
Avonlea who is occasionally suspicious of the wealth and pretensions
of the foreign tourists who stay at the White Sands Hotel, projecting
and discovering the same romantic readings she once put forward. Although these readings of place may seem exotic, revolutionary, and,
yes, foreign to Avonlea, there is absolutely nothing novel or strange
about the way Anne or the tourists interpret their environments. Just
as native islanders in the Caribbean might respond rather sceptically to
pale, sun-burned visitors insisting that their home is a vacation para-
dise, and just as minimum-wage employees in an Orlando theme park
might feel justified in their grumbling evaluations of the working conditions inside 'The Magic Kingdom,' readers of *Anne of Green Gables*
and visitors to the Green Gables Heritage Site must understand that
insider and outsider perspectives on place rarely align and that foreign
readings of social space, even when they are endorsed and carried by
individuals who do not possess significant social power themselves,
still retain that capacity to transform and obliterate long-standing local
traditions. In the end, readers and visitors find themselves in strangely
similar positions and faced with still more difficult questions that can
never be adequately answered. Who will be left to mourn the loss of
Barry's Pond? What kind of deranged local arsonist might have been
deeply motivated to burn down Green Gables in 1997? And what ever
happened to that other place, the world Matthew left behind when he
took that first fateful journey down the road to Bright River and away
from a home he could never return to again?

NOTES

1 Bishop, *The Complete Poems 1927–1979*, 93.
2 'Green Gables House Damaged,' C2.
3 Gallant, 'Copps Presses Flesh,' A1.
4 Gammel, *Looking for Anne*, 156.
5 LMM, 27 Jan. 1911, in *SJ*, 2: 38.
6 De Jonge, 'Through the Eyes of Memory,' 257; see also Fawcett and Mc-Cormack, 'Guarding Authenticity'; Lefebvre, '"A Small World after All"'; Squire, 'Literary Tourism and Sustainable Tourism'; Tye, 'Multiple Meanings Called Cavendish.'
7 Gammel, *Looking for Anne*, 137.
8 LMM, 28 Sept. 1929, in *SJ*, 4: 11; see also Carole Gerson's chapter in this volume.
9 Soja, *Thirdspace*, 74–5.
10 Ibid., 11.
11 Baudrillard, *Simulations*, 1. See Brouse, 'The Maud Squad,' 36; Lefebvre, '"A Small World after All"'; Weber, 'Confessions of a Kindred Spirit,' 54.
12 Squire, 'Literary Tourism and Sustainable Tourism,' 124. For a study of the 'different versions of the "authentic" heritage' that are promoted by competing Anne and Montgomery sites in Cavendish, see Fawcett and Cormack, 'Guarding Authenticity.'
13 Baudrillard, *Simulations*, 1.
14 See, e.g., 'The Gentle Island.'
15 'Green Gables House Damaged,' C2.
16 For a more detailed analysis of this phenomenon, see Sweet, 'Secular Pilgrimages.'
17 LMM, *AGG*, 8, 9.
18 Ibid., 13, 16.
19 Ibid., 22.
20 Ibid., 21.
21 Ibid., 20.
22 Ibid., 22.
23 Ibid., 24, 27.
24 Ibid., 25–8.
25 Ibid., 9–10; original emphasis.
26 Fiamengo, 'Towards a Theory,' 232–3, 235–7.
27 Urry, *The Tourist Gaze*, 2.
28 LMM, *The Annotated Anne of Green Gables*; LMM, *Anne of Green Gables*, ed. Devereux; LMM, *Anne of Green Gables*, ed. Rubio and Waterston.

For a discussion of literary allusions in the novel, see Wilmshurst, 'L.M. Montgomery's Use'; Epperly, *The Fragrance of Sweet-Grass*, 27–38; Epperly, *Through Lover's Lane*, 103–24; Karr, *Authors and Audiences*, 124–37.

29 Squire, 'Literary Tourism and Sustainable Tourism,' 123.
30 See, e.g., Robinson, '"A Born Canadian."'
31 McKay, *The Quest of the Folk*, 37.

9 Anne in a 'Globalized' World: Nation, Nostalgia, and Postcolonial Perspectives of Home

MARGARET STEFFLER

> When she crossed the log bridge over the brook the kitchen light of Green Gables winked her a friendly welcome back, and through the open door shone the hearth fire, sending out its warm red glow athwart the chilly autumn night.
>
> – L.M. Montgomery, *Anne of Green Gables*[1]

When I travelled to Nigeria as an English language and literature teacher with CUSO (formerly Canadian Universities Service Overseas and now CUSO-VSO) in 1981, I chose with great deliberation the few books I would read for pleasure over the next two years.[2] I selected my Norton anthologies of English literature, my Signet edition of *The Complete Works of Shakespeare*, and my paperback copies of *Anne of Green Gables* and *Anne's House of Dreams*. During the rather nerve-wracking days of orientation in Ottawa, filled with workshops on tropical diseases, cultural sensitivity, teaching methods, food and nutrition, motorcycle safety, and Nigerian bureaucracy, I found myself both terrified and excited. In this period of emotional intensity I did not turn to Milton, Donne, or Wordsworth, but took comfort instead in the familiarity of Anne's voice. Shortly after arriving in my Nigerian posting of Gembu, I lent the Anne books to Jessy Reeba Luke, the daughter of a mathematics teacher and an English language teacher from Kerala State in India. I never received them back. Jessy, who was ten years old at the time, read, reread, memorized, recited, and performed Anne. Two years later, when I arrived back home in Canada, one of my first tasks was to send more of Anne to Jessy. I was obviously witnessing the powerful cross-cultural appeal of Anne and of Montgomery's work, and I can still recall the sound of Jessy's voice as she flamboyantly quoted her favourite passages of *Anne* on the Mambilla Plateau in Northeastern Nigeria: '"Oh, Diana, ... do you think – oh, do you think you can like me a little – enough to be my bosom friend?"'[3]

Jessy was particularly drawn to the school scenes in *Anne* and to the female friendships. Jessy and her younger sisters, Jisha and Jyothi, created their own childhood games and education on the surprisingly green and cool hills of the elevated plateau, which looked more like Scotland to me than like any of my preconceived images of West African landscape. Travelling back and forth between India and Nigeria, and living in communities of 'expatriate' teachers from India, Pakistan, the Philippines, Ghana, Cameroon, Ireland, England, and Canada, Jessy was immersed in a multicultural and intercultural way of living. She was curious and excited about every opportunity available to her and exuded confidence, maturity, and resourcefulness. As I remember her now, I realize that in many ways she was not unlike the precocious and articulate Anne Shirley. One of our most memorable occasions was a picnic on the green hills, which seemed bizarrely and anachronistically British and colonial in its domestication of the natural landscape.

Such jolting moments were common for me as a CUSO teacher at GSS (Government Secondary School) Gembu in Nigeria in the early 1980s. Called a 'cooperant' rather than a 'volunteer,' I was well aware of the complexities and problems of our Canadian presence in West Africa. Teaching West African poetry (in English from a British textbook) to Form Five students two months after I arrived in Nigeria was uncomfortable, to put it mildly. The memorization of English idioms required by the West African Examination Council (WAEC) also provided challenges. There were no barns or horses on the Mambilla Plateau, so it took some time and effort to explain 'Do not shut the barn door after the horse is out.' The lively discussion that ensued transformed the irrelevant moralistic idiom into a comic episode or surreal myth. *The Tragedy of Julius Caesar* was a big hit as Shakespearean politics were easily put into a Nigerian context by the students. Halfway through Thor Heyerdahl's *Kon-Tiki Expedition*, however, one student asked what a wave was – not a great book for students who have never seen the ocean or for a teacher who did not notice the disjunction. When I left in 1983, I gave away my books, which had grown in number, to some of my students. I treated the giving away of books as a casual act, but I now wonder about those 'gifts,' their associations, and their repercussions.

One evening in 1980, the year before I travelled to Nigeria, I was made aware of Montgomery's influence within Canada. About twenty English literature graduate students were gathered together in 'The Phoenix,' the graduate pub at McMaster University, when five or six of us discovered that as adolescents we had immersed ourselves in Montgomery's work to the extent that we could quiz one another on the smallest details of plot and character. That evening, this small group of Canadian females broke away from the larger group, which consisted of British and Canadian students, in order to confess that we were still closet Montgomery fans, fitting in Anne, Emily, Pat, Sara, Valancy, and Jane between Edmund Spenser and Virginia Woolf, as time permitted.[4] The strength of numbers gave us the solidarity to depart from our regular game of 'Identify the Norton Anthology Quote' to a subculture of Montgomery trivia: 'Whom did Mrs Spencer adopt from the asylum?' (Lily Jones.) 'What colour was her hair?' (Nut-brown.) 'What was the name of the professional elocutionist at the White Sands Hotel concert?' (Mrs Evans.) The others at the table were understandably mystified.

In 1980 there was not much talk of *Anne* in academic circles. We were still reading Montgomery in the shadow of canonical judgments such as E.K. Brown's 1943 comment that Montgomery, along with Ralph Connor and Robert Service, was 'aggressively unliterary' and 'satisfied to truckle to mediocre taste.'[5] And then there was William Arthur Deacon, a literary critic for the *Mail and Empire* (1928–36) and the *Globe and Mail* (1936–61), a formidable literary nationalist who proclaimed in 1926 that 'Canadian fiction was to go no lower' than *Anne of Green Gables*.[6] Although both he and L.M. Montgomery were active in the Canadian Authors Association and in the promotion of their national literature, he successfully pushed Montgomery to the sidelines, where she more or less remained until the astonishing success of volume 1 of *The Selected Journals of L.M. Montgomery* when it was published in 1985. But in 1980, at the beginning of the decade, we had no idea of the enormous impact Mary Rubio's and Elizabeth Waterston's work would have in the late 1980s and 1990s. Eventually, as Montgomery's popularity became known, the five or six of us at the table that evening discovered that our enthusiasm was actually shared by many of the Canadian writers whose work we had been studying and teaching as graduate students.

I am interested in the comments of these writers as they discuss the delayed establishment of *Anne*'s home in Canadian literature, but primarily I want to tease out some of the possible reasons for Jessy's easy comfort and connection with the novel, read at such a distance from the country in which it was written and set, and also read with an emphasis on the distance of the reading site from her own home in southern India. The insistence on the 'homing' of the novel as Canadian is apparent in the discussion within Canada, whereas Jessy's comments 'unhome' the novel, separating it from its Canadian context. In both cases, there is an emphasis on home – either in the concrete form of Canada as nation and centre or in the more abstract sense of place and text as temporary replacements for what has been left behind. Both of these reactions to home are part of the novel itself: Anne becoming loyal to Avonlea, asserting allegiance and identity in the formation of and attachment to home, and Anne mourning the changes brought about by the passing of time as they affect ideals of origins and home that no longer exist. Postcolonial criticism questions political and cultural assumptions of 'dominant' cultures, working to subvert and overturn entrenched positions of power and marginalization in society. Recent postcolonial interpretations of *Anne*, referred to later in this chapter, reveal its ethnocentricity and other exclusionary representations. My gift of *Anne* to Jessy can be seen in a colonial context as a one-way intersection of cultures in which the book could take on the aura of the norm and the ideal. But Jessy's response uses the pastoral in the novel to inform and clarify her own position and understanding of home. Using this gift of the book as a starting point, then, I want to examine through a critically postcolonial lens the ways in which readings of Montgomery's novel evoke nostalgic ideas and ideals of home in the context of the growing fluidity and nomadism of nation and homeplace in the twenty-first century. In *Ethics and Nostalgia in the Contemporary Novel* (2005), John J. Su argues that the writers in his study 'use nostalgia to envision some degree of solidarity for communities struggling with displacement and cultural differences among their members.'[7] I see a similar 'use' of nostalgia in the reading response and strategy adopted by Jessy.

Anne at Home in Canada

When Canadian women writers are asked about formative literary influences, almost all of them begin their responses with L.M. Montgomery. Comments by Margaret Atwood, Alice Munro, Jane Urquhart, and P.K. Page are now well known through their 'afterwords' to the New Canadian Library editions of Montgomery's work, while others, such as Margaret Laurence, have noted Montgomery's influence elsewhere.[8] The passionate loyalty and debt expressed by these major writers to

Montgomery and her work is astonishing and the acknowledgment of Montgomery's impact continues. Evelyn Lau, for example, when questioned about her literary background, says 'as a pre-adolescent, I was most drawn to the work of L.M. Montgomery, Sylvia Plath, Ray Bradbury and Anais Nin (all very different writers, but I was drawn to their use of language and, in Bradbury's and Montgomery's case, their stories).'[9] Thus readers of literature written by Canadian writers who have been profoundly influenced by Anne and Montgomery also continue to be affected by this iconic character and her creator.

Anne's successors in terms of characters, spanning a century now, are many, as numerous critics have noted. Laura Robinson, for example, explores the qualities of Anne as they manifest themselves in Kathleen, Frances, Mercedes, and Anthony Piper, from Ann-Marie MacDonald's *Fall on Your Knees* (1996). Munro's Del Jordan, Atwood's Joan Foster, and Laurence's Vanessa MacLeod are discussed within the context of *Anne* by Catherine Sheldrick Ross. Jane Urquhart's Esther, in *Away* (1993), carries with her a 'red curtain of hair' and a 'disturbing necessity' for 'passion and pain.'[10] Mary Lawson's orphaned Kate Morrison in *Crow Lake* (2002) should also be mentioned; like Anne, she concentrates on negotiating the space between domestic and natural worlds. Significantly, Lawson lives in England, writing about Ontario characters and landscape from memory and 'from away,' just as Montgomery after *Anne of Green Gables* wrote about Prince Edward Island from the distanced vantage point of Ontario. Writing from a distance resonates with reading from a distance, which is often associated with Montgomery's work, as in Jessy's case. Such distance of time and place can evoke nostalgia.

The pervasive influence of Montgomery and *Anne* on Canadian writers and their characters, as well as on Canadian critics and readers, is remarkable. But *Anne* is surprisingly flexible and becomes powerfully relevant in ways that range far beyond what is expected of a literary text or character. One member of my dragon-boat survivor team, for example, told me that when she was diagnosed with breast cancer, she immediately went home and read *Anne of Green Gables*. The text certainly functions as bibliotherapy, as discussed by Irene Gammel in this volume, but it is Jessy's response that interests me most. What was the basis and power of the attraction to *Anne* for ten-year-old Jessy Luke from southern India reading the novel in Nigeria? It is a question similar to the one that could be asked about M. NourbeSe Philip, who was affected by *Anne* long before she immigrated to Canada. In *A Geneal-*

ogy of Resistance and Other Essays (1997), Philip writes: 'On a tiny tropical island a little Black girl develops an odd affinity with a red-haired girl. On another island. Red-earthed. A feisty girl named Ann [sic] challenging the adult world with her honesty. Many years later Margaret / Harriet Cruickshank in *Harriet's Daughter* would reveal many of the same traits of honesty and feistiness as Ann [sic] did. Decades later, on this red-earthed island, I discover a passion. Shared. For an island – a piece of land surrounded. Prince Edward Island: source of Lucy Maud Montgomery's writing life. Tobago: source of my own writing life.'[11] Jessy was reading *Anne* not only 'from away,' as did. Philip, but also while away from home, introducing homesickness and nostalgia into the process.

To pursue this question of reading *Anne* both *from* away and *while* away, I turn now to an almost opposite experience – that of Adrienne Clarkson, who read *Anne* inside her new home of Canada, specifically in 'Ottawa, then a small white town, filled with snow.' Clarkson writes that 'L.M. Montgomery's world gave me an extended family that taught me about the rivalries of Tory and Grit, Protestant and Catholic, in a highly sophisticated microcosmic way; it was a background, a heritage that I gained literarily and that made my becoming Canadian very easy and attractive.' She explains that 'Anne and Emily, the Story Girl, and all the others were my cousins of the imagination and the spirit, and so what they were, I became also.'[12]

Clarkson's response to the text explains how she made the necessary adjustments in order to fit into the Canadian society and culture depicted in the novel, but it is of course a fictional rather than an accurate depiction she is responding to. Her comment about modelling and duplicating Anne, Emily, and the Story Girl – 'so what they were, I became also' – is understandable but also unsettling in the mimicry and 'becoming' that involve the relinquishment of individual identity. Although Anne was pruned and tamed in order to fit into Rachel Lynde's world, she also imposed form on that world as she named and imaginatively modified it, thus rendering the place familiar and comfortable for herself. Janice Fiamengo notes the ease with which *Anne* 'asserts the effortlessness and harmony of the English and Scots integration into their new land,' pointing out that although Anne's conquest of Avonlea is 'innocent' and 'bloodless,' her narrative still involves the possession of a land that is not her own, erasing Aboriginal and French presences in the process. Similarly, Clare Bradford argues that 'as Anne Shirley makes her first journey to Green Gables in Matthew Cuthbert's buggy, her behaviour mimics British colonial practices of viewing, mapping, and naming,' while Shawna Geissler and Lynn A. Cecil contend that 'Anne becomes Montgomery's fictional colonizer, the appropriator of a land that Montgomery claims for herself through childhood nostalgia, and recreates for the readers of her fiction who may be unfamiliar with the multiculturalism of the real island.'[13] Further colonial activity is emphasized by Alexander MacLeod in his discussion of Anne's disregard and negation of Matthew and his world in the chapter in this volume.

Anne's (and Montgomery's) lack of historical, cultural, and regional sensitivity and awareness is definitely troubling. And yet such attempts on the part of the lonely child, an outsider, to familiarize the 'unhomely' space are understandable, even if excessive and effusive in Anne's case. Such impulses and imprinting are surprisingly absent or muted in Clarkson's arrival narrative, in which 'white' Ottawa serves as a metaphor for a Canada that 'receives' in the sense of swallowing up. The 'becoming Canadian' inspired by the text in Clarkson's reading minimizes the impact of the refugee or newcomer on the 'safe haven that Canada was,' as represented by Marilla and Matthew, although Clarkson does note that the Cuthberts – and by extension Canada – are 'capable of adapting,'[14] presumably demonstrating 'tolerance' for difference, but it is of course a very narrow difference that is tolerated. Clarkson becomes what she reads in her new world, whereas Anne imposes her reading on her adopted place. The text inspires a homing response very different from the one it depicts, but both approaches – assimilation and colonial imprinting – disregard and erase cultures in their application.

After considering *Anne* from a postcolonial perspective and interrogating my own position in Nigeria, I see Anne's assumptions and presumptions in a much less muted and neutral light than I once did. Even though she makes concessions and adjustments, Anne tends to be valorized as the force that provides Avonlea with what has apparently been lacking, and she is thus in danger of being accused of taking on 'saviour' qualities, as were CUSO cooperants in the early 1980s. My own acceptance of insular Avonlea as a place in need of change has been disrupted by a postcolonial understanding of its artificial and exclusionary representation. Both Anne and Montgomery incorporate imaginative reconstructions of what actually exists. The emphasis on Avonlea's insularity serves as a backdrop that highlights and benefits from Anne's imagination. The fictional depiction of place becomes problematic when certain qualities are essentialized to the extent that other elements are minimized, distorted, and lost in the (mis)representation. Whether orchestrated by an author, a fictional character, or an individual in an actual situation, such essentialisms require critical examination.

Whatever we are reading within and exporting outside Canada in the form of *Anne* in the twenty-first century has its origins and appeal in something much larger than our own attempts to articulate a Canadian home, nation, and identity. This brings me back to the main impulse behind this chapter, which I initially thought was Jessy's reading of *Anne of Green Gables* in Nigeria, but I now realize, in my response to postcolonial perspectives of *Anne*, includes my own presence and activity in Nigeria as well. The transnational 'gifting' of books has somehow become part of this discussion as I think about the impulse and effects of my gifts to Jessy and my Nigerian students. An earlier cross-cultural and transnational book-giving of *Anne* in Japan in 1939 provides a worthwhile comparison. I am referring here to Canadian missionary Loretta Shaw's parting gift of *Anne of Green Gables* to her friend, Hanako Muraoka, whose 1952 translation, *Akage no An*, initiated the well-known cultural phenomenon of Anne's popularity in Japan. Muraoka, a teacher, writer, editor, and translator, attended a school similar in its Western emphasis to the one attended by the students at GSS Gembu. Muraoka was educated at 'Toyo Eiwa Jogakuin, a Canadian mission school in Tokyo. She was taught every subject in English while living in an on-campus dormitory as a boarding student on scholarship.'[15] I turn now to a consideration of the cultural exchange between Loretta Shaw and Hanako Muraoka as a way of introducing my ideas about reading *Anne* in Nigeria.

Global Anne: Reading Anne in Nigeria

Although Hanako Muraoka's translation has been a part of Montgomery discussions and scholarship for some time now, Loretta Leonard Shaw's role has only recently begun to receive attention.[16] Danièle Allard notes that Muraoka 'had been given a well-read September 1908 edition of *Anne of Green Gables* as a keepsake, in memory of her friendship with Loretta Shaw, a Canadian missionary, who along with other Canadians, was forced to leave Japan with the impending war.'[17] According to her granddaughter, Mie Muraoka, Muraoka was forty-six years old when she received the book in 1939. Mie Muraoka describes the gift as a 'keepsake' and 'a symbol of friendship,' claiming that as her grandmother translated it in secret, 'she thought of her Canadian friends then so far away.'[18] Mie's sister, Eri Muraoka, refers to the book as 'a farewell gift from her [grandmother's] Canadian colleague Loretta Shaw at their Tokyo publishing company,' and speculates that 'because Shaw was a compatriot of her former Canadian teachers, Hanako must have felt a strong emotional attachment to the book.' In reference to the fact that her grandmother never made it to Prince Edward Island, Eri comments that 'maybe she wanted to keep intact her own image of the island.'[19]

The University of New Brunswick's website includes a discussion of Shaw, describing her as a 'writer, teacher, and missionary' who 'made modernity her mandate, Christian principles her means, and the Far East her field.'[20] Hamish Ion's 2008 essay 'The Canadian Protestant Missionary Movement in Japan, 1873–1951' identifies Shaw as 'the Canadian Anglican [who] was a long-time teacher at the Poole Memorial School for girls in Osaka.' Shaw participated in what Ion identifies as the missionaries' role as 'pioneers in Japanese studies'[21] (from the perspective of outsiders) in her written work, including her published book, *Japan in Transition* (1922), in which, according to the U.N.B. site, she 'spoke sharply but sympathetically of Japan's most troubling issues, which she identified as poverty, weakness in the labour movement, subjugation of women, a persistently feudal social structure, and the degrading influence of legal prostitution.'[22] Although Shaw notes in *Japan in Transition* that 'Japan has become a country of omnivorous readers,' she obviously did not anticipate the extraordinary impact her gift would have on her friend and eventually on an entire nation.[23] The attachment of 'nation' and 'region' to this gift invests it with political and cultural representation, and the spirit in which it was given as an emotional 'farewell' and 'keepsake' permeates with affect its physical materiality as well as its narrative content.

The repercussions are too plentiful to enumerate here, but it is clear that the intention and the spirit with which a book is given and received, as well as the location of the act, can have a significant impact on the way in which it is read. *Anne of Green Gables* was a piece of Shaw and of Canada or the West that was deliberately left behind, and it became a political and cultural connection between past and present, West and East, pre- and post-war, which through translation and publication grew from private to public significance. I now have some idea of the impact of *Anne* on Jessy, but am left to wonder how the gifts of English 'literature' books from a Canadian CUSO teacher have been regarded by my former Nigerian students over the past almost three decades. They no doubt retain some of the colonial flavour that affected the CUSO teacher-Nigerian student relationship at the time.

In conference papers delivered during the 2008 centennial celebrations of the publication of *Anne of Green Gables*, I referred to Jessy Luke's love of *Anne*. Responding to Irene Gammel's suggestion, I subsequently attempted to contact Jessy. Within three weeks of writing to the family home in Kerala State, I received an e-mail from Bahrain, where Jessy – now Jessy Jacob – is currently living with her spouse, her daughter, and her son. Having attained undergraduate and graduate degrees in English literature and language from Indian universities, she is currently teaching English in Bahrain 'in the middle section of a school following the British curriculum,' not unlike my teaching position in Nigeria in 1981.[24] Here are her e-mailed comments from Bahrain:

Anne of Green Gables was the first novel I read when I was 10 years old. Since then I have read so many novels – Indian, British, American, African but the names & characters, the vivid description of the lush green countryside, will always remain evergreen in my mind. I can still mentally visualize Anne's journey to her new home – to Marilla and Matthew, her new caretakers – one silent and one strict, and their first rejection of her because of her femininity, and then accepting her because Matthew says so. I remember Anne meeting Diana, Anne breaking her slate on Gilbert Blythe's head because he called her carrots, descriptions of the beautiful countryside, Matthew's death, Anne finishing her schooling ... I have read all the books and I like *Anne of the Island*, *Anne's House of Dreams* and *Anne of Green Gables* the best.

Jessy's ability to recall the specific episodes reflects the rereading of the books, particularly those read in Nigeria, where children's books were few and 'there was plenty of time to do whatever we liked.'

As for the evocative power of Montgomery's writing, Jessy provides the following analysis:

I feel that this series of books which portrays the life of a girl at different stages – childhood, youth, motherhood, etc. – is a guide and companion for all girls. And more than that, it gives a nostalgic longing for the good old days when people were more innocent, caring about each other, knowing their neighbours so well, having plenty of time for others and themselves. It recalls a time when there was nature with all its beauty around you – no sounds of automobiles or machines – no sights of skyscrapers. That calm and peaceful life we all miss so much can be found in all the books by the author. I think this is the reason I still remember *Anne of Green Gables* and its characters so well even after 27 years!

It is the pastoral that Jessy remembers and describes as the most powerful aspect of *Anne*. Of the Mambilla Plateau, where she first read *Anne*, she says 'how I long for the lonely emptiness in that place,' as she contrasts its 'empty mountains' and green space with the crowds in India and Bahrain. The physical place of reading, the childhood age at which the text was read, the actual story, and the past itself are nostalgically imbued with pastoral qualities.

Now that I have received Jessy's response, I see that the fictional landscape of Prince Edward Island is indeed important, but the Mambilla Plateau where the reader of *Anne* was situated is just as significant. Jessy's solitude within a vast space, which in retrospect she views with affection and nostalgia especially in contrast to the congestion and activity of India and Bahrain, placed her in an 'unhomely' position similar to Anne's. As Montgomery makes clear in her references to the 'orphan asylums in Nova Scotia' and 'Barnado' [*sic*] boys, Anne is part of an identifiable, historical movement, one which involved the 'getting' and sending of orphaned children to homes often distant from their origins, a pattern of movement familiar today.[25] Jessy is also involved in movement patterns, those of contemporary relocations, as she participates in the literal mobility of postmodernity in a so-called globalized world. She has lived for extended periods of time in India, Nigeria, and Bahrain, experiencing different locations and cultures during her childhood, youth, and adulthood, and also participating in expatriate communities. This is a condition that Mavis Reimer, in her discussion of Canadian children's literature in relation to the concept of 'home,' aligns with 'postmodern celebrations of mobile subjectivities.' The possibilities and potential inherent in what Reimer terms the 'unhoming' process and in the condition of 'the migrant, the exile, and the nomad' are elements that perhaps connect the character of Anne to the young reader, who is moving between childhood and adolescence or home and away. In a more general sense, the freedom of Anne's mobility speaks clearly, I think, to postmodern and postcolonial readers, who sense the constrictions and lack of flexibility in 'given bonds of filiation' attached to fixed and established families, homes, and nations. Anne's condition of 'orphanhood' provides her with the opportunity to participate actively in the creation of her home – to choose and influence 'bonds of affiliation' rather than be restrained by 'given bonds of filiation.'[26] Edward Said claims that 'the turn from filiation to affiliation … embodies what Georg Simmel calls the modern process by which life "incessantly generates forms for itself,"' or, to use Said's words, provides 'a kind of compensatory order.'[27] Such generations of form and compensation are provided by nostalgia, according to Su, who argues that nostalgia can inspire important beliefs in alternatives for the future.[28] As family, place, and nation become more fluid, such self-generated, compensatory, and alternative affiliations begin to provide the criteria and definition of home. Nostalgia is capable of playing a constructive role in this process.

When I question myself about why I read *Anne* at the moment of transition between Canada and Nigeria, I realize I was choosing a narrative that spoke to the unhoming and dislocation I was deliberately seeking in a CUSO placement in West Africa. The degree of choice and lack of permanence in this particular movement obviously differentiates it from forced and permanent migrations. Consciously attempting to remove myself from national and natural bonds of filiation, I was trying to immerse myself, albeit in a very artificial and contrived manner, in the mobility and diversity that were part of what I saw as an increasingly open and global world. In a re-enactment of the transition from girlhood to womanhood, I was simultaneously leaving and creating home, perching myself on the edge of the familiar and unfamiliar, home and away, settled and nomadic, student and teacher. The process of unhoming and homing is not a singular occurrence, but is a repetitive and continuous activity. Rereading *Anne* is a way of indulging and validating this process. When my father died in December 2005, initiating profound yearning and homelessness in me, I turned to the chapter of the novel in which Matthew dies, remembering how, as a young reader of these pages, I felt as if I were preparing myself for all the losses that would inevitably occur throughout my life. *Anne* mythologizes the homeless and unhomed figure who manages to participate in homing herself. Rather than losing its relevance, the narrative resonates clearly within the twenty-first century's breakdown of stable territory and settled citizenship.

Like Jessy, I remember Gembu in the early 1980s with nostalgia and retain impressions of its pastoral nature. Similarly, I recognize the nostalgic and pastoral elements of *Anne*. Such nostalgia, literally a 'return home,' is an 'acute longing for familiar surroundings,' encompassing qualities of 'homesickness.'[29] Gammel reminds readers that the 'roots of the word consist of *nostos*, "homeland," and *algos*, "pain" or "longing,"' and 'its German variant is *Heimweh*, literally "home-pain."'[30] In both the real place and the literary space, the power and attraction lie in the exquisite yearning for home. Rereading *Anne* at moments of shock (a diagnosis of cancer), loss (the death of a parent), and displacement (the removal from the familiar) confirms the transition from the comfortable to the strange and validates the intensity and frequency of the unhoming process. In a 'globalized' world, where movement destabilizes the certainty and continuity of home, there is an understanding of the ongoing process of losing and finding home. Jessy and I were both in unhomely states in Gembu, a condition that we look back at with nostalgia. It is important to acknowledge, however, that just as Avonlea is not Cavendish, so the green world as I remember it is one I created for myself and not the actual town of Gembu or the Mambilla Plateau as they existed in the early 1980s. What to me were rolling and scenic hills were also hills suffering from erosion and degradation due to overgrazing. Nostalgia asserts itself, however, and can have positive purposes and effects. As Su argues, 'sentimental and "inauthentic" images' of 'the world as it could have been' are capable of 'establishing some shared goals for the future.'[31]

Conclusion

Gammel demonstrates that Montgomery's writing of *Anne* 'was a nostalgic ode to home and homeland all at once.' She argues that 'in a world experiencing rapid change, fiction accommodated modernization ... by upholding the pastoral ideal' and that 'Maud's longing for home and community was emblematic of a nostalgic undercurrent rippling through an entire era of transition from the Victorian to the modern.'[32] Gammel's explanation of the context of the writing of *Anne* alerts readers to the deep nostalgia that pervades the text itself and calls for critical readings of Montgomery's and our own views of public and private pasts, particularly as they misrepresent place. Reading Anne's renaming and reconstruction of her home through a postcolonial lens exposes it as an intrusive act, no longer a harmless and fanciful activity from which both Anne and Matthew will 'benefit,' as MacLeod notes in this volume. My first reading of *Anne* in 1965, two years before Canada's centennial, was one that incorporated the concept and ideal of Canada as home, while my current reading takes place in the context of Reimer's discussion of homing and unhoming within postmodern mobility and with the knowledge of the authorial nostalgia explained by Gammel. The result is a movement from a nationalistic reading and homing of the text to a more global reading that looks for and values the lack of filiation in the unhoming stage and state of the narrative and character. It is also a reading that sees nostalgia in Su's terms as a 'necessary and often productive form of confronting loss and displacement,' one that offers 'hope that alternatives continue to exist' through its 'refigurative capacity' of pointing out the 'gap between the world as it is and the world as it could have been.'[33]

Montgomery's *Anne* and responses to it continue to provoke animated discussions, not so much about the nation in which it was created or its 'international' popularity, but about the way in which it is read, and specifically about how it continues to update itself or be updated into relevance in unexpected ways. Postcolonial questions and readings of *Anne* in transnational and global contexts expose elements of colonialism as well as misrepresentations resulting from an indulgence in nostalgia and the pastoral. The same questions, however, provide possible explanations concerning its continued popularity and relevance, based on the novel's participation in contemporary ongoing processes of global unhoming and homing through affiliation. In its strangely amorphous way, *Anne* takes on colonial shapes but also elicits postcolonial responses when read in 2008, one hundred years after its publication.

NOTES

I acknowledge with gratitude the generous contributions of Jessy Jacob to this chapter. I also want to thank Irene Gammel for encouraging me to contact Jessy.

1 LMM, *AGG*, 256.
2 For a description and history of this non-profit agency, see CUSO's website at http://www.cuso.org/. According to the website, from 1961 to 2008 CUSO 'sent 11,000 volunteers abroad to work on poverty reduction, human rights, access to justice, health, education and environmental sustainability.' As a teacher in Nigeria from 1981 to 1983, I was paid the same salary as a Nigerian teacher, was provided with transportation to and from my placement, received medical supplies, health insurance, and in-country support, attended orientation sessions in Canada and Nigeria, and was

given a resettlement allowance upon returning to Canada. By 1968, most of CUSO's funding came from the Canadian International Development Agency (CIDA), topped up by donations. CUSO established overseas offices and staff and moved into community-based projects in order to decentralize the organization and respond to local grassroots initiatives. CUSO also established partnerships linking Canadian and overseas groups facing similar challenges and working towards comparable goals. Returned volunteers are important to the organization's aim of encouraging what it refers to as 'global citizens.' The merger of CUSO and VSO in 2008 seems to emphasize the worldwide structure of the VSO network, downplaying the Canadian nationalism inherent in the history and institution of CUSO in favour of the global associations of the VSO organization.

3 LMM, *AGG*, 97.
4 I am not limiting Montgomery's readership in any way, but am simply relating the facts of this event as it occurred.
5 Brown, 'The Problem of a Canadian Literature,' 4.
6 Deacon, *Poteen*, 169.
7 Su, *Ethics and Nostalgia*, 19.
8 'Both Anne and Emily were rebels – intelligent, talented girls who were not about to be put down. Emily had the added appeal of wanting to become a writer – *no*, of actually *being* a writer, as I myself was.' Laurence, 'Books that Mattered to Me,' 241.
9 Lau, 'Author Profile,' *Northwest Passage: Canadian Literature Online*, http://www.nwpassages.com/bios/lau.asp.
10 Robinson, 'Remodeling *An Old-Fashioned Girl*'; Ross, 'Calling Back the Ghost'; Urquhart, *Away*, 8.
11 Philip, *A Genealogy of Resistance*, 28.
12 Clarkson, Foreword, ix–x.
13 Fiamengo, 'Towards a Theory,' 235–6; Bradford, 'The Homely Imaginary,' 180; Geissler and Cecil, 'Lucy Maud Montgomery's Anglocentric Island,' 196.
14 Clarkson, Foreword, ix.
15 Akiro Wada, 'Translating *Anne* Helped Support My Grandmother during the War,' *Asahi Weekly*, http://www.asahi.com/english/weekly/1026/02.html. Thank you to Yuka Kajihara for drawing my attention to this article and for translating the title.
16 Elizabeth Epperly, for example, is currently working with Shaw's papers housed at the University of New Brunswick Archives. See Hanley, 'Following Her Heart,' E1.
17 Allard, 'Hanako Muraoka,' 344.

18 Mie Muraoka, 'Speech at the Reception Held by the Department of Tourism Parks in PEI in 1989,' http://club.pep.ne.jp/~r.miki/speech_j.htm.

19 Wada, 'Translating *Anne*' (see n15, above).

20 University of New Brunswick, '"Compelling the Forces of Conservatism to Yield" … Loretta Leonard Shaw (1872–1940),' Progress and Permanence: Women and the New Brunswick Museum, http://www.unbf.ca/women and museum/bshaw.htm.

21 Ion, 'The Canadian Protestant Missionary Movement,' 13, 16.

22 University of New Brunswick, '"Compelling the Forces"' (see n20, above).

23 Shaw, *Japan in Transition*, 56.

24 Jessy Jacob, e-mail message to author, 19 Aug. 2008. All other quotations of Jessy Jacob are from this communication.

25 LMM, *AGG*, 11, 12. Irene Gammel provides information about the Barnardo children in her discussion of Montgomery's adopted cousin, Ellen Macneill, and also includes important background about 'The Delineator Child-Rescue Campaign,' both of which emphasize the prevalence of the movement of orphans through adoption during the time of Montgomery's writing. Gammel, *Looking for Anne*, 69–70, 238–9.

26 Reimer, 'Homing and Unhoming,' 2.

27 Said, *The World, the Text*, 18–19; Simmel, *The Conflict in Modern Culture*, 12.

28 Su, *Ethics and Nostalgia*, 174–5.

29 Oxford English Dictionary, s.v. 'Nostalgia,' http://www.oed.com/.

30 Gammel, *Looking for Anne*, 155.

31 Su, *Ethics and Nostalgia*, 19.

32 Gammel, *Looking for Anne*, 155, 162, 165.

33 Su, *Ethics and Nostalgia*, 176.

10 An Enchanting Girl: International Portraits of Anne's Cultural Transfer

IRENE GAMMEL WITH ANDREW O'MALLEY, HUIFENG HU, AND RANBIR K. BANWAIT

In the early morning of 20 June 2008, after picking up L.M. Montgomery's granddaughter Kate Macdonald Butler and her brother Deke Macdonald in Charlottetown, I headed to L.M. Montgomery's Homestead Site in Cavendish for the centennial Anne celebration. On that very day, one hundred years earlier, Montgomery had received her first copy of her novel *Anne of Green Gables* and rejoiced in her journal: 'There in my hand lay the material realization of all the dreams and hopes and ambitions and struggles of my whole conscious existence – my first book!'[1] To commemorate this special day (instead of the actual day of the book's first publication in Boston on 13 June 1908, a day conspicuously ignored in Canadian celebrations), a large group of Prince Edward Islanders, visitors, and dignitaries had gathered at the L.M. Montgomery Homestead Site for an early morning CBC Radio special, followed by a communal breakfast and then the much anticipated launch of the new Anne of Green Gables stamps, a joint project between Canada Post and Japan Post. In the white tent where the stamp launch took place with more than one hundred visitors and media representatives in attendance, there were cameras and speeches and applause at the unveiling of the lovely and familiar Ben Stahl image of Anne holding flowers and gazing into the distance. Next came the Japanese stamps amid similar rolling of cameras and clapping of hands, but what struck me as most memorable was the spontaneous 'Awww' that rippled through the crowd at the moment of the unveiling of the Japanese stamps. Based on the 1979 animated series from Nippon Animation, the unfamiliar image of the Anime Anne clearly belonged to another culture, although her red hair and serious expression set against an undulating green field and a dramatic bluish-purple field of clouds proclaimed her as Anne. We suddenly looked at Anne through Japanese eyes, recognizing the creative adaptation and appropriation.

What is at stake in this cultural transfer when Anne becomes Japanese – or Chinese or German or Iranian? In exploring Anne's remarkable international popularity, earlier scholars have noted Montgomery's sustained power in 'exporting' Canadian literature as a *Kulturträger* of sorts, literally a culture bearer who, like a missionary or cultural ambassador, takes Canada to foreign countries. Other scholars like Cecily Devereux, in contrast, have used Anne's 'longstanding global circulation' to pointedly question her putative Canadianness. After all, Anne and Avonlea are 'portable,' as Jeanette Lynes and Janice Fiamengo have argued by respectively pointing to the Anne dolls and the Avonlea landscape, which, despite its P.E.I. locale, are not always recognized as Canadian by readers in other countries.[2] With a remarkable thirty-five foreign-language translations, Anne has developed new roles and identities abroad, proving stunningly adaptable to new cultural contexts and functioning smoothly in the iconographies of other nations, such as Japan. Within each cultural system, Anne seems to act as a super-fractal containing multitudes of self-similar smaller Annes, somewhat like the fractural whirls of cloud in the new Japanese stamp.

Many prior critics have assumed that people of a certain country may find *Anne of Green Gables* so appealing precisely because they *lack* something in their own culture that they find in *Anne*.[3] However, the authors of this essay suggest that, in fact, several countries seem to like her because they have found ways to make the protagonist accord with their prior belief systems. Thus the goal of this chapter is to take a step forward in theorizing moments of cultural transfer as they relate to Anne's journey around the globe by probing some of the ideological functions and the shifting values that are attached to Anne as she crosses cultural boundaries. Thus Doris Bachmann-Medick understands translation as a *'cultural technique'* that always involves the adaptation of cultural concepts to the target readership so the text can be enjoyed and understood,[4] or as Zohar Shavit observes: 'If the model of the original text does not exist in the target system, the text is changed by deleting or by adding such elements as will adjust it to the integrating model of the target system.'[5] Yet, unlike translations for adults, translations of children's literature often feature dramatic changes in order to render a translated text more familiar – 'more like home' – for the child reader.

In fact, the authors of this essay take as their critical starting point the fact that there appears to be little impulse to make translations of *adult* books 'more like home.' That this impulse is common in translations of children's books is highly revealing, we propose, pointing to an *adult* desire to avoid the overly exotic for children, to give them familiarity rather than difference. Why, for example, is it necessary for Swedish children to see the characters of a book they read drink coffee instead of tea, as translator Karin Jensen has done in her Swedish translation of *Anne of Green Gables*, *Anne på Grönkulla*, in 1909? 'In Sweden people drink more coffee than in any other country in the world,' explains Gabriella Åhmansson in her article '"Mayflowers Grow in Sweden Too,"' noting that one reason that 'Montgomery's book was so readily accepted by Swedish readers could be the fact that both the climate and the landscape are very similar in the two countries,' so that the landscape itself is not perceived 'as being specifically Canadian.'[6] Åhmansson recalls that she 'had never really thought about Anne inhabiting a foreign country or a landscape as being specifically Canadian. "The rose and saffron of a winter sunset" – that description is as evocative and as accurate to a Swede as to a Canadian.'[7] In other words, Canada is already enough like Sweden that such incidental changes as changing coffee for tea would suffice to make Swedish readers think of Anne as someone who could live on a nearby farm.

In contrast, Iranian readers and viewers appear to be doing something different, as Andrew O'Malley argues below by discussing *Anni in Green Gables*, the novel's Farsi translation. A Canadian with close family ties to Iran, O'Malley argues that Iranian readers are not witnessing or imagining a 'sameness with a few small differences' with Anne; instead, they are experiencing a difference, coming from a 'dominant' and sought-after culture, that they can claim and transform into their own cultural property. Following O'Malley's argument, Chinese scholar Huifeng Hu explores the process of cultural acceptance of Anne in China. Staying in the Far East, Ranbir Banwait sheds light on the propagandist dissemination of democratic cultural values in Japan after the Second World War, in which *Akage no An* played an important role as a vehicle for a gendered form of cultural censorship. Finally, my own vignette discusses the case of the belated translation of *Anne of Green Gables* in Germany, the country in which I grew up, returning in 2001 to teach *Anne of Green Gables* to a new, post-Communist generation of university students for whom Anne represented North-American values in a period of transition. Since each of the authors below also draws on personal experiences, we have preserved distinctive sections for each author. With the spotlights turned on, the curtain rises on a new cast of culturally diverse Annes, as we begin with 'Anni' in Iran, who appears very different from the Canadian Anne.

Anni in Green Gables in Iran, by Andrew O'Malley

When I agreed to write this short piece about the popularity of *Anne of Green Gables* in Iran, I was not aware of the kinds of obstacles such research would present. Looking for such standard indicators as sales records or reviews of the book and its sequels in newspapers, for instance, proved a task I could not meet. Iran's publishing industry, especially for translated foreign texts, operates to a considerable degree illegitimately, with loosely enforced copyright regulations and a large black market of pirated editions of books (among other media) that does not keep, let alone publish, detailed records.[8] Publishing houses appear and disappear very quickly in an often unstable economic environment, and can be closed down by the government with little notice or explanation. This is even truer of the newspaper industry. Furthermore, according to Leili Hayeri Yazdi, cultural adviser at the Institute for the Intellectual Development of Children and Young Adults (*Kanoon*) in Iran, no survey or review of *Anne of Green Gables* and its circulation and reception in Iran has ever been undertaken domestically.[9] What follows, then, are remarks and observations, by necessity largely anecdotal, that I have been able to cobble together from a variety of sometimes unconventional sources.

The evidence I have gathered suggests an Anne who is appreciated in Iran for reasons often quite different from the mischievousness, individualism, and 'iconoclastic spirit' (as Shirley Foster and Judy Simons describe it) that many Western readers and critics have tended to celebrate.[10] Rather, Anne's main appeal seems to come from the close familial and community bonds she forges and maintains in her new environment. Indeed, the qualities that would mark her as a good and dutiful Iranian daughter are often favourably noted by viewers of Sullivan Entertainment's first two *Anne* miniseries, which aired on the Islamic Republic of Iran Broadcasting (IRIB) station in the 1990s. This was clear from my own conversations with Iranians who watched these programs and from Geoffrey York's article in the *Globe and Mail* on the success of Canadian television programming in Iran; as one young Iranian woman observed to York, 'The character of Anne – she's a very kind daughter, thinking of everyone, not just herself.'[11] Intriguingly, what connects with viewers in Iran is almost the opposite of the proto-feminist independence that Anne is much celebrated for by Western audiences. This difference in how *Anne* is read in Iran suggests more broadly how these print and televisual texts circulate in cultural contexts outside their place of origin.

As John Fiske has remarked of popular culture texts generally, these are 'open' or 'producerly' texts that take on their meanings depending on how they are consumed and in what contexts.[12] Rather than representing, as a number of critics have suggested, the successful exportation of Canadian/Western cultural values or of early twentieth-century feminist sensibilities, the popularity of the Anne books and shows in places such as Iran and Japan is based on an appropriation of these narratives to fit existing cultural expectations. In fact, how the very question has been framed in the case of the much studied phenomenon of Anne in Japan – 'Anne of Red Hair: What Do the Japanese See in *Anne of Green Gables*?' as Calvin Trillin phrased the title of his contribution to the discussion – tends to assume that Anne carries with her some quality absent in and desired by the (non-Western) places to which she travels. Certainly Iranians have a keen interest in the cultural products of the West, access to which has been restricted since the revolution. However, as I will argue below, Anne's success in Iran has primarily to do with how readers and viewers adapt her so that she conforms to their existing cultural needs and expectations.

The publication history of *Anne of Green Gables* and its sequels in Iran has proven difficult to piece together, despite its brevity. According to Leili Hayeri Yazdi, the first Farsi translation available in Iran was published by Soroosh Publishing House in 1996, under the title *The Girl in the Green House*, with a first edition print run of 3,000 copies and two second edition runs of 2,000 and 3,000 copies respectively. Noghteh Publishing House released another edition of 2,000 copies that same year, using a title closer to Montgomery's: *Anni in Green Gables*. Several other editions followed in 1997 (*Anni of Green Dreams* by Peykan Publishing), in 2000 (*Anni Shirly with Red Hair* by Rayhaft Publishing and *The Stories of the Island* by Namira Publishing), in 2001 (*Anni, A Girl From Green Gables* by Golban Publishing), and in 2003 (*Anni with Red Hair* by Banafsheh Books), all with printings of 1,500 to 3,500 copies. Montgomery's sequels have also been printed numerous times.[13] Virtually all Farsi translations alter the spelling of Anne's name to some variation of 'Anni' – pronunciation in the dubbing of the television miniseries is similarly adjusted – for good reason. As the title page of the Ghadyani edition (a 2007 reissue of a 1997 edition) indicates in a small text box in the bottom left corner, 'In this series of books, the character's name, "Anne," has been changed to "Anni" because of its similarity to the word "that" in Farsi.' As my Iranian father-in-law Iradj Naghibi wryly remarked when he translated this notice for me, the word 'An' (with a short 'a' sound) is also a vulgar Farsi word for excrement.[14]

An edition published by Ghadyani, the only Farsi translation of *Anne of Green Gables* that I have been able to consult directly, provides in its back cover blurb some intriguing insights into how the text circulates in Iran as well: 'Anni Shirly, a freckled girl with red hair, was brought up in an orphanage. She is clever and has a boundless imagination. With hope and kindness, she tries to build a new life for herself, even though to fulfil her desire she must face many difficulties. But the future looks so beautiful and promising to her that, to reach her goal, she bears all difficulties and adapts to all situations' (translation by Iradj Naghibi). Striking to many anglophone readers of Montgomery's book would be the absence of any mention – with the exception of the reference to 'imagination' – of the qualities Anne often embodies for Westerners: an at times subversive unconventionality and non-conformity, as well as an endearing free-spiritedness and eccentricity of character. Instead, the focus here is on *Anne* as a story of perseverance and survival in the face of difficult circumstances. It is also a story of hope for a more promising future following an unhappy past and for readjustment after upheaval and dislocation. This reading of the text would understandably resonate in a culture still traumatized by the experience of revolution and by a devastating eight-year war with Iraq that left many in positions similar to Anne's: as orphans.

While I am leery of making comparisons between the responses to *Anne* of very different cultures to explain Iran's enthusiastic embrace of Anne, there are parallels and precedents in places that similarly have endured major traumas. Barbara Wachowicz's sensitive and thoughtful account of the long-standing and profound affection that Polish readers have had for the *Anne* books connects their phenomenal popularity to a national psyche damaged by the horrors of war and by the cultural dislocation caused by the installation of a Communist state. She cites a 1946 reviewer of the book who saw in it potentially therapeutic power for young readers: it 'would bring back life and joy to youngsters after all those horrible years which devoured so many young lives, and had taken away youth and joy from those who survived.'[15] Similarly, Yuko

Katsura (among others) has pointed to the timing of *Anne*'s publication in Japan as a partial explanation for the intensity of the Japanese response to it: '*Anne* was introduced to Japan seven years after the end of the war ... Anne was an ideal heroine who showed the readers how to live in such difficult circumstances with hope and cheerfulness.'[16]

To my mind, the shared experience of social upheaval – the real and symbolic orphanhood all three of these cultures experienced – offers more satisfactory insights into Anne's popularity than many of the prevailing theories about Anne in Japan. Too often when critics have puzzled over why the Japanese are so fanatical over Anne, their conclusions have tended to assume it is because Anne has something the Japanese admire *but don't have*. Judy Stoffman, for instance, is compelled to think of Japanese devotion to Anne as a '*yearning* in the Japanese soul [that] *our Anne* answers.'[17] More strikingly, Linda Ghan paints – in broad strokes indeed – a picture of Japanese girlhood, womanhood, and childhood defined by absence: 'Historically, women, little girls, have had limited dreams in Japan. In many of the folktales, the message is clear: children are to be obedient, to respect their parents, to care for them ... There is no disobedience. There is no "character." The children are faceless and personalityless. They are the child [*sic*] every child is supposed to be. They are a burden.' The Japanese response to this awful state of affairs is, for Ghan, an unsettlingly excessive devotion to a character so opposite to Japanese girls themselves: 'when one recognizes the need – the hunger, even – that Anne as a character fulfils, it is disturbing.'[18] There is a discomforting colonial echo to this formulation of Western culture bringing to non-Western cultures that which they lack. Cecily Devereux suggests that, instead of approaching the puzzle of Anne's popularity in non-Western cultures 'within a putative westernizing impulse ... to promote the advancement of women in non-western cultures,' we could consider Anne as a globalized commodity that is 're-shaped in every location.'[19] By following her reformulation, we can avoid pursuing the question of her popularity through a discourse of absences in favour of an approach that tries to understand the adaptive and appropriative readings of Anne generated in the contexts of cultures elsewhere.

Among the sources I have found, the adaptation and appropriation of Anne into Iranian culture is perhaps most evident in the postings left by Iranian fans in the guestbook of a British website devoted to Megan Follows, who played the lead role in Sullivan Entertainment's *Anne of Green Gables* miniseries. There are a disproportionate number of post-ings by Iranian fans, and interestingly there are almost as many post-ings by male viewers as by females, which suggests that consumption of these texts is not as gendered in Iran as it is in North America. Iranian fans are often effusive in their praise and affection, which is characteris-tic of the Iranian style of speaking and expressing fondness, but which might strike Western readers as 'over the top.' Along with the praises of Follows's acting, the expressions of love, desires for communication with her through e-mail, and the claims to watch her videos avidly are two oft-repeated and highly revealing sentiments: a partly joking re-fusal to accept that Megan Follows is not actually Anne, and a desire for her to be Iranian. Borhan (male) from Ilam writes: 'Hey Anne, I never beleive [sic] that you've got some name like Megan, I dont wanna ac-cept this ... you'll remain my poet Anne in my dreams, in my poems, in my life ... I've lived with your smiles, your words, your eyes, and of course yor hair for nights ... Please be Anne forever, please please' (30 April 2005). Hamed (male) writes: 'made wish you was Iranian' (8 October 2005). Maryam (female) from Tehran writes: 'dear megan dear megan I love you and for me you will always be anne I love you for-ever thank you and bye!' (5 April 2007). And Kamran (male) writes: 'I love you. After to many years you are my dreams girl. Thank you for anne of green gables. Oh, no, I started to cry because I remember my childhood memorys. Thank you' (6 April 2007).[20] The intensity of the emotional connection for these fans is evident and, combined with the half-serious conflation of Follows with Anne, speaks to how real and complete the character's integration into their experiences is. The post-ings of these Iranian fans also suggest a claiming of Anne into their own personal lives and experiences as well as into their cultural contexts.

'Ghost with Red Hair' in China, by Huifeng Hu

Chinese fans of Anne range from elementary to high school students, from teenage girls to middle-aged women who live in all regions of the country and who report a similar integration of Anne into their experi-ences. They give expression to their love of Anne on online message boards.[21] They talk about where to access Anne movies, animation, books, and regularly post pictures from the movies. They debate which Chinese version is the best. They express their love for Anne or show a special preference for Gilbert, and they debate whom Anne should marry. Like the Iranian fans above, they focus on elements of personal transformation, as expressed, for example, by a girl who calls herself 'fan of the green': '*Anne of Green Gables* is the most favorable book of my life, Anne is my best love, the reading experience greatly changed me, before I was introversive with few words, now I am a girl with cheerful disposition.' Other Chinese fans gain new perspectives of their own lives, and find in Anne an affirmation of their own individuality, as this female reader from the northern province of Hebei suggests: 'Like Anne, we are supposed to hold to our intimate feelings and make decisions and never be unrepentant and enjoy the simplest happiness in imagination, ideals, work and friendship.'[22] Some readers connect with Anne in a highly personal way, even naming themselves Anne or Cordelia. There are numerous idols in China, such as Yuchun Li in the *Superstar Girl Show* and Ziyi Zhang in the 2000 movie *Crouching Tiger, Hidden Dragon*, but Anne is a true soulmate of teenaged girls. As an unidentified girl writes, 'Reading a good book is just like talking with numerous great minds, it will have deep impact upon one's life and change one's destiny. *Anne of Green Gables* is such a book.'[23]

My first encounter with *Anne of Green Gables* occurred in 1993, when I was hunting up teaching references in the library of the English Department at Lanzhou University, in Northwest China, where I studied and also taught English language and literature. Growing up in Lanzhou, in Gansu province, I had read classic Chinese fairy tales such as Youjun Sun's *Little Butou's Adventure* and Tianyi Zhang's *The Secret of Magic Gourd*. I also loved Bingxin's *To Young Readers* with its elaborate and refined literary style thought to be the foundation stone of Chinese children's literature. Equally influential for me and my generation were a number of Red Classics such as Luo's *Hongyan*, Yang's *Song of Youth*, and Li's *Shining Red Star* with their focus on faith, devotion, and perfect love.[24] But when I read *Anne of Green Gables* in its original English as an adult, I was carried away by Anne, who seemed to me very different from, but at the same time similar to, the characters I had grown up with.

Anne of Green Gables was introduced into China during the early stages of China's reform and opening-up, as our society negotiated which elements of the 'Western way' to incorporate and which to avoid. In fitting popular children's culture into mainstream Chinese culture at that time, the reception of Anne in China comes down to a question of values. In the story there is no violence, no sex, and the love narratives are largely implied and pure, all of which conforms well to Chinese values. As well, the community where the 'rural girl' Anne lives does not display overt capitalist characteristics that might alienate Chinese readers. At the same time, the book satisfied readers' curiosity about a different – Western – culture.

In 1987, the Press of China Federation of Literary and Art Circles (CFLAC) introduced the first Chinese edition of *Anne of Green Gables* in mainland China with 19,000 copies. Ainong Ma, who later translated the Harry Potter books into Chinese to great acclaim, translated the book. The late 1990s were a golden age in China's literary world, when a large number of children's classics from Western countries were introduced into China. Since then, several more publishers have taken interest in *Anne of Green Gables*, targeting adolescent girls as their main readership. There are now over thirty Chinese versions of *Anne of Green Gables* published by renowned presses, such as Yilin Press, People's Literature Press, and China Children's Press and Publication Group. There are diversified Chinese versions: complete, simplified, adapted, annotated, illustrated, and comic books for young children appealing to an increasingly stratified readership that reflects the increasing fragmentation of mass communication (in contrast to the formerly homogenized mass communication before China's opening-up and reform). In 2002, translations of *Anne of Avonlea*, *Anne of the Island*, and *Anne of Windy Poplars* were published by Zhejiang Publishing United Group, the first to publish later books in the Anne series. Three years later, it published *Emily of New Moon*, *Emily Climbs*, and *Emily's Quest*. In 2005, to commemorate the thirty-fifth anniversary of the establishment of diplomatic relations between China and Canada, Huawen Press published the first edition of *Anne of Green Gables* authorized by Montgomery's heirs and co-prefaced by the cultural councillor of the Canadian Embassy in Beijing and the secretary of the Chinese Central Communist Youth League. The complete Anne series is expected to be launched in Chinese translation by Chongqing Publisher in 2010. In the last few years, *Anne of Green Gables* has been on the list of readings recommended by the Ministry of Education of China for elementary and high school students. The books are readily available in bookstores. E-text books are available on a range of websites.

Ainong Ma's translations, which were retained in a number of successive editions by different publishers, are regarded as the best and are widely used as the standard version. The translator has also been praised for the way in which she makes the foreign Canadian culture familiar to Chinese readers. For instance, Gilbert Blythe's addressing Anne Shirley as 'carrots' is translated as 'Hong Mao Gui,' meaning 'ghost with red hair,' which will certainly offend a teenaged girl very much. Likewise, in chapter 14, when Marilla's 'dishes were washed and her bread sponge set,' Ainong Ma skilfully changed 'bread sponge,' which is difficult to understand in China, into 'famian,' meaning 'to activate dry yeast for steam buns,' a principal food in North China.[25] In fact, the translation is colloquial and localized, and conversations are natural and vivid, so that Chinese readers feel like they are reading the story of a girl in the rural neighbourhood.

National and local newspapers, including *Renmin Daily*, *China Education Daily*, *Chinese Reading Weekly*, *Literature Newspaper*, *Wenhui Bao News*, *Shanghai Evening Post*, *Tianjin Daily*, *Zhejiang Daily*, and *Qianjiang Evening News* announced the arrival of Anne in China with headlines such as 'Anne: Lighten Up Our Heart,'[26] 'Thoughts on Anne of Green Gables,'[27] and 'What Can't Be Missed of Being.'[28] In 1998 and 1999, Channel 8, China Central Television (CCTV) aired the Canadian TV series *Road to Avonlea*, and in 2006, China's Children's Channel (CCTV) broadcast *Anne of Green Gables: The Animated Series* from Sullivan Entertainment. While the interest in them is palpable, the Anne books and films in Chinese translation have not achieved the phenomenal commercial success that they have had in Japan,[29] for a number of reasons. Following China's opening to the outside world, there has been a flood of children's classics such as Alcott's *Little Women* (1868), Spyri's *Heidi* (1880), Porter's *Pollyanna* (1913), and Montgomery's *Anne*, while Chinese children have also been bombarded with Western fantasies, detective stories, and horror stories, all of which have collectively, if not individually, been extremely popular and commercially successful.

The reception of foreign classics has much to do with the receiving culture's values, tastes, and aesthetic standards. Anne's tomboyish, chatty, and quick-tempered character does not quite accord with the Chinese conception of a girl's mind and character. Even in twenty-first-century China, Confucian ethics continues to uphold that children should have self-restraint or 'neilian' (内敛). Since Chinese etiquette rejects wild fantasy – 'don't think wildly' (不要胡思乱想) is what parents often tell their children – daydreaming Anne is not immediately attractive to mainstream readers. By contrast, Diana Barry is more acceptable to our readers, since she conforms to conventional Chinese femininity as a quiet, shy, more restrained and 'graceful' girl. The novel's message that girls are as important as boys doesn't quite strike the same chord for Chinese readers as it does for North Americans. After the founding of the People's Republic of China in 1949, women were granted equal rights and were regarded as 'the half sky' (半边天), that is, as important as men. Equality between the genders was promoted with equal pay for equal work and equal opportunities for employment and promotion. The majority of urban women have their own profession, income, public name, and economic independence, and therefore most of my points apply to urban readers. For a variety of reasons, foreign literature classics like *Anne of Green Gables* are not readily accessible for children in some rural areas where gender discrimination still exists. The most typical example is that many rural families, like Marilla and Matthew who desire a boy helper in the story, want a baby boy as an heir to continue the family line.

In spite of the differences in cultural values, *Anne of Green Gables* resonates with Chinese culture in several important areas. Even today, girls doing house chores or neighbours helping each other is highly promoted in Chinese communities. Like the Iranian readers, so the Chinese readers value the focus on family ties, filial piety, and loyalty, as seen at the ending of the story when Anne puts off her dreams of college to remain on the farm and care for Marilla, who had cared for her. Having respect for the elders, supporting and waiting upon one's parents as they get old and sick is highly valued in traditional Chinese morality. Anne started as a rebel and returned to tradition, conforming to society's expectations.

Akage no An and Censorship in Japan, by Ranbir K. Banwait

Andrew O'Malley reminds us of the ideological dimensions involved in the translation of *Anne of Green Gables* from Canada into new international target systems. But who would have thought that the translation of *Anne* into Japanese would take us straight into the office of American General Douglas MacArthur (1880–1964), who implemented Japan's education policies in the years immediately following the Second World War? What has never been considered in research into the immense popularity of *Akage no An* is the genealogy of cultural censorship in the country. As we shall see, the text's readership was, ironically, constructed at least in part by the Supreme Commander for the Allied Powers (SCAP) of Japan's occupational policies in the country, whose promotion of translated juvenile literature was a component of the reform of education in the process of Japanese democratization.

While scholars such as Jay Rubin have debated the impact of the Allied Occupation on postwar literature, variously asserting the liberating or oppressive function of SCAP's censorship policies, what is clear is that General MacArthur installed a surveillance system whose task was twofold: the Civil Censorship Detachment's strict regulation of '*everything* published or performed in Japan' and the Civil Information and Education Division's simultaneous promotion of American democracy through the circulation of everything permissibly democratic.[30] The Occupation's work thus extended beyond the censorship of Japanese cultural production to the opening up of Japanese borders to the influx of transnational influences. The significance of this lies not so much in determining which aspect of the Occupation's program of reform influenced the output of literature the most. Rather, it suggests the necessity of providing an adequate account of the conditions that made possible the immense popularity in Japan of Western works of adolescent fiction, such as *Anne of Green Gables*, in the first place.

According to historian Marlene J. Mayo, in 'Literary Reorientation in Occupied Japan: Incidents of Civil Censorship,' the U.S. government initiated a wide-ranging set of policies and programs from September 1945 to April 1952. Under the jurisdiction of General MacArthur, the concrete aim of the surveillance operation was to reorient Japan along 'political, economic, and psychological' lines, in order to 'foster new beliefs, labelled as democracy, individual responsibility and fair dealing.'[31] Surveillance of Japan's 'schools, mass media, postal services, and telecommunications' was set in place to ensure the eradication of ideologies such as nationalism and communism that were hostile to American interests.[32] This system of surveillance was uniquely gendered in its approach; indeed, MacArthur's project of countering militarism involved an investment in gendered tropes and a literary culture that contested Japan's pre-war nationalistic culture.

A number of historians have detailed how, despite the fact that the postwar literary period was heavily determined by U.S. censorship, the war years were marked by an even greater degree of censorship for cultural producers in Japan. But even before the onset of surveillance practices, 'media control was a long-established practice in Japan,' as Takemae Eiji observes in *Inside GHQ: The Allied Occupation of Japan and Its Legacy*.[33] From the 1930s onwards, American popular culture and literature in Japan were increasingly censored, along with the work of Japanese writers with leftist or Marxist leanings. Nonetheless, it was with the onset of the Pacific War that media control became ubiquitous. During the Second World War the further suppression of 'Western' translated texts (largely excluding German and Russian books) ultimately led to the removal of most titles even from Japanese libraries. Yet, even prior to the Second World War, the censorship of juvenile literature was of primary importance to the state; in 1938, state control over the publication of children's literature tightened even further with the beginning of the Sino-Japanese War. Specifically, the Japanese government was attentive to the contents of girls' literature because, as Hiromi Tsuchiya Dollase suggests, young girls were considered essential reserves for the future stability of the nation.[34] Their roles in this literature as future patriotic wives and mothers complemented the samurai novel, which also featured as a narrative for adolescent readers.[35]

Since the Japanese government so severely regulated the movement of any external influences into the country (alongside its rigorous regime of internal censorship), it stands to reason that after Japan's defeat, the Allied Occupation undertook a project of disarmament that included the domain of cultural and social production, as Takemae notes: 'Washington ascribed the popular acceptance of Japanese militarism to ideological manipulation in three areas: education, religion and information. Since the Meiji era, the explicit purpose of formal instruction had been to serve the Imperial state, and children were taught absolute loyalty to the Emperor, love of country and devotion to duty. Girls and young women learned "national morality and womanly virtues"; boys were inculcated with martial values and received paramilitary training.'[36] In keeping with such observations, the Occupation's policies in Japan essentially implemented a wide-scale program of reorientation that included both the systemic scrutiny of the media's dissemination of information and the methodical reorganization of the Japanese education system. As a consequence, the conclusion of the Second World War brought dramatic changes in media control to Japan: the Civil Information and Education Division's deployment of a cultural project of re-education was both broadly aimed at the mass public, and more narrowly targeted at various demographic groups, such as women, children, and adolescents.

The re-education of Japan occurred on several different fronts, one of which involved disseminating American ideas to the public by reorganizing Japan's literary culture, which took the form of extensively 'expanding the flow of foreign books to Japan.'[37] In licensing the cultural materials deemed appropriate for reorientation, the Civil Information and Education Division provided Japanese editors with suitable publishable imports,[38] but also established libraries in 'major universities across the country' and employed American librarians who circulated

American values and culture through Western literature and the organization of concerts and lectures.[39]

In 1946, an interdepartmental agreement between the Civil Information and Education Division and the State Department's worldwide information and propaganda network ensured that the latter passed along its media directives through a network of affiliated organizations: 'The War Department's Civil Affairs Division ... established a New York Field Office to supply CI&E with carefully selected books, magazines, newspaper editorials, model radio scripts, feature films, documentaries, plays and musical recordings.'[40] The U.S. Library provided occupied peoples with materials representing a positive view of American life.[41] Indeed, the Civil Information and Education Division played a substantial role in circulating translated adolescent girls' literature in Japan.[42] *Akage no An* must be situated in this historical milieu.

In examining the construction of a readership for *Anne of Green Gables*, it is imperative to consider the nature of the 'positive American values' that the organization hoped to transmit to Japan, and the case of the dissemination of Laura Ingalls Wilder's *The Long Winter* (1940) to libraries across Japan provides an instructive study. Upon MacArthur's personal recommendation, the text was published for use in Japanese schools because, as Noriko Suzuki asserts, he saw *The Long Winter* 'as an effective educational apparatus for inculcating American democracy in Japanese schoolchildren.' Since MacArthur was a believer in the frontier theory that the American West originated the 'American principles of democratic living,' he envisioned the Little House books as tools for spreading America's democratic vision of individualistic determination in the education system.[43] The publication history of *Anne of Green Gables* in Japan can be seen as implicated in the same ideological mechanism.

By 1950, publishers in Japan had, with the establishment of the SCAP Translation Program, begun to select 'American' books for publication. That SCAP encouraged the translation and publication of juvenile literature comes as no surprise. Listed among some fifty-seven books published in a series of translated literature for girls from Mikasa-shobou, a publishing house renowned for its translated literature, more than thirty were American titles. Of these, fourteen were foremost American classics for girls (including, for example, Alcott's *Little Women*, Webster's *Daddy-Long-Legs*, Coolidge's *What Katy Did*).[44] It was in 1951 that the editor of the Mikasa-shobou publishing house approached translator Hanako Muraoka for new material for young readers.[45] At this point, Muraoka's translated *Anne of Green Gables* was ready to be submitted since she had completed her translation by the end of the war. Published in 1952, *Akage no An* was subsequently accompanied by the other eight Montgomery books to be published in the Mikasa-shobou series.[46]

By the time the translated *Anne of Green Gables* was published, it fit into an already determined corpus of adolescent girls' literature, catering to postwar ideals of family and womanhood. In a crucial analysis of the text's dissemination in Japan, Hiromi Ochi also suggests that *Anne* was a means of introducing Japanese girls to U.S. domestic culture and its understanding of gender norms within the democratic American family unit.[47] That *Anne* lends itself to such a reading suggests that gender became a primary site of articulation for U.S. Cold War politics, as Mire Koikari argues: Not only were Japanese women the ideal 'students' in the 'American school of democracy'; they 'were perfect poster girls for selling American democracy internationally.'[48] Yoshie Kobayashi similarly notes that women's emancipation was central to the Allied Occupation's reform policy. Indeed, gender reform was a major focus for CI&E promotional activities because SCAP saw Japanese womanhood as crucial in 'civilizing' the nation in its drive to democracy.[49]

Akage no An was included in the national school curriculum in 1953 upon Muraoka's recommendation. As Yuko Katsura has noted, along with Kathleen A. Miller, the reading patterns of children from the 1950s to the 1980s in Japan indicate that *Anne* remained on the curriculum for junior high school children during those three decades.[50] Moving from SCAP's general principles of literary dissemination in Japan, it remains to be seen what influences, if any, Muraoka exerted on her translation of the text. Since Muraoka served a public role in the cultural life of the nation, participating in the public domains of pedagogy and language reform before, during, and after the Second World War, her translation of *Anne* lends important insights into how language policy informs the text. By extension, we may also consider what impact the text had in configuring gendered social relations in Japan. Certainly, we may infer from the fact that the translation was completed by the end of the war that Muraoka may have attempted to conform (superficially at least) to wartime censorship practices.[51]

Japan's investment in preserving gender norms both before and during the war took place at the level of language use. Indeed, in the years leading up to the Second World War, state efforts to standardize women's speech intensified; such efforts were sustained by the Ministry of Education's output of programs and policies. In an important study of 'women's language' in Japan, Rumi Washi traces the implementation of language policy in education noting that 'the establishment of norms of language for women ... were fostered through education.' According to Washi, *Reehoo yookoo*, a manual of good manners compiled as a textbook for the secondary level and released in 1941 by the Ministry, offers one example of various policy attempts to standardize 'gendered forms of ... speech.'[52] This policy was implemented through the work of Japan's National Language Association (NLA), an organization established to sustain the Ministry's language policies. In the latter part of the 1930s, the NLA recruited a number of female educators and writers to advance the goals of language standardization (and, more specifically, to disseminate the principles of *Reehoo yookoo* in their own work). In collaboration with the women who joined the organization, NLA sought to expound an exemplar of speech as an index of an individual's gendered social identity.[53] Muraoka was one of several women involved in the organization.[54] But in reality, it was only after the war that standardized Japanese speech for women gained widespread currency: 'female speech,' as Washi notes, 'is an artificial construct ... that was developed largely as a state project ... which was also strongly supported by elite women educated during [the pre-war years and the war] period.'[55] It is this cultural work that Muraoka presents in her translation of *Anne of Green Gables*, a literary project that, on the one hand, conforms to U.S. Cold War politics, and on the other, interrupts the democratizing impulse of the language reform policies of the postwar era.

Such an inquiry necessitates a brief look at Sean Somers's insightful reading of *Akage no An*. In referencing *Anne*'s placement in an 'intercultural aesthetic milieu,' he suggests that when Anne becomes An and speaks in Japanese 'she sounds antiquated'; in fact, the translators, he suggests, 'create a voice for Anne by implementing distinctly Japanese stylistics,' using 'verbal registers associated with old-fashioned modes of Japanese speech.'[56] Of course, Anne's dialogue, as English readers have experienced it, also exemplifies elaborate language usage, but *An*'s speech ultimately fits into a previously established lexicon in Japan. This mode of speech, as Somers has suggested, demonstrates an 'education in manners' that belies An's 'low social position.'[57] In other words, it references 'a space of discourse' known as 'women's language' in Japan.[58]

Anne auf Green Gables in Germany, by Irene Gammel

Focusing on cultures whose economic, geopolitical, and linguistic realities are distinctively different from those in the world of *Anne of
Green Gables*, the first two vignettes on Iran and China explore countries where Anne gained very late entrances, in 1996 and 1987, respectively. Although encountering closer economic and political affinities,
Anne also arrived late in Germany, in 1986, seventy-eight years after
the novel was first published and the same year I left Germany to study
in Canada. This belatedness comes as a surprise, given that Germans
are avid consumers of Canadian literature and have an abiding fascination with Canada, a country many Germans associate with expansive
nature landscapes, wilderness, and freedom. The dense population in a
country a third of the size of Ontario explains in part the appeal of this
cultural fantasy and explains why historically, the most popular stories translated into German were those of Grey Owl and Farley Mowat,
focusing on the manly man's interaction with animals. Montgomery's
Anne of Green Gables was prevented from being translated precisely because in the German imagination, Canada is neither a feminine space
nor an enchanted garden, according to Martina Seifert, a German scholar who has studied the reception of *Anne of Green Gables* in Germany.

As Seifert has noted, Germany's first exposure to *Anne of Green Gables*
occurred through the Kevin Sullivan miniseries for television, which
for many was the first introduction to the story. *Ein zauberhaftes Mäd-
chen (An Enchanting Girl)* was first broadcast over four Sundays on ZDF
television late in 1986. Children's book publisher Loewe capitalized on
its popularity with a timely translation of *Anne auf Green Gables* as a
novel for youth (*Jugendroman*). German translator Irmela Erckenbrecht,
who also translates Margaret Drabble, Edna O'Brien, and Vita Sack-
ville-West, was instructed to shorten the novel by 20 per cent and to
omit any episode not included in the Sullivan miniseries. Excised too
were many passages related to religion, in line with the secular German
education system and society. Other victims of the truncated translation included Montgomery's humour, 'the sights, sounds, smells, the
tastes and textures of Prince Edward Island,' along with many references to Canadian history, politics, and weather.[59] The desire to give
children the familiar and make the text feel 'like home' involved a process of 'changing, enlarging, or abridging it or by deleting or adding
to it,' taking liberties that publishers wouldn't take to quite the same
extent with an adult novel, as Shavit observes.[60] The Sullivan film script

was used to guide the translation, producing a hybrid product that was never acknowledged as such, as Seifert notes: 'The only German language version of *Anne of Green Gables* is nothing but an adaptation of an adaptation, a text produced to accompany the Sullivan series.' Seifert calls the story of this transfer a 'scandal.'[61]

In the spring of 2001, I taught a graduate course on L.M. Montgomery at the Friedrich-Schiller Universität Jena and Universität Erfurt, close to Weimar – the heartland of German Romanticism in the eighteenth century. I moved into the room just vacated by Canadian writer Robert Kroetsch, who had preceded me as the visiting professor at both universities. Beautifully restored after the German reunification, these old historical universities and cities are linked to the names of Romantic poets and writers Johann Wolfgang von Goethe and Friedrich Schiller, who had taught at the same institutions two centuries earlier and had frequented the same pubs that I went to in the evenings. The experience was thrilling, as was the fact that I was teaching the very first generation of German *Anne* readers.

On the last day of class in May 2001, I had my twelve Jena students, all women including two mothers, fill out a questionnaire: *How does Montgomery's writing affect you? What specifically do you find interesting, inspiring or important – and why? Are there aspects that may be less appealing or relevant for German readers?* The answers were illuminating in that many of the students reported first encountering the work when they were about twelve or thirteen years old. 'I was "enchanted" by Anne, and so by and by I read all books of the Anne series and participated in Anne's fate in this way,' as one student put it, translating the movie language (bezaubert). She explains: 'I have seen the movies (Anne) before, and read Anne of Green Gables (in English) to my children. I always thought of it as children's literature though it was fun to read it as an adult too. The warm and lively portrayals, especially of the landscape and childhood struggles were appealing to me.' Several students liked the way Montgomery drew her characters and setting, as one noted: 'they are so vivid and described in detail in such a loving way that the reader can easily relate to the characters and develop a picture of the setting which makes the reading experience most intense and enjoyable.' Thus claiming a presence in the text, some students had incorporated the text into their own repertoire, while also reminding me of Holly Blackford's point in *Out of This World*, that girls read in order to 'to encounter alterity,' or in other words, they read not to instantiate the self, but to 'take a break from and move beyond themselves.'[62]

For another German student, Anne is already so close that little aesthetic transformation is needed: 'I think it is *not* its specific Canadianness that makes [Anne] so appealing to young girls but the fact that growing up is the same everywhere basically and so you can relate to some of their experiences and sometimes wish your life was as interesting as theirs.' Of course, growing up in Sudan or Nigeria or revolutionary Iran or post-Maoist China might not necessarily be the same as growing up in a Western country like Germany, but the student notes: 'I think that when we are growing up and read Anne's and Emily's stories we can relate to them because they are making the same experiences (friendship, "rebellion" against parents) as we do to a certain degree.' The book becomes a relational web, whereby the world of Avonlea is neatly integrated into the German reader's reality.

On the occasion of the 2008 centennial, Titania Medien of Leverkusen produced an audio CD series for *Anne auf Green Gables*, including *Ein Abschied und ein neuer Anfang* (A Farewell and a New Beginning), *Anne auf Avonlea* (fall 2008), and *Anne in Kingsport* (spring 2009). The translator's name is conspicuously absent but prominent attention is given to the German dubbing voices that lend Hollywood cachet to the Anne audio play. The voice of Anne, 'sensitive' and 'exuberantly voluable,' is provided by Marie Bierstedt, the German voice of Kirsten Dunst, familiar to Germans above all through her role in *Spiderman*; Matthew Cuthbert's German lines are spoken by Jochen Schröder, the German voice of Gregory Peck; and Rachel Lynde's by Rigina Lemnitz, the German voice of Whoopi Goldberg and Diane Keaton. Also advertised are the German voices of Nicole Kidman and Katie Holmes. Michael Matzer's review sees some quintessentially American values in the Anne audiotext: 'Instead of economic and political reforms, [Montgomery] relies on the typically American virtue of self-improvement, enabled through love, education and responsibility.'[63] In Matzer's review titled 'Death in August' – Yes, here Matthew dies in August whereas in the novel he dies in June – the power of Anne's story is its tragicomedy (*Tragikomik*). In sexually liberal Germany, where children's books often provide explicit sex education, Matzer notes that Anne's metamorphosis from girl to woman 'never touches on issues surrounding menstruation or sex, for these topics were taboo for the Victorians – at least officially.' The reviewer concludes that 'Anne is above all an idealized and idealizing creature, who is meant to function as a model.' In addition to becoming a lovable member of society, she is, he notes, a *Streberin*, a loaded term that combines *striving* with the more negative associations of being a nerd or careerist, with the qualification that the fact 'that she dares to compete with a man alone is a remarkable step towards emancipation and self-affirmation.'

Ultimately, my semester teaching L.M. Montgomery in Germany made me look at *Anne of Green Gables* through the eyes of Eastern German students, who had first encountered the story after the fall of the Berlin wall. It also made me reconnect with the girl series I had grown up with, *Pucki* (nicknamed after the wild forest Puck – like Anne, Pucki is mischievous and loves the woods). Written by Montgomery's close contemporary Magda Trott (1880–1945) and set in eastern Germany during the 1930s, the series follows the blond and rambunctious Pucki through childhood, adolescence, flapper years, marriage, and motherhood. When I first read Pucki, East Germany (which was then Communist Germany), seemed more distant than France or England from my West German perspective. But in 2001, when I travelled from Frankfurt to Jena, I passed Eisenach and the Wartburg, an old castle connected with Pucki's passion for romantic stories and with her misadventures. It was then, seeing the names on the signs during that drive on the Autobahn, that I experienced a sudden resurgence of childhood memory, an emotional recognition I had never felt in relation to *Anne of Green Gables*, since I had first read that novel as an adult. Like Anne, Pucki is re-educated into 'Pucki-Mütterchen,' modelling the perfect mother. Like Montgomery's writing career, Trott's took off late in life, at age thirty-nine, and like Montgomery she was extremely prolific but dismissed as merely popular. Some of the parallels are intriguing, but in light of the paucity of information, we can only speculate if the feminist Trott knew *Anne of Green Gables*.

Adopting Anne around the World

Ultimately, the adoption of Anne is a profoundly intercultural phenomenon. In a Nordic country like Sweden, with a low population density, Anne is so close to home as to require only few changes to make her Swedish. Since Anne fits seamlessly into the Swedish child-readers' experiences, Swedes may not necessarily 'appropriate' Anne; there's no need to, as the cultures are already similar enough to begin with, and moreover they are on a more even political/economic playing field – in contrast to nations like China or Iran. In fact, in Iran, the claiming of *Anne of Green Gables* ultimately comes out of the opposite sense of 'our cultures are different but I can still make Anne fit my experience.' As

O'Malley documented, the Iranian *Anne of Green Gables* books provide maps, explanatory notes, and so forth, designed to make the foreign accessible; in other words, they don't 'pretend' Anne could be living in a farm outside Shiraz.

Meanwhile in China, the values promoted by the Communist regime in a period of opening its door to Western culture made Anne a strategic text for adoption by the state-controlled publishing industry. While the Maoist period sought 'to level, uniformitize, and homogenize the Chinese public,' as Mayfair Mei-Hui Yang writes, post-Maoist China brought about stratification of the mass public according to class, education, region, gender, and occupation, with the state maintaining strong control over mass culture.[64] And this, in part, is where Anne comes in. 'The famous Canadian fairy tale *Anne of Green Gables* was published in Chinese version last week, to commemorate the 35th anniversary of the establishment of diplomatic relations between China and Canada,' reported People's Daily Online, the largest English-language website in China, in 2005. Turning Anne into a 'fairy tale' is a fascinating reference that links *Anne of Green Gables* to the classic Chinese fairy tales so beloved by Huifeng Hu. One might say that Anne reflects the current Chinese era's tension between holding on to Chinese identity and opening up to the West, which is perhaps one of the reasons Montgomery's books are so heavily championed by the state.

In a densely populated Central European country like the reunified Germany, Anne may not be as seamlessly familiar to readers as she is in Sweden, but she is certainly not as different as she is to readers in Iran or China; most notably, she has a North American rather than a distinctly Canadian flavour. Moreover, in East Germany's transition from forty years of Communist rule to a modern-day consumer society with a high-level social security system, the novel's valuation of family, noted as crucially important for the Iranian and Chinese contexts, interestingly also speaks to the values of a formerly collectivist socialist society (the same values that are celebrated in the hugely popular and nostalgic tragicomedy *Good Bye Lenin!* in which family and the supportive collective play a vital role).

A final reason why Anne is such an 'adoptable' orphan around the world is that 'adoption is by nature intercultural and interfamilial,' as suggested by Carol Singley, who observes that 'even the word *adoption* is highly metaphoric.' She continues: 'Whereas *adoption* refers to the act of taking a child into one's own family through legal means and raising that child as one's own, … [t]o adopt may mean to take and follow a course of action by choice or assent, as in adopting a constitution. It may mean to take up and make one's own, as in adopting an idea, or to take on or assume, as in adopting a certain view.'[65] In this definition, adoption itself becomes a metaphor for the cross-cultural homing of Anne, as she is adopted into different familial and cultural structures, ultimately bringing us full circle to the idea, voiced by Anne, that there are 'many Annes' in Anne, an idea that also unifies the multiple vignettes of this chapter, as the P.E.I. and Canadian Anne proclaims her Iranian, Chinese, German, Japanese, and Swedish identities, as she observes: 'There's such a lot of different Annes in me. If I was just the one Anne it would be ever so much more comfortable, but then it wouldn't be half so interesting.'[66]

NOTES

1 LMM, 20 June 1908, in *SJ*, 1: 335.
2 Akamatsu, 'Japanese Readings'; Devereux, '"Canadian Classic" and "Commodity Export,"' 11; Lynes, 'Consumable Avonlea'; Fiamengo, 'Towards a Theory.'
3 See, e.g., Baldwin, 'L.M. Montgomery's *Anne*'; Stoffman, 'Anne in Japanese Popular Culture'; Trillin, 'Anne of Red Hair.'
4 Doris Bachmann-Medick, 'Cultural Studies: A Translational Perspective,' interview with Boris Buden, trans. Erica Doucette; original emphasis. *Transversal*, Sept. 2008, http://translate.eipcp.net/transversal/0908/ bachmannmedick-buden/en.
5 Shavit, Poetics of Children's Literature, 115.
6 Åhmansson, '"Mayflowers Grow in Sweden Too,"' 18.
7 Ibid., 18–19.
8 For information concerning the Iranian copyright law of 1970, see Unesco, 'Iran – Copyright Law,' http://portal.unesco.org/culture/en/ files/30380/1142169773ir_copyright_1970_en_pdf/ir_copyright_1970_ en.pdf. These regulations, however, do not apply to works originating outside of Iran.
9 I was fortunate to have made contact with Ms. Hayeri Yazdi by e-mail through the Centre for Research in Young people's Texts and Culture (CRYTC) at the University of Winnipeg. Her paper, 'An Overview of Active Iranian Writers of Children's and Young Adult Literature,' was presented by proxy at the 2006 Children's Literature Association conference in Los Angeles. She has been extremely generous with her time

and knowledge and I am deeply indebted to her for her help with this chapter.

10 Foster and Simons, *What Katy Read*, 160.

11 G. York, 'On Iranian TV, Avonlea Rules,' A21.

12 Fiske, *Understanding Popular Culture*, 99–101. Fiske adds that the pleasures of reading popular texts 'derive from the production of these meanings by the people, from the *power* to produce them … out of their resources and from the sense that these meanings are *ours* as opposed to *theirs*' (ibid., 121).

13 The Index Translationum website, maintained by the United Nations Educational, Scientific and Cultural Organization, indicates that Peykan Publishing House released the first four volumes of the Anne series in 1999 and that Heram published *Anne of Avonlea* in 2004. The Ghadyani Publishing House, whose edition of the first book I discuss below, seems to be publishing all eight books, as cover illustrations for all of them are printed in the back pages of the first volume. 'Index Translationum: UNESCO Culture Sector,' http://databases.unesco.org/xtrans/xtra-form.shtml.

14 I am indebted to my father-in-law, Iradj Naghibi, for his careful translation of all the extra-textual information in the Ghadyani translation of the first volume of the Anne series, and for obtaining for me a copy of the text.

15 Wachowicz, 'L.M. Montgomery,' 10.

16 Katsura, 'Red-Haired Anne in Japan,' 59. In the same passage, Katsura also remarks on Anne's sense of duty as an important point of connection for Japanese readers.

17 Stoffman, 'Anne in Japanese Popular Culture,' 54; emphasis added.

18 Ghan, 'Snapshots – Me and Anne,' 80, 82.

19 Devereux, '"Canadian Classic" and "Commodity Export,"' 19.

20 See the 'Guestbook' at 'Megan Follows,' http://www.meganfollows .co.uk/.

21 Online comments by Chinese Anne fans, http://tieba.baidu.com/. All comments have been translated into English by the author.

22 Online comments by Chinese Anne fans, http://www.douban.com/ people/315166/reviews.

23 Online comments by Chinese Anne fans, http://www.douban.com/ people/315166/reviews.

24 Red Classics refer to the Chinese revolutionary history novels published between the 1950s and the 1970s, which best reflect the aesthetic characteristic of collectivism, heroism, and romanticism.

25 LMM, *AGG*, 122.

26 Kangkang Zhang, 'Anne: Lighten Up Our Heart,' *Wenhui Bao News* 4, no. 4

(2003), http://epub.cnki.net/grid2008/Detail.aspx?dbname=CCND2003&
filename=WEHU200304040151.

27 Hu, 'Thoughts on Anne of Green Gables.'

28 Guoping Zhou, 'What Can't Be Missed of Being,' *Chinese Reading Weekly*, 7
    Sept. 2003, http://dlib.cnki.net/kns50/detail.aspx?filename=ZHDS200307
    09ZZ31&dbname=CCND0008.

29 Fu, 'Adoption and Transformation.'

30 Rubin, 'From Wholesomeness to Decadence,' 84; original emphasis.

31 Mayo, 'Literary Reorientation in Occupied Japan,' 135.

32 Ibid., 135–6.

33 Takemae, *Inside GHQ*, 384. In introducing various Japanese critics, this
    paper accedes to whatever practice the scholar has ascribed to in the pres-
    entation of his/her full name. Here, the last name precedes the first.

34 Dollase, 'Girls on the Home Front,' 323–4.

35 Ishihara, *Mark Twain in Japan*, 37.

36 Takemae, *Inside GHQ*, 347.

37 Mayo, 'Literary Reorientation in Occupied Japan,' 136.

38 Editors were provided with 'articles from over 100 middle-range US maga-
    zines, including *Life*, *Newsweek*, *Time* and *Reader's Digest*. Material from
    Allied countries and editorial commentary from UN and SCAP sources
    also were supplied to the Japanese media for priority release. The Division
    circulated from 350 to 400 such items every month. The regular appearance
    of so many foreign articles and news items in the mainstream media of a
    single country was an unprecedented event.' Takemae, *Inside GHQ*, 396.

39 Ibid.

40 Ibid., 395–6.

41 Ochi, 'What Did She Read?' 360.

42 Ibid., 359.

43 Suzuki, 'Japanese Democratization,' 68–9. Likewise, an examination of a
    number of translated texts reveals, as Ochi (What Did She Read?' 360)
    suggests, that only those 'juvenile books which had positive, imaginative,
    and peaceful themes and messages' were translated. Ishihara (*Mark Twain
    in Japan*, 66) makes a similar argument about the corresponding relation-
    ship of CCD's censorship practices to CI&E's promotional activities: 'One
    of the main transformations [in the translations] was the deletion of the
    elements of violence in the originals … GHQ's Civil Censorship Detach-
    ment … strictly censored portrayals of violence in Japanese publication,
    films, theatrical productions, and radio programs.' Before the publication
    of texts such as *Huckleberry Finn* and *Tom Sawyer* could occur, the original
    narratives were transformed to accommodate American occupation
    policies.

44 Ochi, 'What Did She Read?' 360–1.
45 Mie Muraoka, 'Speech at the Reception Held by the Department of Tourism Parks in PEI in 1989,' http://club.pep.ne.jp/~r.miki/speech_j.htm.
46 Ochi, 'What Did She Read?' 361.
47 Ibid., 359.
48 Koikari, *Pedagogy of Democracy*, 51.
49 Kobayashi, *A Path toward Gender Equality*, 39, 89.
50 Katsura, 'Red-Haired Anne in Japan'; Kathleen A. Miller, 'Revisiting *Anne of Green Gables* and Her Creator,' *The Looking Glass: New Perspectives on Children's Literature* 13, no. 2 (May–June 2009), http://www.lib.latrobe.edu.au/ojs/index.php/tlg/article/view/142/141.
51 Muraoka also translated Mark Twain's *The Prince and the Pauper* which, as Ishihara argues, was one of the few English texts that remained in circulation in Japan during the war years. That the narrative of *The Prince and the Pauper* lends itself neatly to an adaptation to a Japanese samurai version suggests that such a conventional re-scripting participated in the text's proliferation in Japan. Ishihara, *Mark Twain in Japan*, 37.
52 Washi, '"Japanese Female Speech,"' 77, 79.
53 Ibid., 82.
54 Muraoka also remained prolific during the war, contributing regularly to magazines such as *Shōjo no tomo* (Girls' Friend), the most popular magazine for girls before the war, and one of two girls' magazines to survive throughout the war period. Magazine culture was under the strict supervision of the state during the war. Dollase, 'Girls on the Home Front,' 324.
55 Washi, '"Japanese Female Speech,"' 88.
56 Somers, '*Anne of Green Gables*,' 43, 46.
57 Ibid., 47.
58 Inoue, 'Gender, Language and Modernity,' 392.
59 Seifert, 'Conflicting Images,' 336.
60 Shavit, Poetics of Children's Literature, 112.
61 Seifert, 'Conflicting Images,' 334, 328.
62 Blackford, *Out of This World*, 19.
63 Matzer, 'Tod im August,' http://www.dooyoo.de/audiobooks/anne-auf-green-gables-ein-abschied-und-ein-anfang-lucy-m-montgomery-cd/1162649/. This and all other Matzer quotations are translated from the German by Gammel.
64 Yang, 'Mass Media and Transnational Subjectivity,' 329.
65 Singley, 'Building a Nation,' 52, 53; original emphasis. See also Singley, 'Teaching American Literature.'
66 LMM, *AGG*, 176.

11 What's in a Name? Towards a Theory of the Anne Brand

BENJAMIN LEFEBVRE

'What's in a name? That which we call a rose
By any other name would smell as sweet.'

– Romeo and Juliet[1]

'I read in a book once that a rose by any other name would smell as sweet, but I've never been able to believe it. I don't believe a rose *would* be as nice if it was called a thistle or a skunk cabbage.'

– Anne of Green Gables[2]

In a 1909 letter to her Canadian correspondent Ephraim Weber, written in the aftermath of the unexpected success of her novel *Anne of Green Gables*, L.M. Montgomery laughed over a card she had received that was addressed to 'Miss Anne Shirley, care of Miss Marilla Cuthbert, Avonlea, Prince Edward Island, Canada, *Ontario*.' Despite her initial delight in the idea of 'some kiddy who fondly imagines that all the people in books live "really and truly" somewhere,'[3] her amusement turned to amazement several decades later when actor Dawn Paris (born 1918), who had been cast to play the lead in the second film adaptation of *Anne of Green Gables* by RKO Radio Pictures in 1934, took 'Anne Shirley' as her stage name after appearing in twenty-six feature films as Dawn O'Day. As Montgomery explained to Weber in 1936, 'She has been in several other plays and you've no idea what an *uncanny* feeling it gives me to walk along the street to see a sign suddenly flash out over a theatre "Anne Shirley in So and So." It's positively ghostly. I feel a bit like Frankenstein!'[4] By the time Montgomery repeated this anecdote in a letter to her Scottish pen pal G.B. MacMillan, this 'uncanny' feeling had become 'the oddest thrill': 'I have the weirdest sensation that *Anne* has really come to life.'[5]

Because Montgomery had no creative involvement in the adaptation of *Anne of Green Gables* for the screen or for the stage,[6] having sold all rights to her novel to her exploitative publisher in 1919, the embodied 'Anne Shirley' literally brought to life aspects of her literary legacy over which she had no control. Indeed, the three film adaptations of her work produced in her lifetime anticipated the plethora of afterlives that circulate in contemporary culture, including telefilms, television series and miniseries, plays, abridgements, commodifications, tourist sites, and websites, all of which capitalize on and add to the popularity of the adapted text. Although Montgomery had been proud to claim the first copies of her book as '*mine, mine, mine* – something to which *I* had given birth,'[7] the protagonist of a literary work for which she felt the attachment of a parent would be ushered into the realm of film and supporting media under the tutelage of a number of corporate stepparents. As Carole Gerson and Jason Nolan have both noted in their discussions in this volume of the dispersal of Montgomery's text in culture, these corporate bodies have used images of Anne Shirley to meet a range of narrative and ideological ends.

While much of the critical scholarship on film and television versions of *Anne of Green Gables* has focused on the process of adapting Montgomery's fiction into screen texts,[8] several scholars have turned their attention to the cultural industries that expand and export Montgomery's work and name to geopolitical contexts all over the globe. These 'supplementary products,' according to Cecily Devereux, 'do not, for the most part, reproduce the text itself,' but 'rely on visual representations of the heroine.' As a consequence, 'we do not need to read the book to recognize the heroine: recognition of her and what she represents is visual.'[9] For Jeanette Lynes, who concentrates on mass-produced objects that extend (and, to a point, replace) the literary text that they depict, Anne 'has entered the virtual market-place,' and Avonlea, the fictional village in which she resides, 'seems to have become a floating signifier.'[10] These critical interventions – part of the larger emphasis on popular culture aspects of Montgomery Studies that were the focus of two special issues of *Canadian Children's Literature / Littérature canadienne pour la jeunesse* on 'L.M. Montgomery and Popular Culture' (1998, 2000) and the collection of essays *Making Avonlea* (2002) – highlight the extent to which the international circulation of 'Anne' encompasses these later cultural texts as much as the actual fiction Montgomery wrote. As Irene

Gammel has noted, 'No other author has had Montgomery's sustained power to export Canadian literature and culture around the world.'[11] But while Montgomery's status as a central Canadian author is indisputable, the cultural production of Anne afterlives has become part of a complex multinational industry.

This chapter proposes a new template for further research by focusing not on the adaptation process itself but on the brand power of 'Anne Shirley' – a figure who, as Faye Hammill notes, 'might be considered a celebrity sign in her own right'[12] – particularly as this figure circulates in a sequence of early Hollywood film texts whose strongest relationship to Montgomery's work is through the name and image of Anne Shirley. In doing so, this chapter probes what film theorist Robert Stam refers to as 'a kind of baggage, a thespian intertext formed by the totality of antecedent roles.'[13] As I show below, this 'baggage' served to use the name Anne Shirley as a link between a series of film texts and a vaguely defined pattern of themes and images that were associated with Montgomery's fiction, a set of characteristics that I refer to as the Anne brand. Bearing in mind Paul Budra and Betty A. Schellenberg's comment about 'the "unkillable" protagonist' in their discussion of the production of book sequels,[14] this chapter seeks to answer the following questions: How do images of Anne Shirley outside of the novel *Anne of Green Gables* contribute to or complicate the Anne brand? Or, to paraphrase the quotation from *Romeo and Juliet* that opens this chapter, would Anne Shirley in any other text be recognizable as Anne Shirley? Because these connections and extensions existed outside of standard copyright law and beyond the actual texts that bear her name as author, Montgomery became demoted from creative parent to passive spectator as the embodied Anne Shirley sought to reinvent herself as a Hollywood star after a career of marginal roles. While both Montgomery and Dawn Paris hoped to gain power and prestige through the Anne brand during this period, their inability to exert control over the name or the identity anticipated the contested ownership of the Anne brand in the twenty-first century.

What's in a Brand?

In *Brand Meaning* (2008), Mark Batey defines 'brand' as '*the consumer perception and interpretation of a cluster of associated attributes, benefits and values.*' He notes that 'brand associations are strengthened and consolidated over time through repetition,' and that as 'connections between brand associations are reinforced ... they effectively come to define the brand in consumers' minds.'[15] Batey's definition also evokes Michel Foucault's notion of the 'author function,' whereby the author's name accrues cultural capital and becomes an ideological entity separate from the individual who bears it: that name, according to Foucault, 'seems always to be present, marking off the edges of the text, revealing, or at least characterizing, its mode of being.'[16] However, the cluster of meanings and associations that builds up over time is not only cultural in Batey's formulation but neurological as well, since each encounter with a brand acts as 'a stimulus that is stored in the brain and adds to the associative network already existing for the brand.'[17] In the case of Anne of Green Gables – in particular the adaptations, images, artifacts, and spin-offs that are available to consumers in addition to the print text called *Anne of Green Gables* – the name can encompass a wide range of abstract concepts depending on the perspective of the consumer, including nostalgia for simpler times, the natural landscape of rural Prince Edward Island, the ugly duckling turned beautiful swan, a chaste heterosexual romance plot, and girl power.

Brands are generally associated with consumer goods and services and with the abstract values that their producers attempt to attach to them ('Think Different,' from Apple Computer, can suggest non-conformity), but cultural studies critics have begun to consider print and media texts in these terms, particularly texts whose popularity has created extensive merchandising opportunities. In *Harry Potter: The Story of a Global Business Phenomenon* (2008), Susan Gunelius traces the history of the Harry Potter franchise in terms of a branding cycle, noting that J.K. Rowling's central role as overseer of adaptations and spin-offs of her literary offspring 'would turn her into a respected brand guardian.' As she suggests, Rowling's contracts for her books allowed her as copyright holder to control how the Harry Potter brand would be exploited into adaptations and spin-offs – the afterlives that constitute the 'brand cycle.' As brand guardian, Rowling was legally entitled to wait until she found a movie studio that would allow her 'to ensure the movies stayed true to the books and to Harry Potter as a whole' and to maintain 'some control over merchandising activities.'[18] In contrast, because such exploitation of print texts was not yet an imaginable phenomenon in 1907, Montgomery's contract for *Anne of Green Gables* contained no such language.[19] L.C. Page's motivation for securing film rights was financial, not artistic, hence Montgomery's claim that he had waited until after she had sold all remaining rights to her first seven books to him for $18,000 before selling the film rights to four of these for $40,000.[20]

Montgomery and Rowling make for contrasting case studies in the history of book publishing, since they are both female authors who, at opposite ends of the twentieth century, became household names due to one successful book that prompted endless afterlives, albeit on much different corporate and remunerative scales. While terms such as 'brand guardian' and 'brand cycle' were obviously not part of Montgomery's professional lexicon, a reading of Montgomery's contract for 'ANNE OF GREEN GABLES A JUVENILE STORY' alongside the handwritten manuscript and the published book reveals the complex relationship between the author and her work. On the one hand, Montgomery retained almost absolute control over her text: as Devereux notes in her critical edition of the novel, the most frequent differences between manuscript and published book concern commas and 'the placement of hyphens in nominal and adjectival compounds,' and the few substantive alterations could have been made by Montgomery either as she typed her manuscript or corrected the proofs, two crucial stages of the book's production that were not preserved.[21] Moreover, the contract stipulates that if changes are made to the proofs 'which are a departure from HER manuscript, said changes shall be at the expense of said L.M. MONTGOMERY,' making substantive changes at the proof stage unlikely.[22] As well, she won out in her insistence that her name as author appear as L.M. Montgomery, 'as all my work has been,' instead of '"Lucy Maud Montgomery" which I loathe.'[23] On the other hand, she appears to have had absolutely no say or involvement in the book's design, illustrations, cover, or marketing – in short, any aspect of book production and distribution in excess of the words themselves – either for the initial 1908 edition or for any edition or printing since. Moreover, since 'said L.M. MONTGOMERY' assigned to Page 'all serial rights, dramatic rights, translations, abridgements, selections and rights therefor of said work, or parts thereof,' all decisions concerning future versions of the text would be made by Page; 'net revenue' from such venues would be 'divided equally between the parties hereto,' but these latter earnings were lost after she sold her remaining rights to him in January 1919.[24]

Although Montgomery was satisfied with Page's marketing campaigns and the overall appearance of the book itself, she disliked the interior illustrations, barely tolerated the cover image ('It isn't "my" Anne,' she told Weber, 'but doesn't glaringly violate what she might be'), and balked at the low royalty of 10 per cent on the wholesale price.[25] As Elizabeth Waterston has noted, 'The terms of the publishers' contract did not include any sliding scale of royalties for this run-away best-seller. If the author wanted to cash in on the "Anne-mania" she must get to work on a sequel.'[26] Moreover, as Gerson points out earlier in this volume, Montgomery had a complicated relationship with much of the 'Anne-mania' that she witnessed during her lifetime, including the enshrining of her favourite P.E.I. haunts by Parks Canada in 1936. In these examples, we see Montgomery picking her battles between aspects of literary production she feels should be under her control (her name and her words) and those she recognizes are beyond her authority. This distinction between the textual Anne and the visual Anne is crucial in terms of branding: if recognition of Anne as protagonist of the book is visual, then even the first visual images of Anne are beyond the text written by Montgomery. In short, the 'Anne' that consumers recognize on book covers, film posters, and souvenirs – the 'Anne' that has prompted international recognition – is not Montgomery's Anne at all, but visual renderings of her created without her input or control. While the words on the page are hers, the cultural capital generated by visual images of the heroine is shaped and disseminated without her.

However, a major instance in which Montgomery refused to submit to the decisions of others over the use of the Anne brand occurred in the lawsuit over *Further Chronicles of Avonlea* (1920), a book of short stories that Page insisted on publishing after she had left his firm. As Montgomery noted in her journal, she reluctantly gave her consent in a futile attempt to retain some control over her own work, realizing that the stories he wished to publish were not protected by copyright law in the United States.[27] While she was enraged by the 'crude interpolations … [that] reflect[] on my literary skill,' ultimately she was more worried about the aspects of the book that were in excess of her actual work, including the 'red-haired girl on the cover as appears on all the Anne books': 'It is got up to resemble the Anne books in every way and is an evident attempt to palm it off on the public as an Anne book.'[28] Part of Page's marketing strategy included issuing new books by an author in quick succession and with a similar visual style to maintain readers' loyalty, as Gerson notes in this volume, even though Montgomery found the repetition of this style to be 'monotonous.'[29] Her anger over the book's appearance anticipates the lawsuit that followed less than two months later (and which was not settled until 1928), including an entire day of wrangling over the definition of 'Titian red' in a Boston courtroom with the aim of establishing that the cover of *Further Chroni-*

cles constituted an 'Anne' book from a legal point of view (and thus was a violation of the conditions of their agreement).[30] This part of the dispute arose over Page's unauthorized use of the Anne brand and by the fact that, unlike copyright law, there was no legal precedent to account for the branding implications of the image of a red-haired woman on the cover of one of her books.

Montgomery's comments about *Further Chronicles of Avonlea* appear less than two months after she recorded her impressions of the 1919 silent film of *Anne of Green Gables*, which featured Mary Miles Minter in the title role. Not only did she have difficulty seeing her own work in the film, but she was also upset over the financial loss: 'The play has had an enormous success and I don't get a cent from it!!'[31] The initial success of the film launched some of the first Anne afterlives, including a 'Mary Miles Minter edition' of the novel with movie stills replacing the original illustrations and a 'film story' published in *Photoplay Magazine* (see colour plate 14),[32] but this phase of 'Anne-mania' was not meant to last. As Clarence Karr notes in his detailed analysis of the film's production and reception, 'In spite of the mixed reviews, the film played to capacity audiences until a scandal involving the director and the star disgraced the production, cut short its run, and prevented its export to Britain and Australia.'[33] This scandal, which Montgomery first learned of in 1929, occurred when Minter's sexual relationship with the film's director, William Desmond Taylor, was revealed during the investigation of Taylor's murder in 1922. Recording the anecdote in almost identical ways in her journal and in her correspondence with Weber and with MacMillan, she turned again to Shakespeare for the appropriate euphemism, this time from *Othello*: 'Mary had loved the handsome movie magnate not wisely but too well.'[34] Importantly, though, the film's removal from circulation was prompted not because Minter was ever suspected of Taylor's murder but because her relationship with him compromised the brand image of the film's protagonist: while the discovery of their relationship could hardly affect Minter's performance in the film retroactively, the rationale for burying the film was that the discovery of Minter's actions had damaged the branding relationship between consumers and the abstract concepts encoded into the brand image, to return to Batey's formulation. The studio destroyed all known copies of the film because of their conviction that consumers would no longer find Minter believable as Anne of Green Gables.[35]

Upon hearing about plans for a new film version of *Anne of Green Gables* from a correspondent in Hollywood in April 1934, Montgomery commented in her journal upon the fact that she would receive no re-muneration for this film either: 'It *is* a shame. But it is my own fault, if that is any comfort.'[36] She did not mention in this entry which produc-tion company was attached to the project, but presumably part of her disappointment stemmed from the fact, revealed only in her surviv-ing business correspondence held at the University of Guelph archives, that she had attempted to place her later novels *Anne's House of Dreams* (1917) and *Rilla of Ingleside* (1921) with RKO Radio Pictures the preced-ing February.[37] Given the gaps in this correspondence, it is entirely con-jectural whether RKO decided against adapting these two book sequels in favour of remaking *Anne of Green Gables* or whether Page had already attempted to sell the moving picture rights a second time. What these decisions show is the extent to which *Anne of Green Gables* possessed a brand power that Montgomery's later books lacked. Given the extent to which Montgomery carefully cultivated and negotiated her own celeb-rity, as scholars such as E. Holly Pike and Lorraine York have shown,[38] she must have had difficulty coming to terms with the fact that her character had greater marketing potential than her own name as author of the book in which Anne first appeared.

Since she would not profit financially from the film or participate in the shaping of its script, Montgomery recorded in her journal that her interest in the project was 'academic' and that she might benefit from 'indirect advertisement.'[39] Her decision ended up coinciding with a be-hind-the-scenes move in Hollywood: the birth of 'Anne Shirley.' Ham-mill suggests that Dawn O'Day 'sought to reinvent herself as Anne by changing her name to "Anne Shirley,"' a claim that emphasizes the agency of a struggling young actor over her career. However, Richard B. Jewell reports a more likely scenario, that 'the studio convinced Miss O'Day to change her professional name' in order to maximize the 'latent publicity value.'[40] This blurring of character and actor into a particular brand image for public consumption is not unique to Anne Shirley – as a child, Mickey Rooney adopted the stage name 'Mickey McGuire' after the character he played in a series of sixty shorts for RKO between 1927 and 1934[41] – but it does point to the ways in which popular actors were being groomed for their star power across what would hopefully be a long series of similar film texts, even if that led to a form of typecasting that could not be creatively rewarding.

In fact, the studio's use of the actor as a live advertisement tool start-ed as soon as filming of the 1934 talkie began. In an article in the *Toronto Daily Star* on 8 September 1934, we see both Montgomery and 'Anne

Shirley' vying for control over the Anne brand. Its title, 'Author to Get No Profit as "Green Gables" Filmed,' points to the slant of the article, which focuses almost entirely on Montgomery's career and professional life and provides no details about the film currently in production. However, in contrast with this focus, the article is accompanied by a montage of photographs of Montgomery, 'Anne Shirley' in costume, O.P. Heggie (who played Matthew Cuthbert in the film, opposite Helen Westley as Marilla), and Montgomery's husband Ewan Macdonald – a curious choice, given that, at the time of the interview, Macdonald reportedly was upstairs in his bedroom in the middle of one of his melancholic episodes, or what Montgomery referred to as 'spells.' As Montgomery reported in her journal concerning the interview, 'I was in torture all the time, not knowing what Ewan might be doing or feeling. [The reporter] asked so many ridiculous questions I would have liked to throw something at him.' Perhaps it was her 'torture' that caused her to be quoted as saying, in response to a question about formulas for successful writing, 'Writing a book and making love are alike in that you don't know how it is done.' Moreover, despite the article's emphasis on the fact that Montgomery was not involved in the movie's casting or script, the photograph of Anne Shirley is accompanied by a signed, handwritten note: 'To L.M. Montgomery with my deepest gratitude for the opportunity to play the heroine of your beautiful book "Anne of Green Gables."'[42] Indeed, while this tribute to Montgomery may have been in keeping with the image of 'Anne Shirley' that RKO sought to cultivate, Montgomery remained committed to her own personal brand, which required her to adopt a public persona that showed her to be gracious, accommodating, and in control despite the many turbulences occurring behind the scenes.

But while Montgomery sought to claim authority over the Anne brand at home, the film itself, which George Nicholls Jr directed from a script by Sam Mintz, nevertheless proceeded without her. Despite having lost all control over her story and her heroine, Montgomery told MacMillan that she saw it four times, finding it vastly superior to the silent film of 1919.[43] Still, some of the changes in plot and characterization puzzled her, such as the screenwriter's decision to alter and expand upon Marilla's revelation, late in the novel, that she had once been 'real good friends' with Gilbert Blythe's father by making Gilbert the son of the woman Matthew had hoped to marry, a change that led to Theodore F. Sheckels's observation that 'the movie's plot becomes *Romeo and Juliet* superimposed upon *Anne of Green Gables*.'[44] For

Montgomery, the one redeeming feature of the film was Anne Shirley herself: as she reported to MacMillan, 'Her *eyes* were good and in the scene where she "floated down to Camelot" she *was* Anne completely and satisfyingly.'[45] Montgomery also went on record with her impressions of the film in an article in the January 1935 issue of *Chatelaine*, which shows her asserting her authority over the Anne brand even as she mentioned in passing that she 'had no "say"' in the script and 'had the sensation of watching a story written by somebody else.' Of Anne Shirley, she added, 'There were many moments when she tricked even me into feeling that she *was* Anne.'[46] The RKO film did quite well at the box office and prompted another edition of Montgomery's novel with a cover image from the film (see colour plate 15), but this success provided both rewards and challenges for author and actor. While Montgomery sought to re-establish her role as brand guardian, Anne Shirley the actor discovered that just as her new name prompted instant recognition from moviegoers of the period, it also led to pressure to play roles that fulfilled the wholesome image of Montgomery's protagonist. The success and the narrative pleasures of the Anne brand would constrain her, just as the success of the novel *Anne of Green Gables* had limited Montgomery's options as a writer almost thirty years before.

Anne Shirley in Hollywood, 1936–1945

The success of Anne Shirley as a lead actress in early Hollywood depended on a number of complicated factors surrounding the Anne brand. Without Montgomery as the brand guardian who would ensure that the uses of 'Anne Shirley' outside the pages of her books maintained consistency and integrity, the dispersal of Anne Shirley in Hollywood, much like the distribution of the book by Page, was shaped largely by commercial interests that were prompted by perceived public desire for more Anne. The response to this perceived desire had important implications, not only in terms of the cultural and neurological components of brands but also the Hollywood systems that typecast its stars. In his theories of repetition in popular film texts, Umberto Eco locates narrative pleasure in viewers' ability to predict narrative outcomes based on recurring generic patterns. For Eco, the presence of a recognizable actor in multiple films becomes a 'form of seriality' that 'succeeds in making, always, the *same* film. The author tries to invent different stories, but the public recognizes (with satisfaction) always and ever the same story, under superficial disguises.'[47] Just as Montgomery's public had clamoured for 'more Anne' in the years following the publication of *Anne of Green Gables*, so did the film public of the 1930s in response to the RKO film adaptation of the novel. As a result, Montgomery, the RKO executives, and Anne Shirley herself went to extraordinary lengths to meet this consumer demand without actually duplicating the text(s) called *Anne of Green Gables*.

Within four months of seeing the *Anne* talkie, Montgomery began work on *Anne of Windy Poplars* (1936), a new novel meant to fill a three-year gap in the original book saga, breaking her 'dark and deadly vow,' made almost fifteen years earlier, that she was 'done with *Anne* forever.'[48] As she told MacMillan, her publishers had 'thought it would be a good commercial venture after the film,' and she was motivated by the need for house-buying funds after her husband's early retirement to Toronto and by the Depression-era downturn of the market.[49] She also sought to sell film rights to her later novels, whose film rights she still controlled, and her surviving business correspondence with her second U.S. publisher, Frederick A. Stokes, reveals her continued attempts to interest Hollywood producers in her work: she suggested *Magic for Marigold* and *Jane of Lantern Hill* as vehicles for Shirley Temple and even recommended a rewrite of *Anne's House of Dreams* that eliminated Anne entirely and made a supporting character, Leslie Moore, the protagonist.[50] Montgomery anticipated and accepted that her novels would need to be rewritten for the screen, but she hoped she could at least approve film scripts based on novels whose rights she retained. Still, her contacts at Stokes advised her against giving RKO the right to create original stories featuring Anne, which would be cheaper for them than exercising their options on her book sequels: as Vernon Quinn, a Stokes company representative, wrote to Montgomery on 24 April 1939, 'They might have something written and produced that would be wholly out of character of *your* Anne Shirley and which, if it were not an actual discredit to you as the creator of Anne and the delightful atmosphere that surrounds her, might be harmful to you as a writer.'[51] Tellingly, while Page controlled the film rights to the text called *Anne of Green Gables*, Vernon Quinn considered that Montgomery, and not RKO, should control the Anne brand.

Meanwhile, by the time *Anne of Green Gables* premiered in December 1934, Anne Shirley the actor was placed under a $75-a-week studio contract and then under a new five-year contract in January 1936,[52] but this form of job security came at a price within the studio contract system of the era. Such contracts 'robbed talent of any rights or control over their own careers, requiring them to work on whatever projects the studio dictated,' as Ina Rae Hark notes. 'If they refused, they were suspended without pay and without any ability to find work elsewhere.'[53] Echoing the definitions of 'brand' and narrative pleasure enumerated above, Jewell adds that 'star development involved building up an actor's status through a series of roles which would establish, stabilize and expand upon an image or persona which moviegoers found appealing. Once the persona was fixed in the public's mind, all publicity and promotional material was designed to complement and magnify this pleasing image.'[54] Perhaps in an attempt to build on Anne Shirley's star power, RKO soon reunited her with director Nicholls and with costars Westley and Heggie for *Chasing Yesterday* (1935), in which Heggie played an elderly archaeologist who adopts the young girl played by Anne Shirley, whose mother he once loved.[55] Given the plot changes made to the script of the *Anne* talkie, the RKO producers likely sought to connect the two films together, through both stunt casting and fairly similar storylines. Nonetheless, while they sought to maintain the image of the *Anne of Green Gables* film, they were not successful in duplicating its popularity.

Under her new stage name, Anne Shirley appeared in thirty-two more films over the next decade, most often in a leading role.[56] The brand power of the name 'Anne Shirley' proved bittersweet, however, given that many of her films were poorly received and that she was frequently miscast and overlooked for parts that would have suited her better.[57] Moreover, in an attempt to develop Anne Shirley's cultural commodity beyond the film texts in which she starred, her face appeared in advertising campaigns that literally contributed to her 'clean' image. In an ad for Lux Toilet Soap appearing in a 1938 issue of *Family Herald and Weekly Star*, a photograph of Shirley is accompanied by the caption 'I've found LOVE': '"With women, Romance comes first. That's why I always advise – GUARD AGAINST COSMETIC SKIN" … "Lovely Skin Wins Romance – and *holds* it," says this charming young screen star. "So don't risk Cosmetic Skin. You can guard against it easily as I do with Lux Toilet Soap."'[58]

But by the time the adaptation of *Anne of Windy Poplars* was made in 1940, advertised as a sequel to RKO's *Anne of Green Gables* film, Anne Shirley did not welcome the opportunity to be reunited with the character whose name had relaunched her career. Married and pregnant at the time of filming, she had more difficulty returning to the world of Green Gables than Montgomery had. 'I'm grown up now. I'm not the sweet girl they make me out to be,' she said in a statement to the press. 'I'd like to make a complete change. Even have another name. Anne Shirley. It just doesn't end. It just sort of dies out.'[59] Anne Shirley's stated position – unhappy in her professional opportunities but powerless to change the terms of her contract – in many ways echoes Montgomery's realization twenty years earlier that her success as a novelist had painted her into a corner, as she recorded upon completion of her fifth *Anne* novel, *Rainbow Valley* (1919): '[it] still averages up pretty well of its kind. But I'm tired of the kind. I've outgrown it. I want to do something different. But my publishers keep me at this sort of stuff because it sells and because they claim that the public, having become used to this from my pen, would not tolerate a change.'[60] For both women, the respective Anne brands they had created ended up taking control of their careers, driven by the capitalist demands of producers, publishers, and public. Perhaps not surprisingly given Shirley's lack of enthusiasm for the material, *Anne of Windy Poplars* was a financial and critical disappointment. A review in the *New York Times* complained about the 'dialogue so laced with bromidic beatitudes and with so much nonsensical gush that one observer at least came away as though he had eaten a box of marshmallows.'[61]

However, like Montgomery, who continued to find a balance between work that satisfied her and met her audience's expectations, Anne Shirley had several opportunities to rise to the occasion when a suitable and challenging role was offered to her. Fortunately, two of her most important films are available on DVD, and her roles in these films are memorable precisely because they go *against* Anne Shirley's image as 'the perfect Louisa May Alcott heroine'[62] and into two decidedly contemporary subgenres: the maternal melodrama, a genre of films that required female protagonists 'to take their obligatory turns through the wringer of masochistically enjoyed self-abnegation,' and film noir, a typology of films defined less by generic patterns than by 'subtle qualities of tone and mood,' but referring largely to films that 'portrayed the world of dark, slick city streets, crime and corruption.'[63] Like the 1934 *Anne of Green Gables*, both films – *Stella Dallas* (1937) and *Murder, My Sweet* (1945) – were based on a print text and were remakes of earlier films, meaning that these stories were already familiar enough to moviegoers to warrant high expectations.[64] For the former, Shirley was 'loaned out' to MGM Studios (an expression that heightens the actor's status as a commodity) to appear alongside Barbara Stanwyck, with whom she had worked before. But while Shirley received rave reviews and an Academy Award nomination for Best Supporting Actress, these accolades proved less beneficial to her career than they should have been. On 22 August 1937, less than three weeks after *Stella Dallas* premiered and twenty months after she signed a five-year contract that included 'a standard cancellation clause should she wed,' the nineteen-year-old Shirley married the twenty-five-year-old actor John Payne (they divorced in 1943).[65] According to James Robert Parish, Shirley 'seemed so different since her *Stella Dallas* loan-out,' preferring short skirts and eye makeup over her 'modest little country-girl guise,' but RKO ended up renewing her option despite their uncertainty of which roles would be most appropriate for 'Anne Shirley.' Although she was one of many young actors in serious consideration for the role of Melanie in *Gone with the Wind* (1939), Shirley ultimately never received the role that would catapult her into the realm of a serious adult actor. Although she continued to work fairly steadily – she signed a new seven-year contract with RKO in November 1941 – the majority of her films prompted either indifference or contempt from the public.[66]

Perhaps not unexpectedly, one of Shirley's most successful film roles was her last, although it was not the role she had wanted to play. In *Murder, My Sweet*, about a private eye who descends into 'a nether world of homicide, blackmail, charlatanism, thievery, sadistic violence, sexual enslavement and, above all else, mystery,'[67] Anne Shirley played Ann Grayle opposite Dick Powell, whose career as a 1930s song-and-dance man was in serious jeopardy. Casting him in this new role was a risk, as Jewell notes in his discussion of the pressures of stars' screen image, but RKO aggressively advertised the 'NEW Dick Powell' featured in the film in an attempt to rebrand their leading man.[68] Perhaps motivated by the producers' willingness to repurpose the film's male lead, Anne Shirley devised a plan after discovering that both she and her co-star, Claire Trevor, longed to play each other's roles: 'Claire and I put our heads together and conspired to reverse the femme casting. We even ganged up on the producer and director, probably giving better performances for their benefit than we did in the film. But it all did us no good. Claire went back to being bad and fascinating and I went back to being good and dull.'[69] Although *Murder, My Sweet* gave new life to Dick Powell's career, Anne Shirley subsequently decided to retire from show business and married the film's producer, Adrian Scott, a month before it opened in March 1945 (they divorced in 1948).[70] Despite the quiet years that followed, the 'baggage' (to use Stam's term) of the Anne brand that had both helped and hindered her acting career followed her throughout her life, and in July 1993, the *Globe and Mail* reported that 'Anne Shirley ... has died of lung cancer. She was 74.'[71]

As for the original author of *Anne of Green Gables*, Montgomery continued to maintain her hold on the Anne brand by adding two more books to the Anne library: *Anne of Ingleside*, published in 1939, backtracked to Anne as a young mother, and *The Blythes Are Quoted*, submitted to her publishers the day she died in 1942, contained an experimental blend of poems, short stories, and vignettes that she had reworked to include Anne and her family, from the period covered in *Rainbow Valley* to the beginnings of the Second World War. It was not published in its entirety until 2009 – perhaps because some of its contents clashed too much with the Anne brand she had created.[72] And while she did express feelings of other-worldliness in seeing 'Anne Shirley' come to life and appear in a range of films that were not connected to her body of work except through name branding, she did not dwell too long on this bizarre blending of fiction and reality. In January 1936, she mentioned in a journal entry of scattered jottings that '"Anne Shirley" sent me a box of candied fruit and nuts for an Xmas present. Owing to wrong address and customs delays it did not reach me in time for Christmas.'[73] Towards the end of a career that included bitter lawsuits, the pressures of genre, and the trappings of fame, perhaps the idea of receiving a Christmas present from her own character no longer seemed so strange after all.

Conclusion

'I had another letter from a little U.S. girl,' Montgomery recorded in her journal in 1920, 'asking the old, old question, "Is Anne a real girl?" I must have been asked that literally a thousand times since *Green Gables* was published.'[74] While Montgomery's designation of this as an 'old, old question' only a dozen years after the novel's publication shows the extent to Montgomery's surprise and weariness, the question continues to prove relevant in the decades since because the Anne brand continues to grow strong. Half a century after the RKO talkie made a hit in Hollywood and beyond, the rewards and challenges of portraying Anne Shirley on screen were passed down to a new actor, Megan Follows, who received rave reviews for her portrayal of Anne in Sullivan Entertainment's *Anne of Green Gables* (1985) and *Anne of Green Gables: The Sequel* (1987). Like Anne Shirley, Follows eventually returned to the role of Anne for *Anne of Green Gables: The Continuing Story* (2000) after over a decade of other roles in film, television, and theatre. And, also like Anne Shirley, Follows had difficulty shedding the Anne brand. As Donna Danyluk reported in an article aptly titled 'The Girl They Call Anne,' 'She will always be Anne Shirley … the name Megan Follows is synonymous with Anne Shirley. In fact, it's Follows' face that pops into one's imagination when remembering that "Anne girl."'[75]

But while she may not be a 'real girl' in a human sense, and while Montgomery's heirs have taken on the role of brand guardians since the 1990s by registering key names and phrases as trademarks (including 'Anne of Green Gables™' and 'L.M. Montgomery™'), Anne of Green Gables is also an entity that goes beyond the control of any one individual. In 2008, the year of the centenary of the novel's publication, two major new Annes appeared without Montgomery: in *Before Green Gables*, a prequel by Nova Scotia children's writer Budge Wilson, and in Kevin Sullivan's CTV telefilm *Anne of Green Gables: A New Beginning*, both a prequel and a sequel to his earlier miniseries, with Barbara Hershey and Hannah Endicott-Douglas replacing Follows as the adult and the child Anne.[76] As well, on 29 November 2008, Toronto's Buddies in Bad Times Theatre staged an interactive comedy show called 'Anne Made Me Gay,' advertised as 'a night of corsets, currant wine and more gossip around the punchbowl than a Ladies Aid Society bazaar' (see colour plate 16). Curated by Moynan King and Rosemary Rowe, this 'evening of song, recitation, literary exploration and hot girl-on-girl action' sought to widen the boundaries of what is possible to read into Anne's world, a reclaiming of the text by a community of readers whose responses to the text are usually dismissed or silenced.[77] Ultimately, then, those who keep the Anne brand relevant into the twenty-first century are the public, who continue to read, watch, and engage with various incarnations of Anne. The text of Montgomery's novel has not changed in one hundred years, but Anne's world has proven endlessly adaptable, endlessly extendable, and endlessly relevant to readers all around the world.

NOTES

I gratefully acknowledge the Social Sciences and Humanities Research Council of Canada for a postdoctoral fellowship that helped make this research possible. My thanks as well to Kevin Pighin for several enjoyable conversations about film theory and thespian intertextuality.

1 Shakespeare, *Romeo and Juliet*, 2.2: 43–4.

2 LMM, *AGG*, 38.

3 LMM to Ephraim Weber, 2 Sept. 1909, in *The Green Gables Letters*, 93; original emphasis.

4 LMM to Weber, 22 June 1936, in *After Green Gables*, 223.

5 LMM to G.B. MacMillan, 27 Dec. 1936, in *My Dear Mr M.*, 179.

6 In addition to the films discussed in this chapter, *Anne of Green Gables* and *Anne of Avonlea* were adapted into three-act plays in 1937 and 1940, respectively. See Chadwicke, *Anne of Green Gables*; Carlisle, *Anne of Avonlea*.

7 LMM, 20 June 1908, in *SJ*, 1: 335; original emphasis.

8 See, e.g., Dickinson, *Screening Gender, Framing Genre*, 22–3; Drain, '"Too Much Love-making"'; Frever, 'Vaguely Familiar'; Hersey, '"Tennyson Would Never Approve"'; Lefebvre, 'Stand by Your Man'; Poe, 'Who's Got the Power?'

9 Devereux, '"Canadian Classic" and "Commodity Export,"' 12–13.

10 Lynes, 'Consumable Avonlea,' 270.

11 Gammel, 'Making Avonlea,' 3.

12 Hammill, *Women, Celebrity, and Literary Culture*, 100.

13 Stam, 'Beyond Fidelity,' 60.

14 Budra and Schellenberg, Introduction, 8.

15 Batey, *Brand Meaning*, 6; original emphasis.

16 Foucault, 'What Is an Author?' 211.

17 Batey, *Brand Meaning*, 5. For more on the neurological aspects of branding, see Gordon and Ford-Hutchinson, 'Brains and Brands'; Schachter, *Searching for Memory*, 59, 71.

18 Gunelius, *Harry Potter*, 8–9.

19 See Karr, *Authors and Audiences*, 171–2.

20 LMM, 18 Dec. 1919, in *SJ*, 2: 358.

21 Devereux, 'A Note on the Text,' 48.

22 'Agreement between L.M. Montgomery.'

23 LMM to MacMillan, 8 Jan. 1908, in *My Dear Mr M.*, 37. While L.C. Page's rationale for preferring 'Lucy Maud' to the more androgynous 'L.M.' is open to conjecture, it is worth noting that Rowling's British publisher, Bloomsbury, suggested that she change her authorial name from 'Joanne' to 'J.K.' 'under the assumption that boys wouldn't read a book written by a woman.' Gunelius, *Harry Potter*, 6.

24 'Agreement between L.M. Montgomery.'

25 LMM to Weber, 2 Sept. 1909, in *The Green Gables Letters*, 90; see also LMM, 16 Aug. 1907, in *SJ*, 1: 331.

26 Waterston, 'Lucy Maud Montgomery 1874–1942,' 204.

27 LMM, 19 Jan. 1919, in *SJ*, 2: 286; see also LMM to MacMillan, 10 Feb. 1929, in *My Dear Mr M.*, 140–7.

28 LMM, 10 Apr. 1920, in *SJ*, 2: 376.

29 See LMM, 27 Sept. 1913, in *SJ*, 2: 134.

30 LMM, 18 June 1920, in *SJ*, 2: 382.

31 LMM, 22 Feb. 1920, in *SJ*, 2: 373.

32 Boone, 'Anne of Green Gables.'

33 Karr, *Authors and Audiences*, 173.

34 LMM to MacMillan, 11 Aug. 1929, in *My Dear Mr M.*, 154; LMM, 15 Oct. 1929, in *SJ*, 4: 20; LMM to Weber, 8 June 1930, in *After Green Gables*, 175. See Shakespeare, *Othello*, 5.2: 340.

35 For more on Minter, Montgomery, and Anne, see Hammill, *Women, Celebrity, and Literary Culture*, 100–23.

36 LMM, 28 Apr. 1934, in *SJ*, 4: 260.

37 F.A. Stokes, letter to Mrs L.M. Macdonald, 8 Feb. 1934, in LMM, 'Business and Lawsuit Correspondence.' For more on the history of RKO Radio Pictures, see Lasky, *RKO*; Jewell with Harbin, *The RKO Story*; and Neibaur, *The RKO Features*.

38 Pike, 'Mass Marketing, Popular Culture'; L. York, *Literary Celebrity in Canada*, 75–100.

39 LMM, 22 Aug. 1934, in *SJ*, 4: 291.

40 Hammill, *Women, Celebrity, and Literary Culture*, 118; Jewell with Harbin, *The RKO Story*, 78. Parish (*The RKO Gals*, 340) also suggests that this name change was not simply professional but legal.

41 Jewell, *The Golden Age of Cinema*, 284.

42 LMM, 4 Sept. 1934, in *SJ*, 4: 295–6; 'Author to Get No Profit,' 27. In summer 1934, Ewan Macdonald's suffering from depression and religious melancholia reached the point that he was hospitalized in a mental institution in Guelph, Ontario, for six weeks. Macdonald's religious melancholia was a constant worry for Montgomery, given the threatened impact it could have on his career as a Presbyterian minister.

43 LMM to MacMillan, 27 Dec. 1936, in *My Dear Mr M.*, 179.

44 LMM, *AGG*, 320; Sheckels, 'Anne in Hollywood,' 185.

45 LMM to MacMillan, 27 Dec. 1936, in *My Dear Mr M.*, 179.

46 LMM, 'Is This My Anne,' 22; see also LMM, 29 Nov. 1934, in *SJ*, 4: 325–6.

47 Eco, 'Innovation & Repetition,' 196–7.

48 LMM, 24 Aug. 1920, in *SJ*, 2: 390.

49 LMM to MacMillan, 1 Mar. 1936, in *My Dear Mr M.*, 177; see also Waterston, *Magic Island*, 189; LMM, 9 Mar. 1935, in *SJ*, 4: 356–7.

50 Vernon Quinn to Mrs Macdonald, 5 June 1939; VQ [Vernon Quinn], 'Memo

to Mr Stokes: Mrs Macdonald's letter of July 19, 1935,' both in LMM, 'Business and Lawsuit Correspondence.'

51 Vernon Quinn to Mrs Macdonald, 24 Apr. 1939, in LMM, 'Business and Lawsuit Correspondence.'

52 Parish, *The RKO Gals*, 345, 349.

53 Hark, 'Movies and the 1930s,' 8.

54 Jewell, *The Golden Age of Cinema*, 258.

55 Parish, *The RKO Gals*, 347.

56 For Anne Shirley's filmography, see Parish, *The RKO Gals*, 370–84.

57 Lasky, *RKO*, 133; Jewell with Harbin, *The RKO Story*, 81, 97, 100, 106, 130, 189.

58 'I've found LOVE,' 35.

59 Shirley, unsourced, quoted in Parish, *The RKO Gals*, 360.

60 LMM, 26 Dec. 1918, in *SJ*, 2: 278.

61 'At the Palace,' 13; see also Jewell with Harbin, *The RKO Story*, 149.

62 Parish, *The RKO Gals*, 348.

63 Hark, 'Movies of the 1930s,' 12; Schrader, 'Notes on *Film Noir*,' 150.

64 Olive Higgins Prouty's novel *Stella Dallas* (1923) was made into a film in 1925. Raymond Chandler's *Farewell, My Lovely* (1940) was adapted as *The Falcon Takes Over* (1942).

65 Parish, *The RKO Gals*, 349–50, 354, 363.

66 Ibid., 354, 356, 363.

67 Jewell with Harbin, *The RKO Story*, 200.

68 Jewell, *The Golden Age of Cinema*, 263.

69 Shirley, unsourced, quoted in Parish, *The RKO Gals*, 367.

70 Parish, *The RKO Gals*, 367.

71 'Actress Took Green Gables Name,' C1.

72 See Lefebvre, '"That Abominable War!"'

73 LMM, 11 Jan. 1936, in *SJ*, 5: 54.

74 LMM, 26 July 1920, in *SJ*, 2: 387.

75 Danyluk, 'The Girl They Call Anne,' 19.

76 Shortly thereafter, American author M. Carol Coffey published her first novel, *Zoe Lucky and the Green Gables' Mystery* (2009), featuring the image of a red-haired pre-adolescent on the front cover but with no overt link to Montgomery's internationally recognized creation.

77 See the description of 'Anne Made Me Gay' at the Buddies in Bad Times theatre, http://artsexy.ca/show.cfm?id=242. The international response to Laura Robinson's initial exploration of a lesbian subtext in the Anne series became a cultural phenomenon in its own right, revealing the ways

in which twenty-first-century readers and academics place borders around the Anne brand. See Robinson, 'Bosom Friends'; Devereux, 'Anatomy of a National Icon'; White, 'Falling out of the Haystack'; Robinson, 'Big Gay Anne'; Robinson, '"'Outrageously Sexual' Anne."'

Afterword: Mediating *Anne*

RICHARD CAVELL

'There's such a lot of different Annes in me.'

– Anne of Green Gables[1]

L.M. Montgomery began writing *Anne of Green Gables* in 1905,[2] the year that Einstein published his special theory of relativity. The following year, German hairdresser Karl Nessler introduced the permanent wave in Britain. In 1907 the Hurley Machine Corporation launched the first electric washing machine, the first portable vacuum cleaner went on sale, and Florenz Ziegfeld's *Follies of 1907* introduced the fashion for the slim-figured girl. In 1908, when *Anne* was published in Boston, two-sided phonograph discs were made available by the Columbia Phonograph Company, and a French art critic coined the term 'cubism' to describe the work of Braque and Picasso.[3]

Anne was very much a product of these times, a 'mechanical bride' half a century before Marshall McLuhan wrote his study of the way in which mediated reproductions were governed by an economy of desire that was challenging norms of gender and sexuality, and undermining ideas of the authentic self.[4] The image of Anne on the first edition of the novel is itself the reproduction of a picture on a magazine, *The Delineator*,[5] produced in offset by the thousands, and Anne's mechanical reproduction is reflected in the cubistic montage of the initial chapter headings: 'Mrs Rachel Lynde is Surprised'; 'Matthew Cuthbert is Surprised'; 'Marilla Cuthbert is Surprised.' An avatar of the serial publications that Maud read and reread, *Anne* is herself a media effect, the girl whose image, like that of television, also comes from afar, and it is through television that Anne would have one of her most lasting incarnations. This is how we first meet her, not directly, but at a distance, through the optic of Mrs Rachel Lynde.

Anne is intimately identified with Marilla and Matthew's house, whose 'green gables' design was sold in pattern kits throughout North America.[6] The house also recalls that other gabled house in North American literature, *The House of the Seven Gables* (1851), Nathaniel Hawthorne's allegory of the anxieties caused by the remediation of print in photography,[7] anxieties suggested by the photograph of Evelyn Nesbit that hovers behind our image of Anne.[8]

Maud negotiated these anxieties by making Anne a free-floating and untrammelled subject. Anne belongs, in the end, neither to Maud nor to us; she is global; she is more than the fifty million copies of the book; she is more than her hundreds of millions of readers; she is more than her adaptations for film, stage, and television; more than her Anne houses.[9] She has myriad progeny in Canadian literature and is by no means delineated by a historical period that was itself becoming post-historical, time fusing with space in the way that Einstein envisioned. We encounter her in Will Aitken's novel *Realia* (2000) as a lusty Albertan, Louise Painchaud, an English language teacher in Japan. Aitken has the genius to cast his story in the mould of Eurydice and Orpheus, reminding us of Gammel's comment that Evelyn Nesbit's pose in that picture was 'a backward glance to the Victorian age.'[10] Then Aitken brilliantly flips the tapestry so that *Anne* itself becomes the classic *point de repère* in one of the most eloquent scenes in Canadian literature – eloquent because this scene speaks of the fact that we *have* a literature, and that our literature is intimately bound to *Anne*:

Mrs Fleeman, Mrs Minato and Mrs Anaka, RN, have joined us and are busy laying out their *realia* on the bare boards. This is an idea I got from a book I found at the English bookshop called *Headway: Principles and Practices of English Language Teaching*:

Realia – one way of presenting words by bringing the things they represent into the room. The teacher, or perhaps student, holds up an object (or points to it), says the word and then gets everyone to repeat it.

Last lesson I told everyone to bring in an object, a *thing*, that in some way represents who they are.

Mrs Minato goes first. She has placed in front of her a leather-bound book. The Gothic gilt lettering spells out *Anne of Green Gables*. She places her small hands on the cover and gently caresses it as she speaks. 'This is first book I read in English. Anne is beautiful character, so warm and full of pure feeling. Her life hard but beautiful too. Very nice. When I first read I am girl and I read to my daughters and they read to their daughters. When there is problems in my life, very sad, I read again. When I am lost I think, "How would Anne go?" She is like a tower for boats to me.'

'A tower for boats,' I repeat, reluctant to interrupt.

'With big light,' Mrs Minato explains.

'A lighthouse. *Anne of Green Gables* is like a lighthouse for you?'

'Yes.' A tear runs down Mrs Minato's plump cheek. 'Please look.' She opens the book to the ornate title page. We all lean forward. A violet-ink signature slants across the page: *Lucy Maud Montgomery.*[11]

Postmodernist fiction in Canada is particularly in love with *Anne* because Anne belongs to no one time and to no one place; her village is global, a product of those international publications that the *Minto* brought to that lonely woman in Prince Edward Island. Anne Carson's *Autobiography of Red* (1998) transforms the famous red hair into the red wings of a boy – Anne, too, was a boy, until she became a girl – called Geryon, who falls in love with Herakles, an even more golden Gilbert. Geryon, like Anne, lives on an island. His story, as Carson suggests, might be framed as 'the victory of culture over monstrosity,' the monstrosity of the colonized, including the libidinally colonized:

Eventually Geryon learned to write.

His mother's friend Maria gave him a beautiful notebook from Japan with a fluorescent cover.
On the cover Geryon wrote *Autobiography*. Inside he set down the facts.
Total Facts Known About Geryon.
Geryon was a monster everything about him was red. Geryon lived on an island in the Atlantic called the Red Place.
Geryon's mother was a river that runs to the sea the Red Joy River Geryon's father was gold.
Some say Geryon had six hands and six feet some say wings.
Geryon was red so were his strange red cattle. Herakles came one day killed Geryon got the cattle.[12]

At the end of *Anne of Green Gables*, with all the power of one of the greatest scenes in American literature – when Toto tips over the screen to reveal the Wizard in his ignominious glory – the country idyll is shown to be a fantasy projection: Matthew has lost his money and Avonlea is made to appear what it always was, an extension of downtown Canada.[13] But Maud has left her greatest surprise to the end, and goes L. Frank Baum one better; the möbius strip turns to the other side of the page, and Anne is taken up by the very institution that gave her life in the first place: she has entered into literature. Anne has become *Anne*.

The history of *Anne* criticism has followed her trajectory beyond Avonlea into the wider world, a trajectory confirmed most recently by the inclusion of *Anne of Green Gables* in the Modern Library Classics series, where she joins a pantheon of international writers. Anne was international before she became national (like Canada itself, which was the product of not one but two empires). The essays in this timely collection thus reach Anne orthogonally, by avenues that, often seeming to take us away from Anne, end up taking us closer. The essays in *Anne's World* also remind us that *Anne of Green Gables* is about the end of a way of life, as well as the beginning of another.

NOTES

This afterword is an expanded version of remarks opening the exhibition and symposium *Anne of Green Gables: New Directions at 100* on the occasion of the 2008 Congress of the Humanities and Social Sciences Federation of Canada, held at the University of British Columbia as part of its centennial celebrations. I am deeply grateful to Professor Irene Gammel for the opportunity to address conference-goers at this event.

1 LMM, *AGG*, 176.
2 Gammel, *Looking for Anne*, 14.
3 I rely here on Williams, *Cassell's Chronology of World History*, 463–9.
4 The automobile was the mechanical bride par excellence. Gammel notes that in the year Montgomery's novel was published, 'the symbols of modernity such as cars and motorboats coexisted with the symbols of romantic nostalgia.' Moreover, 'The advertised magazine was urban, modern, and exotic. Hailing the world of the automobile, the stage, photography, fashion, and money, it represented the opposite of Maud's Cavendish life.' Gammel, *Looking for Anne*, note to illustration following 96, 36.
5 See Gammel, *Looking for Anne*, 231.
6 See, e.g., D.T. Atwood, *Country and Suburban Houses*; and Hodgson, *Common Sense Stair-Building and Hand-Railing*. The latter contains twenty-five turn-of-the-century house plans. See also 'Historic House Floor Plans and

Construction Designs with Vintage Garage Plans,' http://www
.housemouse.net/.

7 Pynchon puns on puncheon, a stamping device; Holgrave makes daguer-
rotypes.

8 Gammel, *Looking for Anne*, 32–4. Evelyn Nesbit was the mistress of prominent New York architect Stanford White.

9 'Atlantic Canada Home Inc., a consortium of 36 builders in Canada's
Atlantic provinces, has recently begun to offer the Japanese market Anne-
style houses, complete with … green gables.' See Murray Whyte, 'Anne of
Osaka,' *Metropolis Magazine*, July 1998, http://www.metropolismag.com/
html/content_0798/jl98osak.htm.

10 Gammel, *Looking for Anne*, 34.

11 Aitken, *Realia*, 49–50.

12 Carson, *Autobiography of Red*, 6, 37.

13 'If there is a truth to the general recognition of modernism as an "art of cities," then a tradition of rural Canadian writing has established its continuity with this urban truth, rather than in nostalgic or pastoral alternatives …
Modern capitalism requires the *production* of nature, and of the country, as
"underdeveloped" regions, as external and internal frontiers in its imperialist expansion … Cities are not one pole of a dichotomy between develop-
ing regions; cities organize the relational structure itself.' Willmott, *Unreal
Country*, 148–51. See also Cavell, '"An Ordered Absence."'

Bibliography

'Actress Took Green Gables Name.' *Globe and Mail*, 8 July 1993, C1.

Advertisement for *Anne of Green Gables*. *Publishers' Weekly*, 26 Dec. 1908, cover.

Advertisement for 'Anne of Green Gables: A Literary Legacy.' Flyer. Royal Canadian Mint, 1994.

Advertisement for Grape-Nuts. *Zion's Herald*, 6 May 1903, 564.

Advertisement for Menstruation Medication. *Zion's Herald*, 15 Feb. 1905, 219.

Advertisement for Postum. *Zion's Herald*, 21 June 1905, 787.

'Agreement between L.M. Montgomery and Her Publisher, L.C. Page and Company.' Library and Archives Canada, MG 30 D 342, v. 1.

Åhmansson, Gabriella. *A Life and Its Mirrors: A Feminist Reading of L.M. Montgomery's Fiction*, vol. 1, *An Introduction to Lucy Maud Montgomery, Anne Shirley*. Studia Anglistica Upsaliensia 74. Ph.D. diss., Uppsala University, 1991.

– '"Mayflowers Grow in Sweden Too": L.M. Montgomery, Astrid Lindgren and the Swedish Literary Consciousness.' In Rubio, *Harvesting Thistles*, 14–22.

Aitken, Will. *Realia*. Toronto: Random House of Canada, 2000.

Akamatsu, Yoshiko. 'Japanese Readings of *Anne of Green Gables*.' In Gammel and Epperly, *L.M. Montgomery*, 201–12.

Alcott, Louisa May. *Little Women*. Oxford: Oxford University Press, 2007 [1868].

Allard, Danièle. 'Hanako Muraoka's Famous and Truncated Translation of *Anne of Green Gables*: Some Lingering Questions.' In Mitchell, *Storm and Dissonance*, 344–50.

– '*Taishu Bunka* and Anne Clubs in Japan.' In Gammel, *Making Avonlea*, 295–309.

Anne: Journey to Green Gables. Dir. Kevin Sullivan. 85 min. Sullivan Entertainment, 2005.

Anne of Green Gables. Dir. William Desmond Taylor. 6 reels. Realart Pictures Corporation, 1919.

Anne of Green Gables. Dir. George Nicholls, Jr. 79 min. RKO Radio Pictures, 1934.

Anne of Green Gables. Dir. Kevin Sullivan. 198 min. Sullivan Films, 1985.

Anne of Green Gables: A New Beginning. Dir. Kevin Sullivan. 143 min. Sullivan Entertainment, 2008.

Anne of Green Gables: The Animated Series. DVD boxed set. Sullivan Entertainment, 2008.

Anne of Green Gables: The Continuing Story. Dir. Stefan Scaini. 183 min. Sullivan Entertainment, 2000.

Anne of Green Gables: The Sequel. Dir. Kevin Sullivan. 239 min. Sullivan Films, 1987.

'Anne of Windy Poplars.' *Globe and Mail*, 7 Nov. 1936, 21.

Anne of Windy Poplars. Dir. Jack Hively. 86 min. RKO Radio Pictures, 1940.

Antony, Martin M., and Richard P. Swinson. *When Perfect Isn't Good Enough: Strategies for Coping with Perfectionism*. Oakland, CA: New Harbinger Publications, 1988.

Appadurai, Arjun. *Modernity at Large: Cultural Dimensions in Globalization*. Minneapolis: University of Minnesota Press, 1996.

'At the Palace.' *New York Times*, 23 Aug. 1940, 13.

Atwood, Daniel T. *Country and Suburban Houses*. New York: Orange, Judd & Company, 1871.

Atwood, Margaret. Afterword to *Anne of Green Gables*, by L.M. Montgomery, 331–6. New Canadian Library. Toronto: McClelland & Stewart, 1992.

'Author to Get No Profit as "Green Gables" Filmed.' *Toronto Daily Star*, 8 Sept. 1934, 27.

Bagshaw, Marguerite, and Doris Scott, eds. *Books for Boys and Girls*. 4th ed. Toronto: Ryerson Press, 1966.

Baker, Deirdre, and Ken Setterington. *A Guide to Canadian Children's Books in English*. Toronto: McClelland & Stewart, 2003.

Baldwin, Douglas. 'L.M. Montgomery's *Anne of Green Gables*: The Japanese Connection.' *Journal of Canadian Studies / Revue d'études canadiennes* 28, no. 3 (1993): 123–33.

Batey, Mark. *Brand Meaning*. New York: Routledge, 2008.

Baudrillard, Jean. *Simulations*. Trans. Paul Foss, Paul Patton, and Philip Beitchman. New York: Semiotext(e), 1983.

Beckett, Sandra. *Crossover Fiction: Global and Historical Perspectives*. New York: Routledge, 2009.

Belliveau, George. 'Paul Ledoux's *Anne*: A Journey from Page to Stage.' In Gammel, *Making Avonlea*, 201–15.

Berg, Temma F. '*Anne of Green Gables*: A Girl's Reading.' In Reimer, *Such a Simple Little Tale*, 153–64.

Bieling, Peter J., and Martin M. Antony. *Ending the Depression Cycle: A Step-by-Step Guide for Preventing Relapse*. Oakland, CA: New Harbinger Publications, 2003.

Bingxin. *To Young Readers*. Beijing: People's Literature Press, 2000.

Bishop, Elizabeth. *The Complete Poems 1927–1979*. New York: Farrar, Straus and Giroux, 1983.

Blackford, Holly. Introduction to Blackford, *100 Years of Anne*, xi–xxxviii.

– *Out of This World: Why Literature Matters to Girls*. New York: Teachers College Press, 2004.

– ed. *100 Years of Anne with an 'e': The Centennial Study of 'Anne of Green Gables.'* Calgary: University of Calgary Press, 2009.

Bolger, Francis W.P. *The Years before Anne: The Early Career of Lucy Maud Montgomery*. Halifax: Nimbus Publishing, 1991.

Books for Boys and Girls, Being a List of Two Thousand Books Which the Librarians of the Boys and Girls Division of the Toronto Public Library Deem to Be of Definite and Permanent Interest. Toronto: Boys and Girls House, Public Library of Toronto, 1927.

Books to Read. London: Library Association, 1931.

Boone, Arabella. 'Anne of Green Gables.' *Photoplay Magazine*, Jan. 1920, 52–5, 126.

Booth, Wayne. *The Company We Keep: An Ethics of Fiction*. Berkeley: University of California Press, 1988.

Boucher, François, ed. *Le vêtement chez Balzac: Extraits de la Comédie humaine*. Paris: Éditions de L'Institut français de la Mode, 2001.

Bradford, Clare. 'The Homely Imaginary: Fantasies of Nationhood in Australian and Canadian Texts.' In Reimer, *Home Words*, 177–93.

Breward, Christopher, Becky Conekin, and Caroline Cox, eds. *The Englishness of English Dress*. Oxford: Berg, 2002.

Brink, Carol Ryrie. *Caddie Woodlawn*. New York: Simon & Schuster, 1973 [1935].

Brouse, Cynthia. 'The Maud Squad.' *Saturday Night*, Sept. 2002, 32–4, 36, 39–40.

Brown, E.K. 'The Problem of a Canadian Literature.' In *Responses and Evaluations: Essays on Canada*, ed. David Staines, 1–23. New Canadian Library. Toronto: McClelland & Stewart, 1977.

Bruce, Lorne. *Free Books for All: The Public Library Movement in Ontario, 1850–1930*. Toronto: Dundurn Press, 1994.

Budd, Louis J. 'Mark Twain as an American Icon.' In *The Cambridge Compan-

ion to Mark Twain, ed. Forrest G. Robinson, 1–26. Cambridge: Cambridge University Press, 1995.

Budra, Paul, and Betty A. Schellenberg. Introduction to *Part Two: Reflections on the Sequel*, ed. Paul Budra and Betty A. Schellenberg, 3–18. Toronto: University of Toronto Press, 1998.

Burgess, Gelett. *Goops and How to Be Them*. London: Methuen, 1900.

Burnett, Frances Hodgson. *The Secret Garden*. New York: HarperCollins, 1998 [1911].

Burns, David D. *Feeling Good: The New Mood Therapy*. New York: William Morrow and Company, 1980.

Butler, Kate Macdonald. 'The Heartbreaking Truth about Anne's Creator.' *Globe and Mail*, 20 Sept. 2008, F1, F6.

Buxton, Bonnie. *Damaged Angels: A Mother Discovers the Terrible Cost of Alcohol in Pregnancy*. Toronto: Alfred A. Knopf Canada, 2004.

Cadogan, Mary. *Mary Carries On: Reflections on Some Favourite Girls' Stories*. Bath, UK: Girls Gone By, 2008.

Card, Claudia. *Feminist Ethics*. Lawrence: University Press of Kansas, 1991.

– *On Feminist Ethics and Politics*. Lawrence: University Press of Kansas, 1999.

Careless, Virginia. 'The Highjacking of Anne.' *Canadian Children's Literature / Littérature canadienne pour la jeunesse* 61 (1992): 48–55.

Carlisle, Jeanette [James Reach]. *Anne of Avonlea*. New York: Samuel French, 1940.

Carroll, Lewis. *Alice's Adventures in Wonderland and Through the Looking-Glass*. Ed. Hugh Haughton. London: Penguin Classics, 1998 [1865/1872].

Carson, Anne. *Autobiography of Red: A Novel in Verse*. New York: Alfred A. Knopf, 1998.

Cavell, Richard. '"An Ordered Absence": Defeatured Topologies in Canadian Literature.' In *Downtown Canada: Writing Canadian Cities*, ed. Justin D. Edwards and Douglas Ivison, 14–31. Toronto: University of Toronto Press, 2005.

Chadwicke, Alice [Wilbur Braun]. *Anne of Green Gables*. New York: Samuel French, 1937.

Chandler, Raymond. *Farewell, My Lovely*. New York: Random House, 1940.

Chasing Yesterday. Dir. George Nicholls, Jr. 77 min. RKO Radio Pictures, 1935.

'Cheer Up.' *Zion's Herald*, 3 Feb. 1904, 146.

Chung, Grace, and Sara Grimes. 'Data Mining the Kids: Surveillance and Market Research Strategies in Children's Online Games.' *Canadian Journal of Communication* 30, no. 4 (2005): 527–48.

Clarkson, Adrienne. Foreword to Gammel and Epperly, *L.M. Montgomery*, ix–xii.

Coffey, M. Carol. *Zoe Lucky and the Green Gables' Mystery*. Denver: Outskirts Press, 2009.

Cole, Eve Browning, and Susan Coultrap-McQuin. 'Toward a Feminist Conception of Moral Life.' In Cole and Coultrap-McQuin, *Explorations in Feminist Ethics*, 1–11.

– eds. *Explorations in Feminist Ethics: Theory and Practice*. Bloomington: Indiana University Press, 1992.

Coles, Claire D. 'Fetal Alcohol Exposure and Attention: Moving beyond ADHD.' *Alcohol Research and Health* 25, no. 3 (2001): 199–203.

Collins, Carolyn. 'Re-creating the Lost 1919 *Anne of Green Gables* Movie.' Paper presented at L.M. Montgomery, Anne of Green Gables and the Idea of Classic, Charlottetown, 25 June 2008.

Connor, Ralph. *Glengarry Schooldays*. Toronto: Westminster Company, 1902.

Coolidge, Susan. *What Katy Did*. New York: Garland, 1976 [1872].

Cooper, Cynthia. *Magnificent Entertainments: Fancy Dress Balls of Canada's Governor General, 1876–1898*. Fredericton: Canadian Museum of Civilization, 1997.

Creelman, June, and Irene Gammel, curators. *Reflecting on Anne of Green Gables/ Souvenirs d'Anne … La Maison aux pignons verts*. Library and Archives Canada, 4 June 2008 to 30 Mar. 2009.

Cullinan, Bernice, and Lee Galda. *Literature and the Child*. 4th ed. Fort Worth: Harcourt Brace College Publishers, 1998.

Cummins, Maria. *The Lamplighter*. Boston: J.P. Jewett, 1854.

Danyluk, Donna. 'The Girl They Call Anne.' *Examiner* (Barrie, ON), 3 Mar. 2000, 19.

Davey, Frank. 'The Hard-Won Power of Canadian Womanhood: Reading *Anne of Green Gables* Today.' In Gammel and Epperly, *L.M. Montgomery*, 163–82.

Deacon, W.A. *Poteen: A Pot-Pourri of Canadian Essays*. Ottawa: Graphic Publishers, 1926.

Debolt, Donna. 'Fetal Alcohol Spectrum Disorder: Considerations for Educators.' Paper given at FASD Training Day, Owen Sound, Ontario, 19 Sept. 2002.

De Jonge, James. 'Through the Eyes of Memory: L.M. Montgomery's Cavendish.' In Gammel, *Making Avonlea*, 252–67.

Denison, Muriel. *Susannah: A Little Girl with the Mounties*. New York: Dodd, Mead, and Company, 1936.

Devereux, Cecily. 'Anatomy of a National Icon: *Anne of Green Gables* and the "Bosom Friends" Affair.' In Gammel, *Making Avonlea*, 32–42.

– '"Canadian Classic" and "Commodity Export": The Nationalism of "Our" *Anne of Green Gables*.' *Journal of Canadian Studies / Revue d'études canadiennes* 36, no. 1 (2001): 11–28.

– Introduction to Montgomery, *Anne of Green Gables*, ed. Devereux, 12–38.
– 'A Note on the Text.' In Montgomery, *Anne of Green Gables*, ed. Devereux, 42–50.
– '"not one of those dreadful new women": Anne Shirley and the Culture of Imperial Motherhood.' In *Windows and Words: A Look at Canadian Children's Literature in English*, ed. Aïda Hudson and Susan-Ann Cooper, 119–30. Ottawa: University of Ottawa Press, 2003.
Dewey, John. *Moral Principles in Education*. Boston: Houghton Mifflin, 1909.
Dickinson, Peter. *Screening Gender, Framing Genre: Canadian Literature into Film*. Toronto: University of Toronto Press, 2007.
Dollase, Hiromi Tsuchiya. 'Girls on the Home Front: An Examination of Shjo no tomo Magazine 1937–1945.' *Asian Studies Review* 32, no. 3 (2008): 323–39.
Doody, Margaret. 'L.M. Montgomery: The Darker Side.' In Mitchell, *Storm and Dissonance*, 25–49.
Doody, Margaret Anne, and Wendy E. Barry. 'Literary Allusion and Quotation in *Anne of Green Gables*.' In Montgomery, *The Annotated Anne of Green Gables*, 457–62.
Douglas, Amanda. *A Little Girl in Old Quebec*. New York: Dodd, Mead, and Company, 1906.
Dovercourt Children's Room Daybook, Toronto Public Library [1918–1926]. Baldwin Room, Canadiana Department, Toronto Reference Library.
Drain, Susan. 'Community and the Individual in *Anne of Green Gables*: The Meaning of Belonging.' In Reimer, *Such a Simple Little Tale*, 119–30.
– '"Too Much Love-making": *Anne of Green Gables* on Television.' *Lion and the Unicorn* 11, no. 2 (1987): 63–72.
Eco, Umberto. 'Innovation & Repetition: Between Modern & Postmodern Aesthetics.' *Daedalus* 134, no. 4 (2005): 191–207.
Egoff, Sheila. *The Republic of Childhood*. Toronto: Oxford University Press, 1967.
Eisner, Elliot. *The Educational Imagination: On Design and Evaluation of School Programs*. New York: Macmillan, 1999.
Ellis, Sarah. 'News from the North.' *Horn Book Magazine*, Sept.–Oct. 1988, 663–4.
Entwistle, Joanne. *The Fashioned Body: Fashion, Dress and Modern Social Theory*. Cambridge: Polity Press, 2000.
Epperly, Elizabeth Rollins. *The Fragrance of Sweet-Grass: L.M. Montgomery's Heroines and the Pursuit of Romance*. Toronto: University of Toronto Press, 1992.
– *Imagining Anne: The Island Scrapbooks of L.M. Montgomery*. Toronto: Penguin Canada, 2008.
– *Through Lover's Lane: L.M. Montgomery's Photography and Visual Imagination*. Toronto: University of Toronto Press, 2007.

– curator. *Imagining Anne: Celebrating the Creation and Centenary of L.M. Montgomery's Classic, Anne of Green Gables*. Confederation Centre of the Arts, Charlottetown, June to Oct. 2008.

Ewing, Juliana Horatia. *Jackanapes*. Illus. Randolph Caldecott. London: S.P.C.K., 1883.

The Falcon Takes Over. Dir. Irving Reis. 65 min. RKO Radio Pictures, 1942.

Fall and Winter Catalogue, 1903–1904. Toronto: T. Eaton Company, n.d.

Fall and Winter Catalogue, 1907–1908. Toronto: T. Eaton Company, n.d.

Fawcett, Clare, and Patricia Cormack. 'Guarding Authenticity at Literary Tourism Sites.' *Annals of Tourism Research* 28, no. 3 (2001): 686–704.

Fiamengo, Janice. '"… the refuge of my sick spirit …": L.M. Montgomery and the Shadows of Depression.' In Gammel, *The Intimate Life*, 170–86.

– 'Towards a Theory of the Popular Landscape in *Anne of Green Gables*.' In Gammel, *Making Avonlea*, 225–37.

Fiftieth Annual Report for the Year 1933. Toronto: Toronto Public Library, 1934.

Finley, Martha. *Elsie Dinsmore*. New York: Dodd, Mead, and Company, 1867.

Fiske, John. *Understanding Popular Culture*. London: Routledge, 1989.

'Fitness and Fashion.' *The Magazine of Art* 5 (1882): 339.

Foster, Shirley, and Judy Simons. *What Katy Read: Feminist Re-readings of 'Classic' Stories for Girls*. Iowa City: University of Iowa Press, 1995.

Foucault, Michel. *Discipline and Punish: The Birth of the Prison*. New York: Pantheon, 1977.

– 'What Is an Author?' Trans. Josué V. Harari. In *Aesthetics, Method and Epistemology*, ed. James D. Faubion, vol. 2 of *Essential Works of Foucault 1954–1984*, 205–22. New York: The New Press, 1998.

Frever, Trinna S. 'Anne Shirley, Storyteller: Orality and *Anne of Green Gables*.' *Studies in Canadian Literature / Études en littérature canadienne* 30, no. 2 (2005): 115–41.

– 'Vaguely Familiar: Cinematic Intertextuality in Kevin Sullivan's *Anne of Avonlea*.' *Canadian Children's Literature / Littérature canadienne pour la jeunesse* 91–2 (1998): 36–52.

Fryatt, Norma R. 'A Second Look: Emily of New Moon.' *Horn Book Magazine*, Mar.–Apr. 1986, 174–5.

Frye, Northrop. *The Bush Garden: Essays on the Canadian Imagination*. Toronto: House of Anansi Press, 1971.

Fu, Jun. 'Adoption and Transformation of Cultural Heterogeneity: Analysis of Phenomenal Success of Anne in Japan.' *Foreign Literature Studies* 4 (2001): 133–6.

Gallant, Doug. 'Copps Presses Flesh with Island Voters.' *Charlottetown Guardian*, 29 May 1997, A1.

Gammel, Irene. *Looking for Anne: How Lucy Maud Montgomery Dreamed Up a Literary Classic*. Toronto: Key Porter Books, 2010 [2008].

– 'Making Avonlea: An Introduction.' In Gammel, *Making Avonlea*, 3–13.

– curator. *Anne of Green Gables: A Literary Icon at 100*. Installations at Spadina Museum: Historic House and Gardens, City of Toronto, 19 Apr. to 2 Sept. 2008; Irving K. Barber Learning Centre, University of British Columbia, and Humanities and Social Sciences Federation of Canada, 31 May to 8 June 2008; Hamilton Galleria, University of Winnipeg, 9 Sept. to 31 Oct. 2008; and Parks Canada Green Gables Heritage Site, Cavendish, P.E.I., 15 May to 30 Nov. 2008.

– ed. *The Intimate Life of L.M. Montgomery*. Toronto: University of Toronto Press, 2005.

– ed. *Making Avonlea: L.M. Montgomery and Popular Culture*. Toronto: University of Toronto Press, 2002.

Gammel, Irene, and Ann Dutton. 'Disciplining Development: L.M. Montgomery and Early Schooling.' In Gammel and Epperly, *L.M. Montgomery*, 106–19.

Gammel, Irene, and Elizabeth Epperly. 'L.M. Montgomery and the Shaping of Canadian Culture.' Introduction to Gammel and Epperly, *L.M. Montgomery*, 3–13.

– eds. *L.M. Montgomery and Canadian Culture*. Toronto: University of Toronto Press, 1999.

Geissler, Shawna, and Lynn A. Cecil. 'Lucy Maud Montgomery's Anglocentric Island: (I) Anne as Colonizer (II) Commodification and False Memories.' *CREArTA* 5 (2005): 196–208.

'The Gentle Island.' Tourist map. Government of Prince Edward Island, 2005.

Gerson, Carole. '*Anne of Green Gables* Goes to University: L.M. Montgomery and Academic Culture.' In Gammel, *Making Avonlea*, 17–31.

– 'Anne's Anniversary.' *Canadian Children's Literature / Littérature canadienne pour la jeunesse* 34, no. 2 (2008): 98–111.

– '"Dragged at Anne's Chariot Wheels": The Triangle of Author, Publisher, and Fictional Character.' In Gammel and Epperly, *L.M. Montgomery*, 49–63.

– Introduction to Saunders, *Tilda Jane*, v–xiv.

Ghan, Linda. 'Snapshots – Me and Anne: An Album.' *Canadian Children's Literature / Littérature canadienne pour la jeunesse* 91–2 (1998): 78–82.

Gilbert, David, and Christopher Breward, eds. *Fashion's World Cities*. Oxford: Berg, 2006.

Gillen, Mollie. *The Wheel of Things: A Biography of L.M. Montgomery*. Don Mills, ON: Fitzhenry & Whiteside, 1975.

Gilligan, Carol. *In a Different Voice: Psychological Theory and Women's Development*. Cambridge: Harvard University Press, 1982.

Gladwell, Malcolm. *The Tipping Point: How Little Things Can Make a Big Difference*. Boston: Little, Brown, 2000.

Glass, Loren. *Authors Inc.: Literary Celebrity in the Modern United States, 1880–1980*. New York: New York University Press, 2004.

Goddard, Peter. 'The Genesis of Anne.' *Toronto Star*, 19 Apr. 2008, E15.

Gone with the Wind. Dir. Victor Fleming. 226 min. Selznick International Pictures, 1939.

Good Bye Lenin! Dir. Wolfgang Becker. 121 min. Sony Pictures Classics, 2003.

Goodrum, Alison. *The National Fabric: Fashion, Britishness, Globalization*. Oxford: Berg, 2005.

Gordon, Wendy, and Sally Ford-Hutchinson. 'Brains and Brands: Rethinking the Consumer.' *Admap*, Jan. 2002, 47–50.

Grahame, Kenneth. *The Wind in the Willows*. London: Methuen, 1908.

'Green Gables House Damaged in Fire.' *Globe and Mail*, 24 May 1997, C2.

Grenby, M.O. Introduction to *Popular Children's Literature in Britain*, ed. Julia Briggs, Dennis Butts, and M.O. Grenby, 1–20. Aldershot: Ashgate, 2008.

Grimes, Sara. 'Kids' Ad Play: Regulating Children's Advergames in the Converging Media Context.' *International Journal of Communications Law and Policy* 8, no. 12 (2008): 162–78.

Gubar, Marah. '"Where Is the Boy?" The Pleasures of Postponement in the *Anne of Green Gables* Series.' *Lion and the Unicorn* 25, no. 1 (2001): 47–69.

Gunelius, Susan. *Harry Potter: The Story of a Global Business Phenomenon*. Houndmills: Palgrave Macmillan, 2008.

Hammill, Faye. *Literary Culture and Female Authorship in Canada*. Amsterdam: Rodopi, 2003.

– '"A New and Exceedingly Brilliant Star": L.M. Montgomery, *Anne of Green Gables*, and Mary Miles Minter.' *Modern Language Review* 101, no. 3 (2006): 652–70.

– *Women, Celebrity, and Literary Culture between the Wars*. Austin: University of Texas Press, 2007.

Hanley, Glenna. 'Following Her Heart.' *Daily Gleaner*, 23 Aug. 2008, E1.

Harbour, J.L. 'Lucy Ann.' *Zion's Herald*, 29 July 1903, 956–7.

– '"Saddeners of Life."' *Zion's Herald*, 7 Sept. 1904, 1137.

Hark, Ina Rae. 'Movies and the 1930s.' Introduction to *American Cinema of the 1930s: Themes and Variations*, ed. Ina Rae Hark, 1–24. New Brunswick, NJ: Rutgers University Press, 2007.

Haste, Helen, and Salie Abrahams. 'Morality, Culture and the Dialogic Self:

Taking Cultural Pluralism Seriously.' *Journal of Moral Education* 37, no. 3 (2008): 377–94.

Haweis, Eliza. *The Art of Beauty and the Art of Dress.* New York: Garland Publishing, 1978 [1878–1879].

Hawthorne, Nathaniel. *The House of Seven Gables.* New York: Penguin Books, 1981 [1851].

Hayeri Yazdi, Leili. 'An Overview of Active Iranian Writers of Children's and Young Adult Literature.' Paper presented at the Children's Literature Association conference, Los Angeles, 8 June 2006.

Held, Virginia. *Feminist Morality: Transforming Culture, Society, and Politics.* Chicago: University of Chicago Press, 1993.

'A Heroine from an Asylum.' *New York Times Book Review*, 18 July 1908, 404.

Hersey, Eleanor. '"It's All Mine": The Modern Woman in Sullivan's *Anne of Green Gables* Films.' In Gammel, *Making Avonlea*, 131–44.

– '"Tennyson Would Never Approve": Reading and Performance in Kevin Sullivan's *Anne of Green Gables.*' *Canadian Children's Literature / Littérature canadienne pour la jeunesse* 105–6 (2002): 48–67.

Hilder, Monika B. '"That Unholy Tendency to Laughter": L.M. Montgomery's Iconoclastic Affirmation of Faith in *Anne of Green Gables.*' *Canadian Children's Literature / Littérature canadienne pour la jeunesse* 113–14 (2004): 34–55.

Hodgson, Fred T. *Common Sense Stair-Building and Hand-Railing.* New York: Radford, 1902.

Hoffman, Eva. *Lost in Translation: A Life in a New Language.* New York: Penguin Books, 1989.

Hoffman, Heinrich. *Struwwelpeter, or, Merry Rhymes and Funny Pictures.* London: Blackie & Son, 1903 [1848].

Howey, Ann F. '"She look'd down to Camelot": Anne Shirley, Sullivan, and the Lady of Shalott.' In Gammel, *Making Avonlea*, 160–73.

Hu, Huifeng. 'Thoughts on Anne of Green Gables.' *Literature Newspaper*, 18 Aug. 2007, 4th section.

Hubler, Angela E. 'Can Anne Shirley Help "Revive Ophelia"? Listening to Girl Readers.' In *Delinquents and Debutantes: Twentieth-Century American Girls' Cultures*, ed. Sherrie A. Inness, 266–84. New York: New York University Press, 1998.

Huffman, Louise. 'Canadian Titles of Value in the Children's Room.' *Ontario Library Review*, Feb. 1923, 76–9.

Hughes, Clair. *Dressed in Fiction.* Oxford: Berg, 2005.

Hughes, Thomas. *Tom Brown's Schooldays.* London: Macmillan, 1857.

Hunter, Bernice Thurman. 'Inspirations.' *Canadian Children's Literature / Littérature canadienne pour la jeunesse* 84 (1996): 87–9.

Hutton, Jack, and Linda Jackson-Hutton. 'Images of Anne throughout the Years.' In *The Lucy Maud Montgomery Album*, comp. Kevin McCabe, 200–5. Toronto: Fitzhenry & Whiteside, 1999.

– 'Take Your Girlie to the Movies.' Performance at L.M. Montgomery, Anne of Green Gables and the Idea of Classic, Charlottetown, 26 June 2008.

Inoue, Miyako. 'Gender, Language and Modernity: Toward an Effective History of Japanese Women's Language.' *American Ethnologist* 29, no. 2 (2002): 392–422.

Ion, Hamish. 'The Canadian Protestant Missionary Movement in Japan, 1873–1951.' In *Contradictory Impulses: Canada and Japan in the Twentieth Century*, ed. Greg Donaghy and Patricia E. Roy, 10–28. Vancouver: UBC Press, 2008.

Ishihara, Tsuyoshi. *Mark Twain in Japan: The Cultural Reception of an American Icon*. Columbia: University of Missouri Press, 2005.

'I've Found LOVE.' *Family Herald and Weekly Star*, 30 Mar. 1938, 35.

Jackson, Philip. *Life in Classrooms*. New York: Holt, Rinehart & Winston, 1968.

Jameson, Fredric. *Postmodernism, or, the Cultural Logic of Late Capitalism*. Durham: Duke University Press, 1991.

Jamison, Kay Redfield. *Exuberance: The Passion for Life*. New York: Alfred A. Knopf, 2006.

Jauss, Hans Robert. *Toward an Aesthetic of Reception*. Trans. Timothy Bahti. Minneapolis: University of Minnesota Press, 1982.

Jewell, Richard B. *The Golden Age of Cinema: Hollywood, 1929–1945*. Malden, MA: Blackwell Publishing, 2007.

Jewell, Richard B., with Vernon Harbin. *The RKO Story*. New York: Arlington House, 1982.

Johnson, W.B., C. Hillman, and W.L. Johnson. 'Toward Guidelines for the Development, Evaluation, and Utilization of Christian Self-Help Materials.' *Journal of Psychology and Theology* 25, no. 3 (1997): 341–53.

Johnston, Julie. *Adam and Eve and Pinch-Me*. Toronto: Tundra Books, 2003 [1994].

Johnston, Sheila M.F. *Buckskin & Broadcloth: A Celebration of E. Pauline Johnson – Tekahionwake 1861–1913*. Toronto: Natural Heritage / Natural History, 1997.

Jones, Raymond E., and Jon C. Stott. *Canadian Children's Books: A Critical Guide to Authors and Illustrators*. Don Mills: Oxford University Press, 2000.

Karr, Clarence. 'Addicted to Reading: L.M. Montgomery and the Value of Reading.' *Canadian Children's Literature / Littérature canadienne pour la jeunesse* 113–14 (2004): 17–33.

– *Authors and Audiences: Popular Canadian Fiction in the Early Twentieth Century*. Montreal: McGill-Queen's University Press, 2000.

Katsura, Yuko. 'Red-Haired Anne in Japan.' *Canadian Children's Literature / Littérature canadienne pour la jeunesse* 34 (1984): 57–60.

Kiger, Gary. Introduction to *Disability Studies: Definitions and Diversity*, ed. Gary Kiger, Stephen C. Hey, and J. Gary Linn, 1–4. Salem, OR: Society for Disability Studies and Willamette University, 1994.

Kingsley, Charles. 'A Farewell.' 1858. In *The Home Book of Verse, American and English, 1580–1920*, selected by Burton Egbert Stevenson, 6th ed., 125. New York: Henry Holt & Company, 1926.

Kitch, Carolyn. *The Girl on the Magazine Cover: The Origins of Visual Stereotypes in American Mass Media*. Chapel Hill: University of North Carolina Press, 2001.

Kobayashi, Yoshie. *A Path toward Gender Equality: State Feminism in Japan*. New York: Routledge, 2004.

Koikari, Mire. *Pedagogy of Democracy: Feminism and the Cold War in the U.S. Occupation of Japan*. Philadelphia: Temple University Press, 2008.

Korda, Michael. *Making the List: A Cultural History of the American Bestseller, 1909–1999*. New York: Barnes & Noble, 2001.

Kornfeld, Eve, and Susan Jackson. 'The Female *Bildungsroman* in Nineteenth-Century America: Parameters of a Vision.' In Reimer, *Such a Simple Little Tale*, 139–52.

Kotsopoulos, Patsy Aspasia. 'Avonlea as Main Street USA? Genre, Adaptation, and the Making of a Borderless Romance.' *Essays on Canadian Writing* 76 (2002): 170–94.

Lash, Joseph P. *Helen and Teacher: The Story of Helen Keller and Anne Sullivan Macy*. Reading, MA: Addison-Wesley, 1997.

Lasky, Betty. *RKO: The Biggest Little Major of Them All*. Englewood Cliffs, NJ: Prentice-Hall, 1984.

Laurence, Margaret. 'Books that Mattered to Me.' In *Margaret Laurence: An Appreciation*, ed. Christl Verduyn, 239–49. Peterborough: Broadview Press, 1988.

Lawson, Mary. *Crow Lake*. Toronto: Vintage Canada, 2002.

Lears, T.J. Jackson. *No Place of Grace: Antimodernism and the Transformation of American Culture, 1880–1920*. New York: Pantheon Books, 1981.

Lefebvre, Benjamin. 'L.M. Montgomery: An Annotated Filmography.' *Canadian Children's Literature / Littérature canadienne pour la jeunesse* 99 (2000): 43–73.

– '*Road to Avonlea*: A Co-Production of the Disney Corporation.' In Gammel, *Making Avonlea*, 174–85.

– '"A Small World after All": L.M. Montgomery's Imagined Avonlea as Virtual Landscape.' In *The International Handbook of Virtual Learning Environments*, ed. Joel Weiss et al., 1121–40. Dordrecht: Springer, 2006.

- 'Stand by Your Man: Adapting L.M. Montgomery's *Anne of Green Gables*.' *Essays on Canadian Writing* 76 (2002): 149–69.
- '"That Abominable War!" *The Blythes Are Quoted* and Thoughts on L.M. Montgomery's Late Style.' In Mitchell, *Storm and Dissonance*, 109–30.
- ed. 'Reassessments of L.M. Montgomery.' Special issue, *Canadian Children's Literature / Littérature canadienne pour la jeunesse* 113–14 (2004).

Li, Xintian. *Shining Red Star*. Beijing: People's Literature Press, 1972.

'Library Notes and News.' *Ontario Library Review*, Nov. 1923, 37–41.

Lipson, Eden Ross, ed. *The New York Times Parent's Guide to the Best Books for Children*. 3rd ed. New York: Three Rivers Press, 2000.

Little, Jean. 'But What about Jane?' *Canadian Children's Literature* 1, no. 3 (1975): 77–81.

Ljunggren, David. 'New Exhibit Reveals "Anne of Green Gables" Secrets.' *Reuters*, 3 June 2008.

'L.M. Montgomery and Popular Culture.' Special issue, *Canadian Children's Literature / Littérature canadienne pour la jeunesse* 91–2 (1998).

'L.M. Montgomery and Popular Culture II.' Special issue, *Canadian Children's Literature / Littérature canadienne pour la jeunesse* 99 (2000).

Luo, Guangbin. *Hongyan*. Beijing: China Youth Publisher, 1961.

Lynes, Jeanette. 'Consumable Avonlea: The Commodification of the Green Gables Mythology.' In Gammel, *Making Avonlea*, 268–79.

MacDonald, Ann-Marie. *Fall on Your Knees*. Toronto: Vintage Canada, 1997 [1996].

MacLaren, Eli. 'The Magnification of Ralph Connor: *Black Rock* and the North American Copyright Divide.' *Papers of the Bibliographical Society of America* 101, no. 4 (2007): 507–31.

MacLellan, Carrie. 'Snapshot: Listening to the Music in *Anne of Green Gables: The Musical*.' In Gammel, *Making Avonlea*, 216–22.

MacMurchy, Helen. *The Almosts: A Study of the Feeble-Minded*. Boston: Houghton Mifflin, 1920.

MacMurchy, Marjorie. *The Child's House: A Comedy of Vanessa from the Age of Eight or Thereabouts until She Had Climbed the Steps as Far as Thirteen*. London: Macmillan, 1923.

Maitland, M.A. 'Charity Ann: Founded on Facts.' *Godey's Lady's Book*, Jan. 1892, 70–3.

Malbin, Diane. *Trying Differently but Not Harder*. 2nd ed. Portland: FASCETS, 2002.

- *Fetal Alcohol Spectrum Disorders: A Collection of Information for Parents and Professionals*. 2nd ed. Portland: FASCETS, 2007.

Mayo, Marlene J. 'Literary Reorientation in Occupied Japan: Incidents of Civil

Censorship.' In *Legacies and Ambiguities: Postwar Fiction and Culture in West Germany and Japan,* ed. Ernestine Schlant and J. Thomas Rimer, 135–61. Baltimore: The Johns Hopkins University Press, 1991.

McClung, Nellie L. *Sowing Seeds in Danny.* Toronto: William Briggs, 1908.

McGrath, Leslie Anne. 'Service to Children in the Toronto Public Library: A Case Study, 1912–1949.' Ph.D. diss., University of Toronto, 2005.

McKay, Ian. *The Quest of the Folk: Antimodernism and Cultural Selection in Twentieth-Century Nova Scotia.* Montreal: McGill-Queen's University Press, 1994.

McKinney, Victoria, Linda La Fever, and Jocie DeVries. *Nurture: The Essence of Intervention for Individuals with Fetal Alcohol Syndrome.* Lynnwood, WA: FAS Family Resource Institute, 2005.

McLuhan, Herbert Marshall. *The Mechanical Bride: Folklore of Industrial Man.* New York: Vanguard Press, 1951.

McMaster, Juliet. 'Taking Control: Hair Red, Black, Gold, and Nut-Brown.' In Gammel, *Making Avonlea,* 58–71.

McQuillan, Julia, and Julie Pfeiffer. 'Why Anne Makes Us Dizzy: Reading *Anne of Green Gables* from a Gender Perspective.' *Mosaic* 34, no. 2 (2001): 17–32.

McRuer, Robert. *Crip Theory: Cultural Signs of Queerness and Disability.* New York: New York University Press, 2006.

Milne, A.A. *Winnie-the-Pooh.* New York: E.P. Dutton, 1926.

Mitchell, Jean, ed. *Storm and Dissonance: L.M. Montgomery and Conflict.* Newcastle: Cambridge Scholars Publishing, 2008.

Monod, David. *Store Wars: Shopkeepers and the Culture of Mass Marketing, 1890–1939.* Toronto: University of Toronto Press, 1996.

Montgomery, L.M. *After Green Gables: L.M. Montgomery's Letters to Ephraim Weber, 1916–1941.* Ed. Hildi Froese Tiessen and Paul Gerard Tiessen. Toronto: University of Toronto Press, 2006.

– *The Alpine Path: The Story of My Career.* Toronto: Fitzhenry & Whiteside, 1974.

– *Anne auf Green Gables* [Anne of Green Gables]. Trans. Irmela Erckenbrecht. Bindlach: Loewe, 1986. German translation of *Anne of Green Gables.*

– *Anne of Avonlea.* Toronto: Seal Books, 1996 [1909].

– *Anne of Green Gables.* New Canadian Library. Toronto: McClelland & Stewart, 1992 [1908].

– *Anne of Green Gables.* Ed. Cecily Devereux. Peterborough: Broadview Editions, 2004 [1908].

– *Anne of Green Gables.* Ed. Mary Henley Rubio and Elizabeth Waterston. New York: W.W. Norton, 2007 [1908].

– *Anne of the Island*. Toronto: Seal Books, 1996 [1915].
– *Anne of Windy Poplars*. Toronto: Seal Books, 1996 [1936].
– *Anne på Grönkulla* [Anne of Green Hills]. Trans. Karin Lidforss Jensen. Lund: C.W.K. Gleerups, 1909. Swedish translation of *Anne of Green Gables*.
– *Anne's House of Dreams*. Toronto: Seal Books, 1996 [1917].
– *The Annotated Anne of Green Gables*. Ed. Wendy E. Barry, Margaret Anne Doody, and Mary E. Doody Jones. New York: Oxford University Press, 1997.
– *The Blythes Are Quoted*. Ed. Benjamin Lefebvre. Toronto: Viking Canada, 2009.
– 'Business and Lawsuit Correspondence including Much on Movie Contracts, 1928–1935.' L.M. Montgomery Collection, University of Guelph Library, XZ1 MS A098011.
– *Chronicles of Avonlea*. Toronto: Seal Books, 1987 [1912].
– *Further Chronicles of Avonlea*. New York: Bantam Books, 1993 [1920].
– *The Golden Road*. Toronto: Seal Books, 1987 [1913].
– *The Green Gables Letters: From L.M. Montgomery to Ephraim Weber, 1905–1909*. Ed. Wilfrid Eggleston. Ottawa: Borealis Press, 1981 [1960].
– 'Is This My Anne.' *Chatelaine*, Jan. 1935, 18, 22.
– *Jane of Lantern Hill*. Toronto: Seal Books, 1988 [1937].
– *Kilmeny of the Orchard*. Toronto: Seal Books, 1987 [1910].
– 'L.M. Montgomery.' In *The Junior Book of Authors*, ed. Stanley J. Kunitz and Howard Haycraft, 261–2. New York: The H.W. Wilson Company, 1934.
– *Magic for Marigold*. Toronto: Seal Books, 1988 [1929].
– *My Dear Mr M: Letters to G.B. MacMillan from L.M. Montgomery*. Ed. Francis W.P. Bolger and Elizabeth R. Epperly. Toronto: Oxford University Press, 1992 [1980].
– 'Polly Patterson's Autograph Square.' *Zion's Herald*, 3 Feb. 1904, 146.
– *Rainbow Valley*. Toronto: Seal Books, 1996 [1919].
– *Rilla of Ingleside*. Toronto: Seal Books, 1996 [1921].
– *The Selected Journals of L.M. Montgomery*, vol. 1, *1889–1910*; vol. 2, *1910–1921*; vol. 3, *1921–1929*; vol. 4, *1929–1935*; vol. 5, *1935–1942*. Ed. Mary Rubio and Elizabeth Waterston. Toronto: Oxford University Press, 1985, 1987, 1992, 1998, 2004.
– *The Story Girl*. Toronto: Seal Books, 1987 [1911].
– سبز خانه در دختری [The Girl in the Green House]. Tehran: Soroosh Publishing House, 1996. Farsi translation of *Anne of Green Gables*.
– گـبـلز گـرین در آنی [Anni in Green Gables]. Tehran: Noghteh Publishing House, 1996. Farsi translation of *Anne of Green Gables*.
– سبز رویای با آنی [Anni of Green Dreams]. Tehran: Peykan Publishing, 1997. Farsi translation of *Anne of Green Gables*.

– آنی شرلی با موهای قرمز [Anni Shirly with Red Hair]. Tehran: Rahyaft Publishing, 2000. Farsi translation of *Anne of Green Gables*.

– قصه ها ی جزیره [The Stories of the Island]. Tehran: Namira Publishing, 2000. Farsi translation of *Anne of Green Gables*.

– آنی ، دختری از گرین گیبلز [Anni, A Girl from Green Gables]. Tehran: Golban Publishing, 2001. Farsi translation of *Anne of Green Gables*.

– آنی با موهای قرمز [Anni with Red Hair]. Tehran: Banafsheh Books, 2003. Farsi translation of *Anne of Green Gables*.

– آنی شرلی در گرین گیبلز کتاب اول [Anni Shirley in Green Gables, Book 1]. Trans. Sara Ghadyani. Tehran: Ghadyani Publishing House, 2007 [1997].

– 《绿山墙的安妮》 [Anne of Green Gables]. Trans. Ainong Ma. Beijing: People's Literature Press, 1999. Chinese translation of *Anne of Green Gables*.

– 《绿山墙的安妮》 [Anne of Green Gables]. Trans. Ainong Ma. Nanjing: Yilin Publisher, 2001. Chinese translation of *Anne of Green Gables*.

– 《绿山墙的安妮》 [Anne of Green Gables]. Trans. Ainong Ma. Hangzhou: Zhejiang Art and Literature Press under Zhejiang Publishing United Group Company, 2003. Chinese translation of *Anne of Green Gables*.

– 《绿山墙的安妮》 [Anne of Green Gables]. Trans. Shanshan Ren. Beijing: Huawen Press, 2005. Chinese translation of *Anne of Green Gables*.

– 《绿山墙的安妮》 [Anne of Green Gables]. Trans. Ainong Ma. Beijing: China Children's Press, 2006. Chinese translation of *Anne of Green Gables*.

– 《少女安妮》 [Teenage Girl: Anne]. Trans. Ainong Ma. Hangzhou: Zhejiang Art and Literature Press, 2003. Chinese translation of *Anne of Avonlea*.

– 《女大学生安妮》 [College Girl Student: Anne]. Trans. Huo Li. Hangzhou: Zhejiang Art and Literature Press, 2003. Chinese translation of *Anne of the Island*.

– 《风吹白杨的安妮》 [Anne of Windy Poplars]. Trans. Jinghai Shi. Hangzhou: Zhejiang Art and Literature Press, 2002. Chinese translation of *Anne of Windy Poplars*.

– 《新月的艾米莉》 [Emily of New Moon]. Trans. Min Wen. Hangzhou: Zhejiang Art and Literature Press, 2005. Chinese translation of *Emily of New Moon*.

– 《艾米莉的诗样年华》 [Youthful Days of Emily]. Trans. Xiadan Wang. Hangzhou: Zhejiang Art and Literature Press, 2005. Chinese translation of *Emily Climbs*.

– 《艾米莉之恋》 [Love of Emily]. Trans. Jinghai Shi. Hangzhou: Zhejiang Art and Literature Press, 2005. Chinese translation of *Emily's Quest*.

Moran, Joe. *Star Authors: Literary Celebrity in America*. London: Pluto Press, 2000.

Moran, Mary Jeanette. 'Telling Relationships: Feminist Narrative Ethics in the Nineteenth-Century British Novel.' Ph.D. diss., University of Iowa, 2006.

Morse, Barbara A. 'Information Processing: Identifying the Behavioral Disorders of Fetal Alcohol Syndrome.' In *Fantastic Antone Succeeds! Experiences in Educating Children with Fetal Alcohol Syndrome*, ed. Judith Kleinfeld and Siobhan Wescott, 23–36. Fairbanks: University of Alaska Press, 1993.

Moulson, Margaret C., Nathan A. Fox, Charles H. Zeanah, and Charles A. Nelson. 'Early Adverse Experiences and the Neurobiology of Facial Emotion Processing.' *Developmental Psychology* 45 (2009): 17–30.

Munro, Alice. Afterword to *Emily of New Moon*, by L.M. Montgomery, 357–61. New Canadian Library. Toronto: McClelland & Stewart, 1989.

Murder, My Sweet. Dir. Edward Dmytryk. 94 min. RKO Radio Pictures, 1945.

Neibaur, James L. *The RKO Features: A Complete Filmography of the Feature Films Released or Produced by RKO Radio Pictures, 1929–1960.* Jefferson, NC: McFarland & Company, 1994.

Nell, Victor. *Lost in a Book: The Psychology of Reading for Pleasure.* New Haven: Yale University Press, 1988.

Nelson, Claudia. *Boys Will Be Girls: The Feminine Ethic and British Children's Fiction, 1857–1917.* New Brunswick, NJ: Rutgers University Press, 1991.

Newton, Adam Zachary. *Narrative Ethics.* Cambridge: Harvard University Press, 1995.

Noddings, Nel. *Caring: A Feminine Approach to Ethics and Moral Education.* Berkeley: University of California Press, 1984.

Nodelman, Perry. 'Progressive Utopia: Or, How to Grow Up without Growing Up.' In Reimer, *Such a Simple Little Tale*, 29–38.

Nodelman, Perry, and Mavis Reimer. *The Pleasures of Children's Literature.* 3rd ed. Boston: Allyn and Bacon, 2003.

Nolan, Jason, Jeff Lawrence, and Yuka Kajihara. 'Montgomery's Island in the Net: Metaphor and Community on the Kindred Spirits E-mail List.' *Canadian Children's Literature / Littérature canadienne pour la jeunesse* 91–2 (1998): 64–77.

Nolan, Jason, Steve Mann, and Barry Wellman. 'Sousveillance: Wearable and Digital Tools in Surveilled Environments.' In *Small Tech: The Culture of Digital Tools*, ed. Byron Hawk, David Rieder, and Ollie Oviedo, 179–96. Minnesota: University of Minnesota Press, 2008.

Nolan, Jason, and Joel Weiss. 'Learning in Cyberspace: An Educational View of Virtual Community.' In *Building Virtual Communities: Learning and Change in Cyberspace*, ed. Ann K. Renninger and Wes Shumar, 293–320. Cambridge: Cambridge University Press, 2002.

Ochi, Hiromi. 'What Did She Read? The Cultural Occupation of Post-War Japan and Translated Girls' Literature.' *F-GENS Journal* 5 (2006): 359–63.

Osler, Ruth, Lorraine Vincente, and Marian Scott, eds. *Favourite Books for Boys and Girls, 1912–1987*. Toronto: Toronto Public Library, 1987.

Ouzounian, Richard, and Marek Norman. *Emily*. Toronto: McArthur & Company, 2000.

Page, P.K. Afterword to *Emily's Quest*, by L.M. Montgomery, 237–42. New Canadian Library. Toronto: McClelland & Stewart, 1989.

Palmer, Alexandra. *Couture and Commerce: The Transatlantic Fashion Trade in the 1950s*. Vancouver: UBC Press, 2001.

– ed. *Fashion: A Canadian Perspective*. Toronto: University of Toronto Press, 2004.

Parenting Children Affected by Fetal Alcohol Syndrome: A Guide for Daily Living. Vancouver: B.C. Ministry for Children and Families, 1999.

Parish, James Robert. *The RKO Gals*. New Rochelle, NY: Arlington House Publishers, 1974.

Patmore, Coventry. *The Angel in the House*. London: Macmillan, 1863 [1858].

Phelan, James. *Living to Tell about It: A Rhetoric and Ethics of Character Narration*. Ithaca: Cornell University Press, 2005.

Philip, M. NourbeSe. *A Genealogy of Resistance and Other Essays*. Toronto: Mercury Press, 1997.

– *Harriet's Daughter*. Toronto: Women's Press, 1988.

Piaget, Jean. *The Language and Thought of a Child*. New York: Routledge, 1926.

Picken, Mary Brooks. *A Dictionary of Costume and Fashion*. Mineola: Dover, 1999.

Pike, E. Holly. 'Mass Marketing, Popular Culture, and the Canadian Celebrity Author.' In Gammel, *Making Avonlea*, 238–51.

Pitt, James. *Instructions in Etiquette*. Manchester: published by the author, ca. 1830.

Poe, K.L. 'The Whole of the Moon: L.M. Montgomery's *Anne of Green Gables* Series.' In *Nancy Drew and Company: Culture, Gender, and Girls' Series*, ed. Sherrie A. Inness, 15–35. Bowling Green: Bowling Green State University Popular Press, 1997.

– 'Who's Got the Power? Montgomery, Sullivan, and the Unsuspecting Viewer.' In Gammel, *Making Avonlea*, 145–59.

Porter, Eleanor H. *Pollyanna*. London: Puffin Classics, 1994 [1913].

Potter, Beatrix. *The Pie and the Patty-Pan*. London: Frederick Warne, 1905.

Prouty, Olive Higgins. *Stella Dallas*. New York: Perennial Library, 1990 [1923].

Pullman, Philip. *The Subtle Knife*. His Dark Materials 2. London: Scholastic UK, 1997.

Reimer, Mavis. 'Homing and Unhoming: The Ideological Work of Canadian Children's Literature.' In Reimer, *Home Words*, 1–25.

– ed. *Home Words: Discourses of Children's Literature in Canada*. Waterloo: Wilfrid Laurier University Press, 2008.

– ed. *Such a Simple Little Tale: Critical Responses to L.M. Montgomery's 'Anne of Green Gables.'* Metuchen: Children's Literature Association / Scarecrow Press, 1992.

Richards, Frank. *The Making of Harry Wharton*. London: Howard Baker, 1975.

Robertson, Catherine C., et al., eds. *Books for Youth: A Guide for Teen-Age Readers*. 3rd ed. Toronto: Ryerson Press, 1966.

Robinson, Laura M. 'Big Gay Anne.' In *Canadian Studies: An Introductory Reader*, ed. Donald Wright, 377–85. Dubuque: Kendall/Hunt, 2004.

– '"A Born Canadian": The Bonds of Communal Identity in *Anne of Green Gables* and *A Tangled Web*.' In Gammel and Epperly, *L.M. Montgomery*, 19–30.

– 'Bosom Friends: Lesbian Desire in L.M. Montgomery's Anne Books.' *Canadian Literature* 180 (2004): 12–28.

– '"Outrageously Sexual' Anne": The Media and Montgomery.' In Mitchell, *Storm and Dissonance*, 311–27.

– 'Remodeling *An Old-Fashioned Girl*: Troubling Girlhood in Ann-Marie MacDonald's *Fall on Your Knees*.' *Canadian Literature* 186 (2005): 30–45.

Ross, Catherine Sheldrick. 'Calling Back the Ghost of the Old-Time Heroine: Duncan, Montgomery, Atwood, Laurence, and Munro.' In Reimer, *Such a Simple Little Tale*, 39–55.

– 'Readers Reading L.M. Montgomery.' In Rubio, *Harvesting Thistles*, 23–35.

Rothwell, Erica. 'Knitting Up the World: L.M. Montgomery and Maternal Feminism in Canada.' In Gammel and Epperly, *L.M. Montgomery*, 133–44.

Rubin, Jay. 'From Wholesomeness to Decadence: The Censorship of Literature under the Allied Occupation.' *Journal of Japanese Studies* 11, no. 1 (1985): 71–103.

Rubio, Mary Henley. '*Anne of Green Gables*: The Architect of Adolescence.' In Reimer, *Such a Simple Little Tale*, 65–82.

– '"A Dusting Off": An Anecdotal Account of Editing the L.M. Montgomery Journals.' In *Working in Women's Archives: Researching Women's Private Literature and Archival Documents*, ed. Helen M. Buss and Marlene Kadar, 51–78. Waterloo: Wilfrid Laurier University Press, 2001.

– 'Harvesting Thistles in Montgomery's Textual Garden.' Introduction to Rubio, *Harvesting Thistles*, 1–13.

– 'L.M. Montgomery: Scottish-Presbyterian Agency in Canadian Culture.' In Gammel and Epperly, *L.M. Montgomery*, 89–105.

– *Lucy Maud Montgomery: The Gift of Wings*. Toronto: Doubleday Canada, 2008.
– 'Subverting the Trite: L.M. Montgomery's "Room of Her Own."' *Canadian Children's Literature / Littérature canadienne pour la jeunesse* 65 (1992): 6–39.
– ed. *Harvesting Thistles: The Textual Garden of L.M. Montgomery*. Guelph: Canadian Children's Press, 1994.
Said, Edward. *The World, the Text, and the Critic*. Cambridge: Harvard University Press, 1983.
Saltman, Judith. *Modern Canadian Children's Books*. Toronto: Oxford University Press, 1987.
Sampson, Paul, et al. 'Incidence of Fetal Alcohol Syndrome and Prevalence of Alcohol-Related Neurodevelopmental Disorder.' *Teratology* 56, no. 5 (1997): 317–26.
Saunders, Margaret Marshall. *Beautiful Joe: An Autobiography*. Halifax: Formac, 2001 [1894].
– *Tilda Jane: An Orphan in Search of a Home*. Halifax: Formac, 2008 [1901].
Sayers, W.C. Berwick. *Books for Youth*. Rev. ed. London: Library Association, 1936.
Scaltsas, Patricia Ward. 'Do Feminist Ethics Counter Feminist Aims?' In Cole and Coultrap-McQuin, *Explorations in Feminist Ethics*, 15–26.
Schachter, Daniel. *Searching for Memory*. New York: Basic Books, 1996.
Schrader, Paul. 'Notes on *Film Noir*.' In *Film Theory: Critical Concepts in Media and Cultural Studies*, ed. Philip Simpson, Andrew Litterson, and K.J. Shepherdson, 2: 149–59. London: Routledge, 2004.
Seifert, Martina. 'Conflicting Images: *Anne of Green Gables* in Germany.' In Mitchell, *Storm and Dissonance*, 328–43.
Setoodeh, Ramin. 'It's Still Not Easy Being Green.' *Newsweek*, 28 July 2008, 48–50.
Severa, Joan. *Dressed for the Photographer, 1840–1900*. Kent: Kent State University Press, 1997.
Shakespeare, William. *The Tragedy of Othello the Moor of Venice*. Ed. Alvin Kernan. 2nd rev. ed. New York: Signet Classic, 1998.
– *The Tragedy of Romeo and Juliet*. Ed. J.A. Bryant, Jr. 2nd rev. ed. New York: Signet Classic, 1998.
Shavit, Zohar. *Poetics of Children's Literature*. Athens: University of Georgia Press, 1986.
Shaw, Loretta L. *Japan in Transition*. Toronto: Missionary Society, Church of England in Canada, 1923 [1922].
Sheckels, Theodore F. 'Anne in Hollywood: The Americanization of a Canadian Icon.' In Gammel and Epperly, *L.M. Montgomery*, 183–91.

Shields, Carol. *Swann*. Toronto: Vintage Canada, 1996 [1987].

Simmel, Georg. *The Conflict in Modern Culture and Other Essays*. Trans. K. Peter Etzkorn. New York: Teachers College Press, 1968.

Sinclair, Catherine. *Holiday House*. New York: Garland Publishing, 1976 [1839].

Singley, Carol. 'Building a Nation, Building a Family: Adoption in Nineteenth-Century American Children's Literature.' In *Adoption in America: Historical Perspectives*, ed. E. Wayne Carp, 51–81. Ann Arbor: University of Michigan Press, 2002.

– 'Teaching American Literature: The Centrality of Adoption.' *Modern Language Studies* 34, no. 1–2 (2004): 76–83.

Smith, Lillian H. 'A List of Books for Boys and Girls.' *Ontario Library Review*, Aug. 1917, 11–33.

– *The Unreluctant Years: A Critical Approach to Children's Literature*. Chicago: American Library Association, 1953.

– ed. *Books for Boys and Girls*. 2nd ed. Toronto: Ryerson Press, 1940.

Soja, Edward. *Postmodern Geographies: The Reassertion of Space in Critical Social Theory*. New York: Verso, 1989.

– *Thirdspace: Journeys to Los Angeles and Other Real-and-Imagined Places*. Oxford: Blackwell, 1996.

Somers, Sean. '*Anne of Green Gables / Akage No An*: The Flowers of Quiet Happiness.' *Canadian Literature* 197 (2008): 42–60.

Spyri, Johanna. *Heidi*. Trans. Eileen Hall. London: Puffin Classics, 1995 [1880].

Squire, Shelagh J. 'Literary Tourism and Sustainable Tourism: Promoting "Anne of Green Gables" in Prince Edward Island.' *Journal of Sustainable Tourism* 4, no. 3 (1996): 119–34.

Stage, Sarah. *Female Complaints: Lydia Pinkham and the Business of Women's Medicine*. New York: W.W. Norton, 1979.

Stam, Robert. 'Beyond Fidelity: The Dialogics of Adaptation.' In *Film Adaptation*, ed. James Naremore, 54–76. New Brunswick, NJ: Rutgers University Press, 2000.

Stanley, Barry. 'Attention Deficits and FASD.' Paper given at FASD in Our Schools, Guelph, Ontario, 25 Oct. 2007.

Stanley, Jacqueline. *Reading to Heal: How to Use Bibliotherapy to Improve Your Life*. Boston: Element Books, 1999.

Steele, Valerie. *The Corset: A Cultural History*. New Haven: Yale University Press, 2001.

– *Paris Fashion: A Cultural History*. 2nd ed. Oxford: Berg, 1998.

Stella Dallas. Dir. Henry King. 110 min. Samuel Goldwyn, 1925.

Stella Dallas. Dir. King Vidor. 104 min. United Artists, 1937.

Sterne, Laurence. *A Sentimental Journey through France and Italy*. London: Oxford University Press, 1967 [1768].

Stoffman, Judy. 'Anne in Japanese Popular Culture.' *Canadian Children's Literature / Littérature canadienne pour la jeunesse* 91–2 (1998): 53–63.

Streissguth, Ann. *Fetal Alcohol Syndrome: A Guide for Families and Communities*. Baltimore: Paul H. Brookes, 1997.

Stretton, Hesba. *Jessica's First Prayer*. London: Religious Tract Society, 1867.

– *Little Meg's Children*. London: Religious Tract Society, 1870 [1868].

Su, John J. *Ethics and Nostalgia in the Contemporary Novel*. Cambridge: Cambridge University Press, 2005.

Sullivan, Kevin. *Anne of Green Gables: A New Beginning*. Toronto: Key Porter Books, 2008.

Sun, Youjun. *Little Butou's Adventure*. Beijing: China Children's Press, 1961.

Sutherland, Zena, Dianne L. Monson, and Mary Hill Arbuthnot, eds. *Children & Books*. 6th ed. Glenview: Scott Foresman, 1981.

Suzuki, Noriko. 'Japanese Democratization and the Little House Books: The Relation between General Head Quarters and *The Long Winter* in Japan after World War II.' *Children's Literature Association Quarterly* 31, no. 1 (2006): 65–86.

Sweet, Catherine S. 'Secular Pilgrimages: Vacation as Pilgrimage to Prince Edward Island.' M.A. thesis, McMaster University, 2005.

Takemae, Eiji. *Inside GHQ: The Allied Occupation of Japan and its Legacy*. Trans. Robert Ricketts and Sebastian Swann. London: Continuum, 2002.

Thomson, Jean, ed. *Books for Boys and Girls*. 3rd ed. Toronto: Ryerson Press, 1954.

Thomson, Rosemarie Garland. *Extra-ordinary Bodies: Figuring Physical Disability in American Culture and Literature*. New York: Columbia University Press, 1997.

'Thoughts for the Thoughtful.' *Zion's Herald*, 29 July 1903, 954.

'Translation of Dr William R. Clark.' *Zion's Herald*, 21 June 1905, 774–5.

Tremain, Shelley. 'On the Government of Disability: Foucault, Power, and the Subject of Impairment.' In *The Disability Studies Reader*, ed. Lennard J. Davis, 185–96. 2nd ed. New York: Routledge, 2006.

Trillin, Calvin. 'Anne of Red Hair: What Do the Japanese See in *Anne of Green Gables*?' In Gammel and Epperly, *L.M. Montgomery*, 213–21.

Tye, Diane. 'Multiple Meanings Called Cavendish: The Interaction of Tourism with Traditional Culture.' *Journal of Canadian Studies / Revue d'études canadiennes* 29, no. 1 (1994): 122–34.

Urquhart, Jane. Afterword to *Emily Climbs*, by L.M. Montgomery, 330–4. New Canadian Library. Toronto: McClelland & Stewart, 1989.

– *Away*. Toronto: McClelland & Stewart, 1993.

Urry, John. *The Tourist Gaze: Leisure and Travel in Contemporary Societies*. London: Sage, 1990.

van der Klei, Alice. 'Avonlea in Cyberspace, Or an Invitation to a Hyperreal Tea Party.' In Gammel, *Making Avonlea*, 310–16.

Vasquez, Vivian Mara. *Negotiating Critical Literacies with Young Children*. Mahwah: Lawrence Erlbaum Associates, 2004.

Vipond, Mary. 'Best Sellers in English Canada, 1899–1918: An Overview.' *Journal of Canadian Fiction* 24 (1979): 96–119.

– 'Best Sellers in English Canada: 1919–1928.' *Journal of Canadian Fiction* 35–6 (1986): 73–105.

Vygotstky, Lev Semenovich. *The Mind in Society*. Cambridge: Harvard University Press, 1978.

Wachowicz, Barbara. 'L.M. Montgomery: At Home in Poland.' *Canadian Children's Literature / Littérature canadienne pour la jeunesse* 46 (1987): 7–36.

Wahl, Kim. 'Fashioning the Female Artistic Self: Aesthetic Dress in Nineteenth-Century British Visual Culture.' Ph.D. diss., Queen's University, 2004.

Warner, Susan. *The Wide, Wide World*. New York: Feminist Press at the City University of New York, 1986 [1850].

Washi, Rumi. '"Japanese Female Speech" and Language Policy in the World War II Era.' In *Japanese Language, Gender, and Ideology: Cultural Models and Real People*, ed. Shigeko Okamoto and Janet S. Shibamoto Smith, 76–91. New York: Oxford University Press, 2004.

Waterston, Elizabeth. *Kindling Spirit: L.M. Montgomery's 'Anne of Green Gables.'* Toronto: ECW Press, 1993.

– 'Lucy Maud Montgomery 1874–1942.' In *The Clear Spirit: Twenty Canadian Women and Their Times*, ed. Mary Quayle Innis, 198–220. Toronto: University of Toronto Press, 1966.

– *Magic Island: The Fictions of L.M. Montgomery*. Toronto: Oxford University Press, 2008.

– 'Marigold and the Magic of Memory.' In Rubio, *Harvesting Thistles*, 155–66.

Watkins, Pattie Lou. 'Self-Help Therapies: Past and Present.' In *Handbook of Self-Help Therapies*, ed. Pattie Lou Watkins and George A. Clum, 1–24. New York: Routledge, 2008.

Weber, Brenda R. 'Confessions of a Kindred Spirit with an Academic Bent.' In Gammel, *Making Avonlea*, 43–57.

Webster, Jean. *Daddy-Long-Legs*. London: Puffin Books, 1995 [1912].

Weiss-Townsend, Janet. 'Sexism Down on the Farm? *Anne of Green Gables*.' In Reimer, *Such a Simple Little Tale*, 109–17.

Welters, Linda, and Patricia Cunningham, eds. *Twentieth Century American Fashion*. Oxford: Berg, 2005.

Wendell, Susan. *The Rejected Body: Feminist Philosophical Reflections on Disability*. New York: Routledge, 1996.

White, Gavin. 'Falling out of the Haystack: L.M. Montgomery and Lesbian Desire.' *Canadian Children's Literature / Littérature canadienne pour la jeunesse* 102 (2001): 43–59.

Wiggin, Kate Douglas. *Rebecca of Sunnybrook Farm*. Toronto: William Briggs, 1913 [1903].

Wiggins, Genevieve. *L.M. Montgomery*. New York: Twayne Publishers, 1992.

Wilder, Laura Ingalls. *The Long Winter*. New York: HarperTrophy, 1971 [1940].

William, Norman, ed. 'The Diary of Mary Louise Pickering-Thomson.' In *Canadian Women on the Move, 1867–1920*, ed. Beth Light and Joy Parr, 42–3. Documents in Canadian Women's History 2. Toronto: New Hogtown Press / Ontario Institute for Studies in Education, 1983.

Williams, Hywel. *Cassell's Chronology of World History*. London: Wiedenfeld & Nicolson, 2005.

Willmott, Glen. *Unreal Country: Modernity in the Canadian Novel in English*. Montreal: McGill-Queen's University Press, 2002.

Wilmshurst, Rea. 'L.M. Montgomery's Use of Quotations and Allusions in the "Anne" Books.' *Canadian Children's Literature / Littérature canadienne pour la jeunesse* 55 (1989): 15–45.

Wilson, Budge. *Before Green Gables*. Toronto: Penguin Canada, 2008.

Wilson, Elizabeth. *Adorned in Dreams: Fashion and Modernity*. London: I.B. Tauris, 2003.

Woodruff, Anne Helena. *Betty and Bob*. New York: Frederick A. Stokes, 1903.

Wychwood Daybook, Toronto Public Library. Boys and Girls House Archives, Osborne Collection of Early Children's Books, Lillian H. Smith Branch, Toronto Public Library.

Wynne-Jones, Tim. *Lord of the Fries and Other Stories*. Toronto: Groundwood Books, 1999.

Yang, Mayfair Mei-Hui. 'Mass Media and Transnational Subjectivity in Shanghai: Notes on (Re)Cosmopolitanism in a Chinese Metropolis.' In *The Anthropology of Globalization: A Reader*, ed. Jonathan Inda Xavier and Renato Rosaldo, 325–49. Oxford: Blackwell, 2001.

Yang, Mo. *Song of Youth*. Beijing: People's Literature Press, 1961.

Yonge, Charlotte. *Countess Kate*. New York: Random House, 1960 [1862].

York, Geoffrey. 'On Iranian TV, Avonlea Rules.' *Globe and Mail*, 4 Mar. 2000, A1, A21.

York, Lorraine. *Literary Celebrity in Canada*. Toronto: University of Toronto Press, 2007.

Zhang, Tianyi. *The Secret of Magic Gour*. Beijing: China Children's Press, 1962.

Zipes, Jack. 'The Anne-Girl: She Is What We're Not.' Introduction to *Anne of Green Gables*, by L.M. Montgomery, ix–xxi. New York: Modern Library, 2008.

Contributors

Ranbir K. Banwait is a Ph.D. student at Simon Fraser University working on Asian-North American writing.

Richard Cavell is a professor in the Department of English at the University of British Columbia. He is the author of *McLuhan in Space: A Cultural Geography* (2002), the editor of *Love, Hate and Fear in Canada's Cold War* (2004), the co-editor of *Sexing the Maple: A Canadian Sourcebook* (2006), and has published more than seventy chapters, articles, and reviews. In 2008 he was Academic Convenor of the Congress of Humanities and Social Sciences, the largest conference hosted by UBC and the Humanities and Social Sciences Federation of Canada.

Alison Matthews David is an assistant professor in the School of Fashion at Ryerson University. She holds a Ph.D. in Art History from Stanford University. She has published on the Aesthetic movement, Victorian riding habits, uniforms, and early *Vogue*. She is currently writing *Fashion Victims* (Berg Publishers) on clothing causing bodily harm.

Irene Gammel, a professor of English, holds the Canada Research Chair in Modern Literature and Culture at Ryerson University in Toronto. She is the author, editor, and co-editor of many articles and books including *Looking for Anne: How Lucy Maud Montgomery Dreamed Up a Literary Classic* (Key Porter Books, 2008), *Baroness Elsa: Gender, Dada and Everyday Modernity* (MIT Press, 2002), *The Intimate Life of L.M. Montgomery* (UTP, 2005), *Making Avonlea* (UTP, 2002), and *L.M. Montgomery and Canadian Culture* (UTP, 1999).

Carole Gerson, a professor in the English Department at Simon Fraser University, has published extensively on early Canadian women writers and Canadian literary history. She was a member of the cross-Canada editorial team working on *History of the Book in Canada / Histoire du livre et de l'imprimé au Canada*, for which she co-edited volume 3 (1918–80) with Jacques Michon.

Helen Hoy, a professor of English at the University of Guelph, is the author of *Modern English-Canadian Prose* (1983) and *How Should I Read These? Native Women Writers in Canada* (2001), and co-editor with Thomas King and Cheryl Calver of *The Native in Literature* (1987). She has also taught at the Universities of Toronto, Manitoba, Lethbridge, and Minnesota.

Huifeng Hu is an associate professor of English at the School of Foreign Languages at Guangdong University of Technology in Guangzhou, Guangdong, China. She specializes in Canadian children's literature and has published scholarly articles on L.M. Montgomery and *Anne of Green Gables* in China. She has translated fiction by Canadian authors including Kenneth Oppel into Chinese.

Benjamin Lefebvre has held postdoctoral visiting appointments at the University of Alberta, the University of Worcester, and the University of Prince Edward Island. In addition to directing the L.M. Montgomery Research Group, he recently edited Montgomery's rediscovered final book *The Blythes Are Quoted* (Viking Canada, 2009) and wrote the introduction to a new edition of Montgomery's novel *A Tangled Web* (Dundurn Press, 2009).

Alexander MacLeod is an assistant professor of English at Saint Mary's University, where he is also undergraduate coordinator of the Atlantic Canada Studies Program. His research on the relationship between literary regionalism, postmodernism, and spatial theory has appeared in *Canadian Literature*, *Essays on Canadian Writing*, and *Studies in Canadian Literature*.

Leslie McGrath obtained her Master of Library Science and her Ph.D. in Information Studies from the University of Toronto. She began working at the Toronto Public Library in 1985 and has been the head of the Osborne Collection of Early Children's Books since 1995.

Mary Jeanette Moran is an assistant professor of Adolescent Literature at the College of Staten Island. Her teaching and research interests include eighteenth- and nineteenth-century British literature and contemporary adolescent fiction. She has published on Frances Hodgson Burnett, *Cranford*, and the Judy Bolton series.

Jason Nolan is an assistant professor in the School of Early Childhood Education as well as faculty member of the graduate programs in Early Childhood Studies and in Communication and Culture at Ryerson University. He is co-editor of *The International Handbook of Virtual Learning Environments* (2006) published by Springer and director of the Experiential Design and Gaming Environments (EDGE) lab.

Andrew O'Malley is an associate professor in the English Department at Ryerson University, where he teaches courses on children's literature and culture, as well as on the eighteenth century, and where he is director of the M.A. program in Literatures of Modernity. He is the author of *The Making of the Modern Child: Children's Literature and Childhood in the Late Eighteenth Century* (Routledge, 2003) and of articles on various subjects relating to children's texts appearing in *The Lion and the Unicorn*, *Children's Literature*, and *English Studies in Canada*.

Margaret Steffler is an associate professor in the Department of English Literature at Trent University. Her areas of research, publishing, and teaching include Canadian literature, postcolonial literature and theory, children's literature, Canadian women's life writing, and the construction of girlhood in Canadian fiction.

Kimberly Wahl is an assistant professor in the School of Fashion at Ryerson University. She holds a Ph.D. in Art History from Queen's University, where her dissertation focused on late nineteenth-century aesthetic dress. Her current area of research examines the intersections between feminism and fashion.

Index